Nina-Sophia Miralles is an award-winning London-based writer and editor specialising in the arts, history and lifestyle.

In 2015 she launched *Londnr*, a culture magazine with an elegant twist wich was born online and has since expanded to a print edition and a literary salon. She has also worked for *HARRODS Magazine* and writes for *The Paris Review*.

Praise for *Glossy*:

'Dame Anna Wintour might be one of the best-known and most successful journalists on the planet. But it wasn't always like that. When she started out on *Vogue* she was often so miserable she had to phone her husband for help. This is just one of countless fascinating titbits in this zippy story of dizzying fortune, out-of this-world fashion, ingenuity, passion, sex and power. And, this being fashion, some intense bitchiness too. Started as a gossip magazine for snobbish New Yorkers in 1892, *Vogue* is now one of the most recognisable brands in the world. Spanning London, New York and Paris, this is a high-speed, fun read full of fascinating though not always likeable people'
Daily Mail

'Fashion never seemed more relevant than in this engrossing and unputdownable history of the Queen of them all...the story of Vogue's war years in France is extraordinary . . . wonderful'
Miranda Seymour

'Nina-Sophia Miralles' *Glossy* takes readers on an in-depth voyage through the history and workings of *Vogue*, from the brand's establishment to the people who made it such a success. Branded "the definitive story of *Vogue*", the insightful retrospective details the 129-year-old publication's triumphs and tribulations, from its humble New York beginnings to its international influence today'

Country and Town House

'Full of stories. . ... Miralles has an eye for the telling detail'

Irish Times

'If ever a magazine understood the special relationship between women and shiny paper, it is *Vogue*. Launched as "a dignified authentic journal of society, fashion and the ceremonial side of life," its pages have drawn the curious to its privileged glow since 1892 . . . *Glossy* tells a jaunty story of elite relationships, acute business acumen and some alluringly strange individuals. The great magazine entrepreneur Condé Nast saw its potential when he bought the title in 1909 and aimed it squarely at a market no one had spotted: extremely rich women. The creation of a luxuriant home for advertisers by using the finest editorial ingredients became the Condé Nast brand, and *Vogue* was its flagship. Nast, with his forensic socialising, is deserving of a book on his own, but the real stars are the outré terrors who have plotted their way into the editor's chair. *Glossy* is a vivacious and gossipy history of *Vogue* . . . [with its] philosophy, based on hauteur, social exclusivity, impeccable taste, and editors whose ideas at times verged on the lunatic'

Strong Words Magazine

GLOSSY

the inside story of Vogue

Nina-Sophia Miralles

QUERCUS

First published hardback in Great Britain in 2021 by Quercus Editions Ltd
This paperback edition published in 2022 by

QUERCUS

Quercus Editions Ltd
Carmelite House
50 Victoria Embankment
London EC4Y 0DZ

An Hachette UK company

PB ISBN 978 1 52940 277 3
Ebook ISBN 978 1 52940 275 9

10 9 8 7 6 5 4 3 2 1

Typeset by CC Book Production
Printed and bound in Great Britain by Clays Ltd, Elcograf S.p.A.

Papers used by Quercus Editions Ltd. are from well-managed forests
and other responsible sources.

To Rui with love,
For getting me to the finish line

Contents

American Vogue *Editors-in-chief*

Josephine Redding: 1892–1901
Marie Harrison: 1901–14
Edna Woolman Chase: 1914–52
Jessica Daves: 1952–62
Diana Vreeland: 1963–71
Grace Mirabella: 1971–88
Anna Wintour: 1988–present

British Vogue *Editors-in-chief*

Elspeth Champcommunal & Dorothy Todd, interim editors: 1916–22
Dorothy Todd: 1922–6
Michel de Brunhoff and interim editors: 1926–8
Alison Settle: 1926/8–34
Elizabeth Penrose: 1935–40/41
Audrey Withers: 1941–60
Ailsa Garland: 1960–4
Beatrix Miller: 1964–84
Anna Wintour: 1985–7
Elizabeth Tilberis: 1988–92
Alexandra Shulman: 1992–2017
Edward Enninful: 2017–present

French Vogue *Editors-in-chief*

Cossette Vogel: 1922–7
Main Bocher: 1927–9
Michel de Brunhoff: 1929–54
Edmonde Charles-Roux: 1954–66
Francine Crescent: 1968–87
Colombe Pringle: 1987–94
Joan Juliet Buck: 1994–2000
Carine Roitfeld: 2001–11
Emmanuelle Alt: 2011–present

Proprietors of Vogue

Arthur Turnure and family: 1892–1909
Condé Montrose Nast: 1909–34
Lord Camrose: 1934–58
Newhouse family: 1959–present

Introduction

Vogue magazine started, like so many great things do, in the spare room of someone's house. But unlike other such makeshift projects that flare up then fizzle away, *Vogue* burned itself on to our cultural consciousness.

Since the late nineteenth century it has been the blueprint for a popular magazine, a pioneer of beautiful living. Today, over 125 years later, *Vogue* spans 25 territories, claims an international print readership of 24.9 million monthly, 113.6 million online users monthly and 118.7 million followers across channels. Uncontested market leader for over a century, it is one of the most recognisable brands on the globe and a multimillion money-making machine. It is not just a fashion magazine, it is the establishment. A bible. But what, and more importantly who, has made *Vogue* such an enduring success?

Focusing on the three most important editions – American *Vogue*, the original and still the seat of power; British *Vogue*, the second office opened and the second most influential edition; and *Vogue Paris*, which represents France's legacy as the birthplace of couture – we'll trace a legendary organisation from its inception as a New York gossip rag, to the sleek corporate behemoth we know now. Providing a biography of *Vogue* in every sense of the word we will be taken on a ride through three centuries and two world wars, witness plunging failures and blinding successes, experiencing the dizzying journey of a magazine and those who made it. For the *Vogue* narrative is incomplete without its colourful cast, a unique set of personalities – from editors to owners – who left their personal legacies imprinted in the pages. From the snobbish founder Arthur Turnure, to the rapacious businessman Condé Montrose Nast, to Mitzi Newhouse, the pretty billionaire housewife who induced her husband to buy *Vogue* on a whim over breakfast, each had a different agenda. The editors were just as memorable. Among them was a decorated war hero who'd been in the French Resistance and the daughter of Hollywood royalty who grew up in a pink palace. The editorial staff were an unruly, hugely varied, visionary bunch who deserve to be brought back to life, as do the *Vogue* photographers. From Horst P. Horst to Cecil Beaton to Helmut Newton, they were sometimes vicious, sometimes precious, always geniuses. Yet the ever-present tussle for power between the boardroom and the editorial departments reveals the tricky interplay between creativity and commerce.

The *Vogue* universe is even richer than one could dream of. Some of the lore includes: *Vogue*'s invention of the catwalk during WWI; a scandal in the 1920s when the British editor, a notorious lesbian, seduced her secretary away from her husband; the French editor dancing with the devil in occupied Paris, pulling extraordinary tricks to stop *Vogue* assets being seized by the Nazis; and a slew of drug-related rumours which forced a sober editor to complete a stint in rehab in the 1980s. *Vogue* could be a cruel mistress, and stories of brutal firings reverberate throughout its history. But the opposite has also been true. Rewards for favourites have included solid gold coins and free houses.

Now, especially with social media at play, *Vogue* editors-in-chief have become celebrities in their own right. No longer fashion commentators, they are full-on cultural icons. Anna Wintour, editor-in-chief of American *Vogue*, has reigned supreme for thirty-two years, her fearsome, almighty presence felt by everyone in the sector and beyond. Just as famous is her flame-haired colleague, creative director Grace Coddington, who plays the darling to Wintour's despot.

The British office inspires no less furore. The red-hot debate ignited by Alexandra Shulman's resignation as editor-in-chief in 2017 was fanned into full-blown flames when Edward Enninful, the Ghanaian former male model and stylist, was named her successor, raising the question over whether fashion can – or should – be an agent of social change.

The 2017 death of *Vogue* owner Samuel Irving Newhouse Jr has also served to shine the spotlight on *Vogue*'s past, fuelling speculation of its future. Two Hollywood blockbusters have been based on Newhouse's flagship titles: *The Devil Wears Prada* in 2006 and *How to Lose Friends & Alienate People* in 2008. This adulation, veneration, rumour and gossip only underline what has been true for the last hundred years: people want to hear more and still more about *Vogue*.

Glossy is the story of passion and power, dizzying fortune and out-of-this-world fashion, of ingenuity and opportunism, frivolity and malice. It is the story of *Vogue*.

CHAPTER 1

Once Upon a Time in Old New York . . .

Early *Vogue* as a Home-grown Gazette

The Gentleman Founder

The best stories tend to rely on a fairy godmother to wave her magic wand, but in real life, a well-placed parent can do the trick. This rings especially true for the United States of America, where people like to make their own luck. It was winter in New York and snowfall was coating the steel skeletons of the skyscrapers; they had just started going up in the 1880s. Brand-new department stores like Macy's were conjuring up exquisite Christmas store fronts to lure in shoppers. Factories in the suburbs smoked away, US exports zipped out of the harbour. The place we'd come to call The City That Never Sleeps was already bursting with action. And so was Arthur Turnure. He was preparing to launch his daughter into society and *Vogue*, as he had christened her, embodied the qualities of the perfect debutante. She was pretty, eloquent and informed.

Across Manhattan, polite society madams, misses and gentlemen were eager to welcome her into their homes, introduce her to their neighbours and see what the fashionable little beauty had to say for herself. Those born into privilege are often well positioned for success and *Vogue* was no different, for her advantages in life came courtesy of her very aristocratic father. Turnure was a well-connected gentleman about town, charming, portly, enthusiastic and cosmopolitan – and much of the city's anticipation to meet *Vogue* came down to his popularity. Even the daily press, aware of the surrounding furore, heralded her approach. 'One of the principal debutantes of the week will be Vogue who will be introduced next Saturday under the chaperonage of Arthur Turnure',[1] a bulletin decreed. New York held its breath.

The first edition of *Vogue* hit newsstands across America on 17 December 1892. Priced at ten cents and aptly featuring a debutante on the cover, illustrated by A. B. Wenzel and printed in black and white, the inaugural issue is still stylish. A coy but hesitant smile plays on the face of the deb, who holds in one hand a bouquet of flowers, while with the other she lifts the hem of her gown. Her shoulders are slanted and one foot points forward, as though she is caught mid-step. Her waist is tiny, her cleavage open, her dark bodice offset by the frilly lace garlanding the neckline. Her sleeves are puffed out and topped with bows, her gloves are of the long, evening-dress variety and fluttering around her are a flock of butterflies. Above her, at the top of the cover, the word VOGUE is spelled out on an ornate banner. On either side is a classical muse, one representing harmony and beauty, the other literary tradition, which are accompanied by Grecian columns and a tangle of white blossoms.

Turnure's opening letter to his readers ran:

The definite object [of this enterprise] is the establishment of a dignified authentic journal of society, fashion and the ceremonial side of life.[2]

These are the laws which have arguably governed *Vogue* ever since. A love of beauty, pomp and style are clear, but Turnure's edict means more than just this. In chronicling the life of high society, their ballgowns and their balls, Turnure must have believed – accurately enough – that the general public would also be hankering to read of goings-on in New York's upper echelons. As one of the few publishers who belonged to that lofty strata of society, he was well placed to gather insider knowledge. Not for nothing would *Vogue* be dubbed the magazine 'written by the smart set, for the smart set'.[3]

Arthur Baldwin Turnure, born in 1857, was a native New Yorker. Descended from the original Dutch settlers of the city (known as Knickerbockers), Turnure belonged to the elite whose families had bought up vast swathes of Manhattan and Newport, then sat on the fortune and watched it appreciate for generations. Here was a man perfectly placed to give *Vogue* entrée to the fashionable world. As the only son of old money, Arthur Turnure followed the expected path to an Ivy League college. He graduated from Princeton in 1876 and practised law rather indifferently, before packing it in to address his true passions: typography, publishing and print. For a while he was the art director of Harper & Brothers (now HarperCollins) before branching out on his own, launching two lavishly illustrated art magazines and founding the New York Grolier Club alongside eight friends, which to this day caters to the bibliophiles of America. Little wonder that Turnure became known by the fitting sobriquet 'type-mad Princeton grad'.[4] By his mid-thirties he had tried his hand at a number of publishing roles, some successful, some less so. Yet his zenith was still to come. Few could have imagined his next project would become not only an international fashion bible, but one of the most famous magazines in history.

Turnure had all the shortcomings of a real gentleman. Photos show a heavy-set man with a barrel chest and square jaw, although his charming manner led him to be considered handsome. He was a sociable man who liked a good time and took financial risks – a combination some might call dangerous, and one that would certainly come back to haunt his family after his death.

That is not to say Turnure was all entitlement and idleness. Although he was an ardent elitist, he scorned bad language and remaining accounts underline his gallantry. A zealous and outspoken supporter of women's rights, he believed in women's suffrage, backed the movement and made a point of always giving women fair employment at his magazines. Indeed, *Art Interchange* and *Vogue* set a precedent for women as editors. Women were even allowed rare managerial power over male employees. Unusually, Turnure's female staff were sufficiently well paid so they could support themselves without need of a husband. When one of his employees left her spouse she was able to sustain herself and her young child, and hire help on Turnure's wages. An extraordinary luxury in the 1900s.

There was also a humanity in Turnure. Once, when Woolman Chase, a young staffer, was severely ill, he broke all convention by venturing to the run-down boarding house she was living in at the time. When her landlady informed Woolman Chase her employer was downstairs, she almost fainted in terror, thinking she was about to be fired. Instead she found Turnure in the parlour, looking shell-shocked, with a jar of homemade soup on his knees. 'My wife and I thought you might find it more nourishing than your boarding house fare,'[5] he explained shyly. Though this seems like a small gesture, it was an act that defied the extremely strict boundaries of New York society.

Old Money vs New Money

By the Gilded Age, the old-monied New Yorkers had become bound together by intricate family ties. They lived huddled on the newly minted Fifth Avenue where they built their urban châteaux and occupied brownstones that author Edith Wharton described as coating the city of New York like cold chocolate sauce.[6] Yet the world around them was changing. Eighteen years prior to the birth of *Vogue*, a party was held that would go down in history as a bad omen. The event in question – later dubbed the Bouncer's Ball – was a fancy-dress dance hosted at Delmonico's, the hottest spot in town. The list of invitees for the ball included both old money and new money, a wild move since to mix the groups had hitherto been sacrilege. Little did Delmonico's know their gutsy combination of New York nobility and brash rich newcomers would spark a social war.

The Old New Yorkers were sickened to suddenly find themselves square-dancing side by side with the Bouncers (their nickname for new money), whom they saw as arrivistes with no roots in or right to New York City. One prominent lady went as far as to darkly prophesise that one's place in society would no longer be a case of birthright and would soon be judged by who has the more millions instead.[7] This turned out to be a shrewd prediction, for the nouveaux riches – these tycoons from the Midwest, the Vanderbilts, Carnegies, Fricks and Mellons – were often far, far richer and more dynamic than their old-money counterparts, presiding over estates so big they stretched across state lines, far into America and beyond the limits of imagination. Now, having struck gold with railways and steel mines, they were pouring into New York to conquer the final American frontier – not just Manhattan, but fashionable living itself. Since there could be no peerage in the republic of America, it made sense that the sum of a family's fortune would come to dictate social standing. Without the rigid European institutions of rank to shut out hopefuls, the upper echelons were susceptible to infiltration by any upstart who'd gone and made a killing. In the years following the Bouncer's Ball, the Old New Yorkers' anxieties about new money began to spiral. Somebody had to do something, so *the* Mrs Astor became the self-appointed guardian of Old New York, their customs and their caprices.

Born Caroline Webster Schermerhorn, Mrs Astor was a million-heiress in her own right. Having raised her five children, she began casting around for something new to do and decided her true calling lay in protecting the established hierarchy from the simmering hordes of parvenus clamouring to get in. A dark, forceful, bullish woman, Mrs Astor was already in her forties and still subscribed to po-faced Victorian severity. Straddling two of the most important families in the city, her position in society was guaranteed and she promised to be a formidable gatekeeper. In 1892, the same year *Vogue* launched, it was announced to the press that the Astor brownstone mansion on Fifth Avenue could only accommodate 400 people in its ballroom. This room capacity meant those who were invited by the formidable hostess would be the crème de la crème of New York. How better to keep the newcomers away than to literally shut them out of the best parties? Soon enough, the number became a nickname and the Four Hundred came to symbolise the limit of who the traditional status quo were prepared to recognise as socially relevant.

An ally of Mrs Astor's was Arthur Turnure. One of the Four Hundred himself, he was among those looking for ways to reinforce the class divide. His opening 'Statement' in the first issue of *Vogue* is loaded with meaning, by turns flattering the Old New Yorkers while hinting at the inferiority of the monied Bouncers and the outdated European nobility:

American society enjoys the distinction of being the most pro-
gressive in the world; the most salutary and the most beneficent.
It is quick to discern, quick to receive and quick to condemn. It
is untrammelled by a degraded and immutable nobility. It has in
the highest degree an aristocracy founded in reason and developed in natural order.[8]

He hammers the point home by adding, 'the magazine's wielding
force is the social idea.'[9] He proceeded to fill the pages with stories,
profiles and illustrations of his friends from the Four Hundred.
Bouncers were not featured. In a sense he was bringing his skills as
a publisher to the class war, stepping on the Bouncers' fingers as they
tried to scale the social ladder, reinforcing in the eyes of the public
who really ran the town.

Turnure touched his millionaire Manhattanite friends to help
finance *Vogue*. There were 250 names in 1892 on the original shareholder list including all the oldest city titans such as Astor, Stuyvesant,
Heckscher, Whitney, Van Rensselaer, Cuyler and Ronalds, who came
together to ensure *Vogue* was born with a silver spoon in its mouth.
They also formed the foundation of an exclusive subscriber list that
would carry *Vogue*'s reputation through rocky financial years.

One might say *Vogue* started life as the vehicle for a petty quarrel
between the rich and the rich. Or that the pages were full of gossip
and the proprietor a snob. But that wouldn't be fair. *Vogue*'s concep-
tion is as much a result of positive drives as warring factions. *Vogue*
became Turnure's passion, he almost bankrupted his family to keep
it going. *Vogue* was also a magazine produced by women in a time
when ladies weren't supposed to work. When *Vogue* appeared on
newsstands, it wasn't just an ego stroke to the status quo, it was a
joyful, aspirational read for the middle classes. From the start *Vogue*
was too big an idea to serve one ideal. Whatever else, it was the

foresight, perspicacity, vitality and steely nerve of Turnure and the early editors that has become the mark of *Vogue*'s staff today.

The class-driven turbulence which shook infant *Vogue* shows exactly how much goes on behind the glossy pages. There would always be a complicated web of relationships, politics and belief systems pulling invisible strings behind the scenes. The intrigues of *Vogue* have all the makings of a classic Astor ball: glittering people wearing devilishly expensive garb, elite, prestigious, sought-after, secretive. Now there's one key difference: we're all invited. And it's time to dive between the pages.

Inside the Early Issues

There were a number of other factors that contributed to *Vogue*'s early success in regards to readership. Towards the end of the nineteenth century, great changes were afoot in America. It was a time of great expansion, growing patriotism and mass industrialisation, though nothing was quite as big as the new fortunes being made. During the last three decades of the century, previously unpopulated territories were finally filled up, a ruling class emerged and a flood of 'new immigrants' nearly engulfed the continent.

In this very fertile landscape *Vogue*, like many of her contemporaries, had a decent chance of thriving. But several clever decisions at the outset singled her out. For one, although the general public increasingly consumed the written word, quality monthly magazines like *Harper's* and *Scribner's* were priced beyond their means and edited beyond their understanding.[10] At the other end of the scale stood the cheap weeklies and pulp fictions, which were poorly produced and sensationalist.[11] By making *Vogue* a high-quality weekly journal, Turnure found his audience. With one paper he seduced two social groups: middle-class readers would buy it so they could finally see what the rich and distinguished were up to and upper-class readers would buy it to feed their egos.

The elegant French appellation also served the publication well. Not only did the foreign word 'Vogue' allude to sophisticated Europe, but the insinuation of Paris, capital of couture fashion, was irresistible. In a study of fifty women's magazines of the nineteenth century, twenty-seven used the word 'lady' in the title, while the remaining twenty-three used the word 'house' or 'home' (such as *Ladies' Home Journal*) or 'the fair sex' (such as *Amusements for the Fair Sex*).[12] *Vogue* would have stood out on the shelf, beguiling and novel.

Still, *Vogue* was not an entirely commercial endeavour. It may have been Turnure's magnum opus, but it was also a serious power play; even a cursory glance at the first issue of *Vogue* reflects the founding father's social connections. There are pages full of imminent parties under 'Coming Events' which read like private invitations. Some give no clues whatever regarding the nature of the event: 'Mrs. John Lawrence, 33 West Seventeenth Street'[13] or 'Mrs. F. H. Betts, 78 Irving Place. Thursdays until Lent'.[14] The *right* sort of reader will understand. Others deign to provide a little more information: 'Mrs. Charles G. Francklyn, N. Washington Square. Dance for the younger set'[15] or, 'Mrs. Anson Phelps Stokes. Dinner, followed by cotillon'.[16]

The 'Vogue Society Supplement' provides more detail of past events, giving blow-by-blow accounts of dinners, bulked out with name-dropping. An account of the Prince of Wales runs thus: '[he] is looking anything but well. I saw him the other day, and was particularly struck by the curious appearance of his eyes. The white of the eye at one corner is quite obscured by a dull red film; and his hands also, usually so "well groomed," look dull and heavy in texture'.[17] In fact the Prince of Wales was already dead in December 1892 when *Vogue* came out, having succumbed the previous January.

There is style advice, though *Vogue* was conceived as a society gazette and hadn't yet taken shape as a fashion magazine. One double page entitled 'Floral Garniture' dispenses absurdist commentary such as: 'the fashion of wearing dozens of roses has passed, and it is doubtful if it will ever be revived'.[18] Meanwhile an article on slippers advises: 'with full ball costume they [the slippers] are finished only with the tiniest of buckles'.[19] Best of all is a memorandum concerning a fad for red umbrellas: 'The fin de siècle girl is quick to take an idea, and this fashion of carrying an umbrella which will cast a rosy becoming color on a dull day is clever in the extreme.'[20]

Just as it had not yet become a fashion magazine, *Vogue* had not yet become a women's magazine. This early incarnation featured plenty for male readers including 'As Seen by Him', and 'Le Bon Oncle d'Amérique', a fiction series in which a man living in Paris on his American uncle's dime indulges in all sorts of tomfoolery with French girls.

Other features include meandering discussions on literature and a feature called 'London', supposedly from their correspondent in that city. The column opens with: 'Dogs are the fashionable fad of the moment. Every one who is any one goes about esquired by a canine "follower" and even "church parade" in the park on Sunday is given over to the vagaries of these four-footed types de monde'.[21] This sort of content hotchpotch endured for years. An early employee described *Vogue* as having 'a certain nonchalance about it . . . we once illustrated a love story of a girl on an army post with drawings of plump, belligerent trout on hooks'.[22]

As one might expect from a nineteenth-century journal, the writing is stuffy, muddled and overly elaborate. Descriptions of the fashions are never beside the correct illustrations and are sometimes missing altogether. The layout is haphazard: one editor's letter is flanked by an unfinished piece of fiction, a joke and a gloriously random rhyming couplet, 'Hearts may sometimes rule the land, But diamonds often win a hand'.[23]

Even if this *Vogue* seems incomprehensible now, certain qualities typical of the brand shine through. There is a reverence attached to wealth and luxury, as well as a sense of what is and isn't fashionable, whether this be clothes, cutlery or hair clips. Even some of the advertisers are the same: Tiffany & Co., Veuve Clicquot and Perrier Jouët all bought space in the first issue, occasionally sitting in questionable company next to Marsh Mallow Hair Tonic or Allcock's Porous Plasters. It is in some ways comforting to note that the habits of the ultra-rich haven't changed all that much. The London correspondent writing of the pampered poodle: 'It has, moreover, a trunk all to itself, duly marked with its own initials, in which are collected its multitudinous array of ribbons of all hues and designs, its different bangles for its different legs, and its variety of collars to suit all occasions',[24] sounds remarkably similar to Paris Hilton's famously pampered chihuahuas!

If a lot of the content of *Vogue* seems buddy-buddy, requiring insider knowledge of 'who's hot' and 'who's not', that's because it was largely put together by the well-born friends of Turnure. In her memoir *Always In Vogue*, Edna Woolman Chase – who began as a temp and finished as editor-in-chief – describes the set-up as informal and non-professional, with contributors more likely to be friends of the editor than chosen for their literary repute.

To those used to the glossy, exquisitely art-directed product of today, the first *Vogue* may seem a little grey and chaotic by comparison. Yet it was largely the prestigious staff members, not the content itself, that brokered *Vogue*'s early reputation. Readers everywhere wanted to hear from members of the famous Four Hundred, caring little for what exactly they said. And despite his choice of seemingly inexperienced contributors, Turnure knew that an office bursting with blue bloods was necessary to create a certain status for *Vogue* and he also knew he had to acquire a supervisor for them who could run the place with vision and proficiency. As a result, his founding editor was a happy exception to the rest of his decorative personnel.

An accomplished journalist, Josephine Redding shared Turnure's love of the print medium and had made herself known as both a writer and editor across numerous publications. She had already worked with Turnure as an editor at *Art Interchange* and would later become its owner. She was from his social circle, though this downplays her expertise. Redding was a tremendous asset to Turnure and *Vogue* will carry her legacy for ever. Turnure and his team had been unable to fix upon a title and they turned in desperation to this formidable journalist. It wasn't until they were at a showy affair during which they were expected to announce the name that Josephine Redding appeared, brandishing a dictionary where she'd underlined the word 'vogue'.[25] It was exactly what Turnure had been looking for.

That was a strong start for Redding. Once she became editor-in-chief, Turnure was demoted to a lowly employee in her eyes and treated accordingly (Redding disliked men overall). Her eccentricities did not stop there. She wore a broad-brim hat even when she was sick in bed (a fact that led to endless gossip and excitable speculation in the office[26]) and learned to cycle at night in the dark. She wrote many provocative editorials which fell decidedly outside the remit of *Vogue*, including pieces on women's suffrage, racism and animal rights. This last was a particular favourite and she made it a habit to fill endless spreads with accounts of the lives of various wild beasts and cattle. She was so charmed by a dinner guest's tale of growing up with a pet goose that she commissioned an artist to produce an illustration of this and duly published it in *Vogue* without any context.[27] Her column 'Concerning Animals' managed to survive in American *Vogue* until the 1940s.

Redding's contributions show signs that the earliest version of *Vogue* had multiple dimensions, extending beyond reviews of balls and scandalmongering. Many of her favoured topics toned down the elitism of the other features, rendering early *Vogue* accessible to a wider audience. And although her love for animals and feminist causes made the magazine more approachable, there were other measures she implemented that addressed readers outside of high society. 'Smart Fashions for Limited Incomes' tacitly acknowledged not all the subscribers were rolling in it. Redding also promoted the idea of *Vogue* patterns, thus admitting that a portion of their audience had to make their own clothes at home.

Redding's egalitarian outlook balanced Turnure's snobbism, though her content never alienated the New York socialites *Vogue* claimed to predominantly cater to. It was Redding who created the blueprint for an aspirational paper by ensuring a delicate balance of content appealing across classes, thus extending *Vogue*'s reach. It might be picked up by anyone from the modern female suffragist, to the working milliner girl, to a general's pampered new bride, if they heard Mrs Astor was reading it. Although it established itself on newsstands thanks to Turnure's connections to the Four Hundred, it became a faithful mirror of 'the society and fashions of the nineties,'[28] thanks to Redding and when she chose to retire in 1901, *Vogue* was left rudderless.

After Redding's departure Turnure took the entire assembly and editorship of the periodical upon himself, on top of advertising and business duties, with his junior staff sticking in articles they fancied willy-nilly. He was badly in need of a new leading lady. Casting around within his inner circle for a contender for the job, he alighted on an eminently likeable personage whom he picked even though she was a female golfer with no prior publishing experience. Marie Harrison was Turnure's sister-in-law and though she had none of Redding's know-how, between them Turnure and Harrison managed to cobble together *Vogue* for every print run. What she lacked in skill she made up by building a good rapport with Turnure's other ingénues, showing good leadership. This might have been enough to carry the magazine if only there were other serious journalists on the team, but again, the problem was a dearth of competent writers and well-heeled ad men.

The lax atmosphere went beyond the posh staff. A big problem was that Turnure had no idea how to make money. When illustrations of dresses were printed, the names of the dressmakers were often omitted, so they couldn't target the businesses and sell them ads. Although Turnure was capable of using his connections to get exclusive scoops – such as seeing the trousseau of Consuelo Vanderbilt before her marriage of the century to the 9th Duke of Marlborough – he had no idea how to leverage this into increased profits.

Just as Turnure was beginning to despair, the inexperienced Tom McCready was recommended by a mutual acquaintance. McCready swaggered in and managed to net himself the job as advertising manager of a magazine with virtually no ads. He asked for $9 a week, Turnure promised him a handsome $20. When his first cheque came, it was for $25 – Turnure liked to play such pleasant surprises on his staff. McCready, though barely twenty, was not all talk. He and Turnure began teasing out a pioneering strategy for *Vogue*, planning to abolish selling ads by the line – as was the custom – and instead offer blocks of ad space for a cheaper price. This would encourage advertisers to make the page their own by using the space liberally, providing their own illustrations to boot. If the adverts were beautiful and aesthetic, it saved *Vogue* the expense of producing imagery in-house. Unfortunately, they never got to witness the long-term outcomes of this approach, for their 'just about getting by' state of affairs was about to end.

In 1906, Turnure suddenly died and *Vogue* went on life support. After Turnure's death it became apparent that the journal had been making a considerable loss. Editor Marie Harrison and junior Edna Woolman Chase clung on, determined not to let *Vogue* go under, as it was the bread and butter of Turnure's widow and his young son.[29] Though Harrison never managed to recapture *Vogue*'s earliest glory or even adapt to changing times, she did maintain the interest of their richest readers. This illustrious subscriber base, in turn, caught the attention of a publishing entrepreneur who had been waiting patiently in the wings.

CHAPTER 2

The Second Act

Arrival of Condé Nast: Building a Publishing Empire

The Invisible Man Appears

Before Condé Montrose Nast became a corporate entity with over a hundred magazines churned out monthly under his name, he was a man who fell head over heels. The object of his affections was a comely little number he encountered at a newsagent's one day and he would not rest till he got his hands on her. Their chance meeting sparked a love affair that would consume his life and last till his death. Her name, as you might suspect, was *Vogue*.

The magazine had been on Nast's radar for some time; he was on the hunt for an upmarket periodical and although *Vogue* was losing some of her sparkle, she still had her valuable ties to society. He had already approached Turnure the year before his death, expressing interest in buying him out[30] and after the painful discovery of Turnure's mountainous debts, he approached the widow.[31] This time, Turnure's widow agreed the family were not equipped to carry on running the magazine alone. It had taken four years until the time was right for Nast to put his long-awaited masterplan into action.

When Condé Montrose Nast finally bought *Vogue* in 1909, it was a ramshackle little firm squeezed into a couple of boxy rooms, its staff scribbling peacefully on cheap furniture bought wholesale from office-equipment shops.[32] He slid into their lives almost as though he materialised from thin air. Keen to preserve his anonymity at the offices, then located on 24th Street, he picked a room with a separate entrance so no one would see him coming in or going out.[33] Although his name slipped on to the contents page, printed just below 'The Vogue Company' and just above editor Marie Harrison, no other indication was given in the magazine that it had changed hands. There was no announcement in the press and no introductory letter from the new owner. *Vogue* employees soon nicknamed him the 'Invisible Man' and lived in a deadly tension, waiting for the occasional sudden firings he'd dish out and praying they weren't next.

The rumours which trickled down to his nervous personnel painted a daunting picture of Nast as Machiavellian and his staff spent hours in nervous speculation, wondering whether they'd all be out on the streets.[34] But, far from planning mass firings, Nast had been burying himself in the revenue streams and profits, fixing his strategy for the future. His love of numbers had always been at the core of his approach to business and it served him just as well at *Vogue* as it had at his previous position with *Collier's Weekly*, where he'd effected his first meteoritic success.

Nast, who was most certainly *not* from an affluent background, had studied law at Georgetown University on a bequest from an aunt. It was there that he met Robert Collier, whose friendship turned out to be worth all the degrees in the world. When he graduated in 1895 with an LL.B. and returned home to St. Louis, Missouri, he made no effort to enter the legal profession and instead became more interested in a family concern. Some of his relatives had a small stake in a printing plant which was on the verge of bankruptcy – and the young graduate Nast wanted to turn it around.

He racked his brains for a solution to the plant's financial woes, to no avail, until he noticed Missourians all around preparing for the yearly St. Louis Exposition. Acting fast, Nast made up a list of businesses that might need printing jobs done for the expo and approached them with a special deal if they ordered from his printing plant.[35] It was a complete victory and funds came pouring in. Meanwhile Robert Collier, hearing of his friend's doings and the unlikely turnaround of the printing plant, paid Nast a visit. Collier's father owned a flourishing book business, with a floundering magazine attached entitled *Collier's Weekly*. In the 1890s this dry publication was full of war photographs, college sports news and paltry fiction. Collier took a long hard look at his old university pal and his promotional work for the plant . . . and offered Nast a job in New York as the advertising manager of *Collier's*. He couldn't have made a shrewder business decision, for it was at *Collier's* that Nast's knack for marketing matured into a full-blown superpower.

When a penniless Nast arrived in NYC, he was given a salary of $12 a week and told to increase the magazine's revenue through any means he saw fit.[36] He alighted on a bold strategy, writing an audacious letter to potential clients introducing himself and assuring them that he didn't want their money. He told them *Collier's* was unpopular and overlooked, undervalued and underestimated. He finished up this cryptic piece by asking the proprietor of the business to send him their residence address in order to claim a free subscription, with the final line insinuating big things were coming to *Collier's* which they might want to keep an eye on.[37] This genius bit of reverse psychology meant the companies and tradesmen he approached had their interest piqued. And as they began to watch *Collier's*, it transformed before their eyes.

Nast hired top writers, using their credentials to boost readership. He introduced colour photographs, adjusted the design and padded out the content, all to give the paper a more complete, luxurious feel. His other great invention was the concept of limited editions, which he used to drive mass sales. In 1887, *Collier's* had a dusty circulation of 19,159 and a total advertising income of $5,600.[38] After ten years of Nast's treatment the circulation had shot up to 568,073 with a revenue of $1 million.[39] He would produce detailed accounts and spend hours poring over the data to determine what was and wasn't working. He went so far as to search for correlations between editorial tweaks and any spikes or drops in income. His pay-off for masterminding all of this was an ever-rising salary, which by 1907 was in excess of $40,000 per annum.[40] So grand was this sum that it was heralded in a St. Louis paper as the largest wage ever received by a 35-year-old man and almost that received by the president of the USA.[41] At the height of this triumph he went to Robert Collier and resigned. Nast had decided to strike out on his own.

His next step was to acquire the Home Pattern Company, through which he began franchising patterns for the *Ladies' Home Journal*. Still a largely unexploited market, clothing patterns fascinated Nast. Although it did not turn out to be the big break he'd hoped for, it did awaken him to the needs of the female consumer. American magazines of the time tended to ignore women. Discovering the female buyer was one of Nast's lightbulb moments – and it made him mull over other unexploited areas in the market.

Another common feature of publishing in the early 1900s was its concentration on mass circulation. Publications aimed to make money by building up their subscribers to a point where local tradesmen would be forced to take out ads. Nast felt there was enormous scope for a journal which catered to a narrower market, giving advertisers direct access to a targeted audience – and who'd be prepared to pay higher rates for the privilege. A weekly focused on hunting, for instance, would be a logical place for rifle-makers to advertise. Women were still a vast group, so he decided to subdivide them by demographic. What about those looking to target only extremely rich women? Bespoke milliners, specialist shoemakers and fine jewellers had a far greater struggle finding their audience than soap brands. He figured that giving those businesses direct access to the coveted 1 per cent of wealthy America could be a goldmine. He had arrived at his famous formula: the female-centred, class-based, luxury magazine. He explained his philosophy:

> If you had a tray with two million needles on it and only one hundred and fifty thousand of these had gold tips which you wanted, it would be an endless and costly process to weed them out. . . . but if you could get a magnet that would draw out only the gold ones what a saving![42]

His big idea that anything of high value – grand pianos, emerald brooches, fancy cars – would be best displayed in a magazine read by those with money at their disposal, had crystallised. Now all he needed was to find the quality publication to play guinea pig to this brainwave . . . it was then that his beady eye had fallen upon *Vogue*, and though it would be years before she became his, he'd found his perfect fit.

Vogue 2.0

It took Nast almost a year to evaluate and make changes to *Vogue*. Untangling the remains of Turnure's confusing reign took some doing. His challenge was how to create a standardised format out of the mishmash which made up *Vogue* and how to consolidate their biggest asset: that exclusive readership of affluent Americans. Only in 1910 was he ready to declare his intentions publicly; the issue of mid-February carried the following announcement:

> Beginning with the Spring Fashion Forecast Number of February 15th, Vogue will be issued under a plan that will make for a bigger, a better, a still more attractive Vogue.
>
> [Vogue] will hereafter present the current notes of fashion, society, music, art, books and the drama in two splendid fortnightly numbers, each of them more than twice the size of the present ordinary weekly issue.[43]

From then on all the covers were in colour and the magazine switched from weekly to biweekly.[44] The following issue carried a rise of advertising by fourteen pages compared to the same issue the year before, and the price went from ten cents to fifteen (though subscription rates stayed the same). Nast made it his business to understand the inner workings of every department,[45] but no matter how diligently he investigated every area, it was the advertising men who were his soulmates and his own past as an ad man made him more attuned to their work. Since Nast planned to turn advertising into the main income stream, overtaking subscriptions, they became doubly important. In the Nast business model, circulation would eventually become just a number to throw at advertisers, luring them into spending the big bucks. It is a strategy used everywhere now, though Nast was the pioneer. Sales would count for less and less of the revenue.

This advertising department, as it increased in status, could occasionally butt heads with editorial. The advertising men were known to march into the editors' rooms to try and wrangle fake coverage for merchandise the editorial team considered subpar, to encourage brands to shell out for big advertorial spreads. Why not insert a few nice words about a big client? The editors felt this would grossly compromise the quality of the advice they gave to readers. When one ad man bawled at an editor that his department paid her wages, she coolly replied that if she filled the pages with rubbish products *Vogue* would lose its reputation and then neither of them would have a job.[46] If *Vogue* was packed with paid-for products they would lose the trust of their customers, but if they didn't sell enough ad space, they would lose precious revenue.

Marie Harrison stayed on as editor for the first five years of Nast's reign. But aware that *Vogue* was still an enterprise which might sink or swim, Nast knew his next choice of editor would tip the scales. A native of New Jersey, Edna Woolman Chase was raised a Quaker by strict grandparents. At eighteen she had relocated to New York, in desperate need of a job. Competition was harsh, with many young hopefuls starving to death in boarding houses. Saved by a friend who worked in a minor capacity at *Vogue*, she was brought in to take up a lowly position writing addresses on envelopes.[47] From the beginning she performed all sorts of chores for her privileged colleagues, happy to offload their duties on the keen, hardworking teenager. 'I absorbed Vogue and Vogue absorbed me',[48] she would write. By now she had been at *Vogue* almost twenty years she probably knew more than anybody else about the magazine. Although still technically a junior, subsequent events would soon propel her forward.

When Nast bought *Vogue*, Turnure's widow had played safe and kept her shares in preferred stock, believing this would yield a more stable income for her family.[49] However, as the magazine's profits shot up under Nast's management, the widow began to feel she'd been cheated. She sued Nast and the resulting battle spilled out of the courts and into the company corridors. Since the incumbent editor, Marie Harrison, was the widow's sister, relations between Harrison and Nast became icy. Now was the time for someone sharp and enterprising to make themselves seen. Woolman Chase became the go-between, delivering messages back and forth between her two warring bosses. She was right under Nast's nose.[50]

When Harrison left, Woolman Chase smoothly manoeuvred into her position. She adored *Vogue*, but with Turnure's death and the confusion that followed she had waited for a promotion too long. In fact, she had just begun toying with the idea of leaving[51] when Nast had tapped her on the shoulder to succeed Harrison and in the process clinched for himself the strongest ally a publisher ever had.

Nast and Woolman Chase understood each other implicitly, trusted each other completely and shared the same values, both in personal morals and in business. They built the *Vogue* we know side by side. It's rare for proprietor and editor to work on relatively equal terms, but the years of tremendous success and ferocious expansion were masterminded together. Their pattern of comfortable co-existence included the mundane, such as grabbing 'a quick and dirty'[52] bite to eat at their favourite greasy spoon; and the vaguely devious, such as their tacit agreement to overlook each other's staffing foibles.

Nast would often pick up some pretty young thing at a party and invite her to take up no particular job at *Vogue*. Nast liked attractive girls and some of these would naturally cross over from his editorial department to the romantic one.[53] Woolman Chase would agree to accommodate these neophytes despite the fact that their only contribution was to get under everyone's feet. In return, Nast would respect Woolman Chase's own choice in recruits.

Woolman Chase's fanatical allegiance to *Vogue* was so strong that often those who turned their back on the publication were made to pay. Artists who defected to *Harper's Bazaar* were never forgiven and publicly snubbed. When De Meyer, who had been one of her best photographers, attempted to return to *Vogue* she refused to rehire him.[54] He died destitute as a result. Employees who resigned could receive letters so harshly worded they were terrified of bumping into her in the street.[55]

Compact and birdlike, with a frizz of short, prematurely grey hair, Edna Woolman Chase was already on her way to a fearsome legacy. 'Demanding'[56] and 'hard'[57] are adjectives used against her. One biographer of Condé Nast's goes so far as to accuse her of sadism.[58] At the height of her career at *Vogue* Woolman Chase was the editor-in-chief of four separate editions (American, British, French and German) and in charge of overseeing some 150 permanent employees, plus freelance writers, photographers, artists and illustrators.[59] To expect her to be informal, chatty or forgiving was asking too much. She was exactly what she needed to be: precise, efficient, effective.

True, there were traces of harshness. She made it compulsory for *Vogue* staff to wear black silk stockings with white gloves and hats, tricky for the poorer girls who struggled to afford these items on their meagre salaries.[60] When one of her editors tried to commit suicide by jumping on the subway tracks, Woolman Chase informed her dourly, 'We at *Vogue* don't throw ourselves under subway trains, my dear. If we must, we take sleeping pills.'[61] This said, she supplemented occasional coldness with countless moments of warmth and generosity. Many of her mentees were for ever grateful. Future fashion editor Bettina Ballard recalls their first meeting:

> Everything about her is so familiar to me now, after years of confidence and affection, that I cannot separate from the whole my first impression. I can only remember that she was not terrifying and that she said, 'You have an easy pen, my child, and there is always a place for that on a magazine.'[62]

This tallies with other accounts: Woolman Chase, like Condé Nast, gave people chances. She gave them to sharp minds, while he gave them to soft bodies (rumours even circulated that Nast would occasionally pop down to Grand Central Station to scout out pretty girls moving to the city and offer them jobs[63]).

Aside from her role as mother hen to aspiring writers and personal confidante to Condé Nast, Woolman Chase was also creative, as her many clever editorial and business decisions prove. She consistently broke new ground with *Vogue* and was responsible in no small part for its fame in the late 1910s and early 1920s. Woolman Chase believed her knack for editing was innate. She had the impression that all her life she was secretly critiquing everything, including her friends and her house, to the extent that while she was giving birth to her only child she spent her hours of labour staring at some construction work outside the hospital window and fantasising about how to improve it.[64] In her memoir she admits this is hardly an endearing quality, and one which led her to be constantly dissatisfied with the world around her.[65] But if this quirk of character was damaging in her private life it was the perfectionist streak that kept her pushing *Vogue* to new victories.

Whatever Woolman Chase's personal performance, in general the magazine operated some pretty offbeat company policies. One tactic favoured by both Nast and Woolman Chase was to encourage rivalries among staff to stop them from slacking.[66] They gave only vague instructions to see what the newcomer came up with[67] and though some personalities would thrive, this strategy could backfire. Observing this, Nast claimed the world was split into 'gatherers' and 'scatterers'.[68] The gatherers would always find something helpful to do; while scatterers would never find a function for themselves and soon drop out.

Another of Nast's techniques was his famous open-door policy. He encouraged people to pop in anytime, call him up with a question, ask his advice.[69] He did this himself too. He'd stop unsuspecting passers-by in the corridor and chat idly with them – even if he had no idea who they were or if they even worked for him.[70] It was a way of making himself more approachable, as well as stimulating his own thought process by injecting outside views. Nast kept this up even when the company became a multimillion-dollar success.

By the late 1910s, and throughout the 1920s, *Vogue* began to take on a new and definite shape. It was now earning untold profits – cash was pouring in with all the force of a tropical rainstorm – and it was time for this to be reflected in the surroundings. Early in the *Vogue* takeover, Nast's bored but socially significant wife Clarisse Coudert Nast tried dabbling with the interior design of the magazine's new headquarters on 443 Fourth Avenue. Her office makeover featured a scheme of pastel colours. Other attempts to upgrade included hiring a smart little maid to wheel a wagon of tea and biscuits through the organisation at 4.30 p.m. daily.[71] Edna Woolman Chase would abolish this quaint custom as soon as she could, claiming it distracted everyone from their jobs. 'Only the British can serve tea during business hours without demoralization',[72] was her final remark.

Some years later the offices were redone again by the iconic decorator Elsie de Wolfe, a sure sign that *Vogue* was going up in the world. Bigger and brighter, de Wolfe's *Vogue* offices had curtains of raw silk, the rooms strewn with original art and glass. The reception had a feature wall of fake books although Woolman Chase's office, where she had been installed as editor-in-chief since 1914, retained the pale green chosen by Mrs Nast. The satirist Dorothy Parker (then Dorothy Rothschild), who arrived at *Vogue* in 1915, exclaimed in wicked joy that the décor reminded her of a brothel.[73]

Things were changing at *Vogue* and many of these changes, like the interiors upgrade, were a result of all the money rushing in. As the company grew and turned into this opulent cavern of hard-workers, the core editors wove themselves into groups and schedules were formalised. Much as Nast relished throwing new employees in at the deep end, an HR department slowly emerged and rules appeared. With the arrival of a German vice-president everyone was suddenly obliged to show up at 9 a.m. on the dot. Latecomers were required to fill out a card explaining the reason for their poor timekeeping . . . something that backfired when a sassy illustrator, rolling in around noon, concocted the story that he'd been tardy because a herd of elephants had chased him down Sixth Avenue. Hilarity abounded and instead of a disciplinary for the illustrator the late-cards were abolished.[74] An atmosphere of comradery still existed and staff from this era recalled their 'Vogue family'[75] with affection. A former assistant explained the set-up like this: 'it was a family in which Mr Nast was the father, Mrs Chase the mother . . . Vogue was a democracy and everyone had a voice in it – even the lowest member, which I certainly was.'[76]

For many, the Vogue 'family' spilled outside the premises and became actual family. There were a surprising amount of Vogue employees who married, divorced and remarried each other, often matching with staff from the offices abroad.[77] The further result of this was a great number of Vogue babies born into the fold and used liberally as a source of child models. Teenage daughters were often roped in to be photographed as reluctant brides, with Condé Nast's own daughter, Natica, modelling wedding veils aged fifteen, in 1920.[78]

There were other mouth-watering rewards for a life at Vogue. The company encouraged travel, frequently funding it and allowing staff long and rambling periods of time off for adventure and exploration. The theory was that voyages broadened the mind, exposing it to different cultures, new trends and gossip. The trade-off was this: any truly valuable discovery had to be relayed immediately to Vogue in case it was worth including in the magazine. Few at that time would have had access to far-flung nations, so the staff were eyes and ears, a kind of human database spread across the fashionable world, collecting information to send back to the central office. It kept *Vogue* content fresh and ahead of the curve.

Hard workers were prized, and nobody was more dedicated than Woolman Chase. Nast was sincerely grateful and showered her with lavish presents. During Christmas in the early 1910s he sent her a box of chocolates and under each candy was a solid gold coin, along with a letter informing her of a generous pay rise.[79] Some Christmases later, after Woolman Chase had purchased a house in Brookhaven, Nast sent her a note to say he'd paid off her entire mortgage . . . *and* enclosed a cheque reimbursing her for what she'd paid down.[80] A couple of Christmases after *that*, he sent her a stock certificate with the memo: 'In appreciation of some of the *all* you have done for me and Vogue.'[81] In its second iteration *Vogue* was a jolly, bustling place of real opportunity. The staff were happy, clever, creative, merry, extravagant, well connected and immaculately dressed with a strong sense of team spirit.

The Real Great Gatsby

What Condé Nast achieved for his company in the 1920s has lasted in reputation and revenue streams until 2020. However, his personal biography has been eclipsed by his assets: he blazed such a hot trail across the publishing landscape that he burned his own imprint off it. And yet once Nast had been so famous that people recognised him in the street. By nature Nast was a discreet person, a contradiction since his success was founded on aggressive sales techniques. Precisely attired in a suit and waistcoat, hat and rimless oval pince-nez and with a banker's demeanour, the impression of a financial scion was not totally off the mark. But somewhere under that serious façade was the other side of Nast, the bon viveur and seducer. Despite his reserved manner, he was keen on beautiful women and for a decade threw the most lavish parties in New York. His guests barely knew him but that didn't matter; he was perfectly content to host from the sidelines.

Nast painstakingly recorded who was invited to the revelries at his thirty-room penthouse at 1040 Park Avenue, who attended, any comments guests made, reasons for absence and the cost, down to the last dime. Nast divided potential invitees into A, B and C groups: society, people in the arts and celebrities respectively. These lists had to be monitored and updated for accuracy and his secretaries were kept busy jotting down every bit of hearsay, along with every rumoured marriage and confirmed divorce which might make dinner seating awkward.[82] For several of his secretaries this was a full-time job. Nast was determined to offer five-star service in his home, which was also a stage set, the moving, breathing, dancing version of what was happening in *Vogue*'s pages. It was a virtuous circle which fed into the mystique of his character and of his magazine. F. Scott Fitzgerald had been among the merrymakers more than once; maybe Nast was the real Great Gatsby.

The planning behind these events bordered on the obsessive. Nast's domestic staff were given exacting instructions on how to set up these blowouts in the ballroom, a weekly task which included ferrying cumbersome furniture back and forth. All this hard work just to have a knees-up, but Nast's unobtrusive character was driven by a burning-hot engine of ambition. Having earned a respectable fortune in publishing with *Collier's*, he had risked it all on his theories. His doctrine on advertising and identifying the consumer are now part of the industry canon, but before the glory and the goldmine he was just a nervous man in middle age about to bet everything he'd ever made on a gut feeling. It paid off when his name was first printed in *Vogue* on 24 June 1909. It has never left it.

Today, the multinational that bears his name claims over 427 million consumers in digital, 88 million in print, with online video content generating in excess of 1 billion monthly views.[83] And the purity of *Vogue*'s message – to promote a wonderful world – has been maintained. Yet although he wished to show his readers how to live their best life, Nast worked eighteen hours a day, even after he'd made a fortune. To stop himself from passing out from exhaustion at dinners Nast would draw two baths, one nearly boiling hot, the other freezing.[84] He would get in and out of them alternately to wake himself up before appearing socially, and it has even been suggested this was the root of the heart problems that ultimately killed him.[85] The success he made of *Vogue* was his reward.

CHAPTER 3

Consolidating Condé Nast

Expansion, the British Edition, WWI

Birth of the British Edition

Early during his ownership of *Vogue*, Condé Nast's hunger for expansion became apparent and *Vogue* would not remain his only conquest. In 1911 he bought an interest in *House & Garden*.[86] In 1913 he acquired men's fashion magazine *Dress* and the struggling Broadway sheet *Vanity Fair*, which he merged into *Dress & Vanity Fair*. This instantly bombed, before he dropped the 'dress' to relaunch it in 1914 as just *Vanity Fair*,[87] a literary and current-affairs dynamo headed by legendary editor (and Nast's long-time roommate) Frank Crowninshield.

Having so comfortably set up his interests in the USA, Nast began to lust after foreign shores. His competitor William Randolph Hearst had already begun extending his investments across the Atlantic. Hearst had established the National Magazine Company, a wholly owned subsidiary of the Hearst Corporation, at the end of 1910 to function as his British base for publishing. Aware of this, Nast wanted to beat him to the punch by being the first to publish a foreign version of an American magazine. Hearst was a long-time publisher with a lifetime of experience, just like Nast, though his outlook was totally different. Unlike Nast he had been born to money, having inherited his father's newspaper holdings. The fortune he amassed translated into art collections, a castle in California and numerous attempts at political office.

Despite accumulating a media empire, Hearst is largely remembered for the size of his holdings rather than the quality of his journalism. However, he did buy *Harper's Bazar* (the second 'a' was added later) in 1913 and was determined to turn this quiet, family-oriented periodical into a rival for *Vogue*. At the outset, *Harper's* circulation stood at a superior 65,000, while *Vogue's* was 30,000,[88] though by 1916 Nast's magazine had levelled up: both publications had grown to circulations of 100,000.[89] The feud which would rage between the two proprietors would reach its bitterest, blackest moments in the 1930s. But in the 1910s this competition was just heating up and Nast, having watched the export trade between American and British magazines advance, felt it was time for his coup. Employing William Wood, an energetic Londoner, to operate as his man on the ground, Nast began sending over copies of American *Vogue* for distribution in the UK in 1912.[90] The only tangible difference to the magazine before it hit the newsstands was a change from American spelling to English.[91]

Nast expected Wood to attract local advertisers, but tight-lipped and tight-fisted, British manufacturers still considered the USA their ill-bred little cousin and were unwilling to part with significant portions of their budget for an American publication. Still, the zealous Wood and his team peddled *Vogue* furiously every month and by 1914 the imported edition was selling between 3,000 and 4,000 copies per issue.[92] In 1916, a mere two years later, this number had quadrupled.[93] Now it was Wood's turn to launch a campaign: convincing Condé Nast to create a completely separate edition, revised and printed in the UK. 'Brogue', as British *Vogue* was affectionately known, became official that very same year.

It wasn't just Wood's powers of persuasion that forced Nast's hand. WWI had broken out in 1914 and led to a ban on exports after a slew of German submarine attacks, meaning supplies of *Vogue* could no longer reach London from New York.[94] The resourceful Wood was not put out. A locally produced English-centric edition would keep costs down and allow them to continue selling *Vogue* during the war. He also believed he stood a better chance of galvanising commercial advertising if they could legitimately show British brands that they were inserting original British content. The first London headquarters, presided over by Wood who acted as publisher, manager and managing editor,[95] were studiously low-key. Four rooms in a cramped, dingy building were filled with just a handful of employees.[96] But modest though these beginnings were, the tests they endured were monumental.

Conscription, air raids, rationing, gas masks. Allied Powers, civilian bombings, king and country. It seems a little incongruous to place a fashion magazine in the midst of mass destruction, yet British *Vogue* soared to popularity while the Great War seethed. Its reputation in the trenches was said to be second only to that of the *Saturday Evening Post* and back home women were avidly combing its pages, resulting in huge upticks of circulation.[97] Geopolitical turmoil and economic uncertainty have a curious effect on fashion: research generally shows frivolous non-essentials (beauty products, clothes, make-up) to be in high demand during periods of war, the consensus being that they serve as morale boosters.[98] The established Viennese and Parisian fashion journals had disappeared from newsstands at the outbreak of WWI and so those looking for light reading had to turn to *Vogue*.

WWI came at a critical time for women. The suffrage movement was at its height, but had to be shelved. Men were ushered into the army, meaning women had to mobilise. The homemaker and mother had to set down her needlepoint and march into factories and farms, buckle up her seat belt and uphold stiff British values. Although women were badly needed to take up labour-intensive roles in traditionally masculine environments, such as munition plants, conservative groups often treated them with suspicion. Meanwhile in the media and on propaganda posters female bodies were idealised symbols of victory, purity and beauty; inspiration for soldiers, angels of mercy, appointed guardians of Western morality. It was this conflicted era which *Vogue* had to try and translate for women.

There are distinctly evocative *Vogue* covers which reference the horror of the moment, though there were also covers which continued to emphasise the silliest sides of fashion. The year 1918 is particularly rich in wartime motifs. The January cover shows a lady wearing a sumptuous pink-and-white ballgown, holding one long flickering candle against a stark, unnerving black background.[99] In May, the cover shows a downcast young nurse with a red cross painted on a fluttering grey background and the words 'Les Blesses' (the casualties) behind her.

Three covers show a woman with arms raised in attitudes of glory. One includes British, American and French flags for solidarity;[100] another shows a torn French flag, though the figure holds bouquets of flowers to signal victorious celebration.[101] The last cover before the announcement of the armistice is strangely sad. A tiny person in a plain cream frock holds up a big gold heart with a tricolor cockade left of centre. 'Le Coeur de la France' run the letters above her, while the surrounding landscape is totally bare and very pale.[102] White, of course, is the colour of surrender.

The WWI covers, examined together, seem to include every possible female wartime role, from the practical to the romantic. The woman as an emblem of national triumph was such a widespread motif that the editor's letter of October 1918 ran: 'As this number of *Vogue* goes to press the war news continues to thrill and cheer even the most apathetic pessimists – it looks almost as if the bravery of those first new fashions has proved a lure to victory. And why not? Victory is essentially a feminine goddess.'[103]

And yet, there was still space for the playful and the dreamlike: also included was a cover with a woman sitting astride a huge, white, tiara-wearing peacock.[104]

There are moments in which *Vogue* addresses the conflict through its editorial content. The subhead of one fashion segment is '"If You Can't Be Gay, Be Gallant," Says Paris';[105] another, which touts fur coats, appropriates military vocabulary, running with the header 'These Are the Defences of Paris Against Winter'.[106] An article on the First Aid Nursing Yeomanry opens with 'An Organization of Englishwomen under the Frivolous Title of "Fannies" Is Doing the Man's Size Job of Running First Aid Stations'. Although the regular column 'Smart Fashions for Limited Incomes' was renamed 'Dressing on a War Income', to the modern reader the writing seems cringingly carefree. Midsummer of 1918 it opened: 'With the long hot days of July comes the cooling thought of sheer, very sheer, dresses and big shade hats, as refreshing in themselves as a tall glass of lemonade with cracked ice tinkling'.[107] This '*Vogue* voice' might feel uncomfortably flippant to us, but doubtless provided contemporary readers with a welcome distraction from the grim newsreels.

Adverts – in accordance with the Condé Nast business model – are an unavoidable fixture and in the early days they promised a great deal. Among imported oriental cigarettes and versatile blouses for sunbathing are self-ventilating Aquascutum coats and the lizard-skin shoe of Fortnum & Mason's in infinite styles. Reducing garments (a kind of rubbery corset) are proclaimed 'thoroughly hygienic';

while Clark's Thinning Bath Salts insist: 'do not submit a day longer to the miserable discomfort of being too fat. You can rid yourself of the incubus of disfiguring, unwanted tissue by the method so successfully employed by all lovely-figured Parisiennes',[108] claiming any excess padding will be broken down painlessly in the bath and drawn out through the pores. Omo bleaching detergent apparently also releases oxygen. The back cover constituted prime advertising real estate, though clearly editors had not yet become as discerning as they are now since Bovril frequently filled the slot.

Growth of Runway Fashion

The American edition progressed more glamorously through the war since no battles were fought on their soil. Theirs was a different challenge. In August 1914 the Germans declared war on France, just as Woolman Chase arrived safely back home to New York. She was returning from a couple of months visiting designers in Europe, but she was empty-handed. The war had caught Paris at a bad time for fashion. It was right before the autumn collections; always a city-wide production involving millions of francs, thousands of workers and meticulously orchestrated theatrics. A buyer for an American department store later described his experience of being trapped in the capital during mobilisation and he keenly remembered running around the ateliers trying to score some dress models to haul back home.[109]

Many of the couturiers hadn't completed their designs and while the American buyer witnessed many tender scenes of farewell – including famed designer Paul Poiret in a blue-and-red infantry uniform, surrounded by his adoring female staff – he found few clothes for sale. Part of the problem was that most couturiers were male and were preparing to join the army rather than finishing gowns. Female couturiers largely went ahead with their collections, but they were thin on the ground. For Woolman Chase this was inconvenient news. She had no way of knowing that after the first few months France's haute couture industry would resume business as usual. All she heard from her foreign correspondent in Paris was that a sense of mourning and hopelessness was seeping through the country like a sickness.[110] How on earth was she supposed to fill the pages of her magazine without French fashion? Paris was the centre of style, the one and only authority on clothes.

Mulling this problem over on the bus to work, she suddenly remembered the *Vogue* dolls which had been used as a publicity stunt back in Turnure's time.[111] These figurines had been kitted out in miniature versions of dresses by New York designers and exhibited to a curious public. Woolman Chase had one of her many lightning moments. By the time she got to the office she had a clear idea in her mind which, marching straight to Nast's office, she pitched to him. If they had no clothes to feature in *Vogue* they would have an empty publication. Since there was nothing coming in from Paris why not get a group of New York designers to create original pieces, then show them off to society ladies at a public event? The garments could be displayed on other women selected specially and they could walk, one after the other, in front of the audience. The 'show' could even be sold as a charity benefit with profits going to help the war effort in France. Woolman Chase would have enough fashion designs to print in *Vogue*, solving her editorial problem; American design could be introduced to the world, since up until then France had a monopoly on couture; and they could raise money to support their suffering friends in Europe. Still, Condé Nast was suspicious. He struggled to see the appeal of watching people walk while wearing clothes. Woolman Chase later explained: 'Now that fashion shows have become a way of life, it is difficult to visualize that dark age when fashion shows didn't exist.'[112]

It *does* seem impossible to visualise now, but Woolman Chase had to really fight to convince anyone. Most importantly, she had to persuade someone worthy to act as patroness or Nast wouldn't let her go ahead.[113] New York society was as closed as ever, its door sealed shut against any new ideas, the gaze of the glacial grandes dames who presided over the city ready to freeze out any upstarts. They also refused to be involved with anything commercial. Woolman Chase was determined to push the charity angle, but the involvement of *Vogue* might be enough to alienate since publishing was a business and business was beneath them.[114] In her mission to get her project off the ground Woolman Chase determined to go right to the top and approach the most illustrious and imposing madam of them all. Once that had been Mrs Astor. Now it was Mrs Stuyvesant Fish.

Known as a 'fun-maker',[115] fun she does not look. In photographs Mrs Fish's slab-like bosom is draped in finery, her wide frame squeezed into a frightening corset and her expression would have made Queen Victoria look downright jolly. To get to the assigned meeting on time Woolman Chase had to catch a train before sunrise, making her way to Mrs Fish's mansion with trepidation. Once there, Mrs Fish's secretary came down and told Woolman Chase that Mrs Fish wouldn't see her after all. Unsure what to do next, Woolman Chase lingered in polite conversation with the secretary, who, it turned out, had a son who liked to draw. Wouldn't Mrs Woolman Chase as editor of *Vogue* be able to look at his work and see if it was any good? Graciously agreeing, Woolman Chase commented what a shame it was that nothing could be done to persuade Mrs Fish to hear her out. The secretary took the hint – and went back upstairs to plead with the formidable woman to give the editor a chance.[116]

Once in front of Mrs Fish, Woolman Chase coaxed her round.

The net result was a brimming list of patronesses that was labelled a 'stunner'.[117] With Mrs Fish's help, some of the juiciest names in New York stepped up to the plate, including the likes of Mrs Vincent Astor, Mrs William K. Vanderbilt Jr, Mrs Harry Payne Whitney and Mrs Ogden L. Mills.[118] At the sight of this impressive roll call, Condé Nast completely buckled. With the green light from Nast, Woolman Chase busied herself with other details. She christened the event a 'Fashion Fête'; chose the Committee of Mercy which helped widows and orphans of allied countries as the recipient of the profits; booked the ballroom of the Ritz-Carlton; and hand-picked seven patronesses to act as judges, although this was just a cover. Woolman Chase realised that any dressmakers, boutique owners or department store representatives who paid for advertising in *Vogue* but were not picked to exhibit at the fête might be offended and pull their ads. She didn't want to compromise on the quality of the clothes shown so, craftily, she told each client that she would *love* to show their pieces, but sadly the 'judges' picked out the designs and she had no sway over them.[119]

She performed yet another service to fashion by training mannequins, teaching the carefully selected beauties to strut and pivot professionally. Her goal was to get them to walk in a way that would convince onlookers this was a real art, rather than the random machinations of an ambitious editor. The catwalk strut might well have been popularised here and the Fashion Fête had big consequences for modelling, raising awareness of the profession across the United States.[120]

The evening was a resounding success, starting with a dinner, after which all the smart ladies went up the curving staircase to take their seats for the show. At the time it was so unusual for these mighty New York families to mingle with the common folk that the attending socialites considered themselves quite intrepid for spending a night with models and dressmakers.[121] A number of high-end brands we still know today, such as Bergdorf Goodman, were launched on to the fashion scene that night. The fête took up a good eleven pages in the *Vogue* issue of 1 December 1914. Woolman Chase's fear of empty pages was avoided.

This would not be *Vogue*'s final act of altruism regarding the war. In 1915, Nast wrote an appeal to his readers urging them to donate to the Sewing Girls of Paris Fund. He was genuinely interested in supporting industry workers affected by the ongoing conflict; though this move also fed into his desire to mollify the heavyweights of Parisian fashion. When they got wind of the Fashion Fête the couturiers took it badly, seeing it as a move by the Americans to promote native dressmakers while French design was disrupted due to the war. (*Harper's Bazaar* tried to profit from this scandal by fanning the flames and urging ateliers to blacklist *Vogue* editors from their future shows.)[122] Keen to make amends, Nast offered to host a Paris Fashion Fête in New York, again at the Ritz-Carlton, again for charity, again with lots of coverage in the magazine. This time the names of designers were far better known – Worth, Poiret, Lanvin – but the proceeds were far less. Nast was happy to shoulder the financial burden as it repaired relations with France and satisfied the couturiers.

Whether she'd meant to or not, Woolman Chase had demonstrated that fashion did not have to be French, that dressmakers in New York did not have to ape Parisian models to sell their wares and that Americans could step forward and develop their own style. She also proved the appeal of looking at women wearing new designs – it literally brought clothes to life. As her daughter would say to her years later, 'You and World War One. What a twosome you turned out to be!'[123]

The Brand Gets Big

The Great War might have propelled Nast to expand into Europe, but he knew that to lock down the company's future *Vogue* had to establish itself as the deciding authority in fashion, while Condé Nast Publications had to corner the magazine market. One example of how he leveraged events to his advantage can be seen in the saga of Paul Poiret and Parisian couture.

The hottest designer of the day, Poiret, visited New York in 1914 and saw his name being used without licence in America. In response to these shameless rip-offs, Poiret let up a howl of fury that echoed all the way back to Paris. Laws regarding plagiarism are still pretty hard to negotiate today; back in 1914 it was a free-for-all. Nast understood that *Vogue* relied on having the best clothes to show in its pages. To have access to the latest designs from the greatest designers they needed to maintain friendships among the Parisian couturiers. So, in a bid to get Poiret on side, Nast and Woolman Chase moved to turn what could have been a Greek tragedy into another gainful scheme.

When Poiret returned to France he was planning to blacklist all American editors and buyers from his atelier and was on the verge of persuading all his Parisian colleagues to follow suit. Banning all Americans from their shows meant none of their designs could be stolen and copied in the US, but it would have been disastrous for *Vogue* and every other foreign fashion magazine. Instead, Nast, Woolman Chase and their newly acquired European representative, Philippe Ortiz, convinced Poiret to sit down with them to try to find a solution. Thanks to this, Le Syndicat de Défense de la Grande Couture Française was born, a bombastic title for an association whose aim was to protect the rights of French dressmakers.[124] Officially formed in June 1914, Poiret took seat as president; illustrious designer Jacques Worth became vice-president; and a plethora of other respected fashion veterans became dedicated members.

By patrolling stores, defaming those selling knockoffs in press statements and applying pressure through their numerous industry connections, *Vogue*'s campaign saw that individual names of designers were no longer being used indiscriminately by factory outlets. Poiret and other couturiers would show their gratitude to *Vogue* with special favours including letting them preview collections and allowing them the best seats for shows.

As well as keeping a controlling hand on the fashion sector, Nast also wanted to guarantee the continued quality of all his publications so, following the advice of his vice-president, he purchased his own printing plant at auction in 1921.[125] The site in Greenwich, Connecticut had once been the Douglas McMurtrie Arbor Press and was ideal for production work as it was placed on a high and dry plot, minimising the possibility of dampness so fatal to printing works. Little more than a dirty, deserted track when it was signed over to Nast, he spent a total of some $350,000 just on the landscaping.[126] The buildings were elegantly rendered by a fashionable architect, with vast stone obelisks flanking the entrance by the side of the motorway, to be seen by every passing car. The names imprinted on the minds of those driving past were those ever-grandiose properties of Nast's:

'VOGUE, GLAMOUR, HOUSE & GARDEN, VANITY FAIR, CONDÉ NAST PUBLICATIONS'.

Some 1,600 more Condé Nast employees were based at the printing plant and joyfully made use of further perks, including a cafeteria, recreation rooms and a dispensary complete with the services of a doctor and nurse.[127] There was a spring fashion show, an annual Christmas party and outings in summer to a prestigious country club for all the staff and their families.[128] When Connecticut passed a law allowing women to work nights, Nast's stately printers was quickly populated by female proofreaders.[129] In its heyday, the majestic property included Italian imported sculptures on the grounds, fountains at the entrance and some $25,000 worth of elms which gave the plant the air of a secluded castle. Heavyweight magazines or newspapers frequently build their own printing plants since this allows them to supervise quality control. Even more appealing is the fact they can make extra money by taking on contracts for other publications. Soon other magazines, including *The New Yorker*, were printing at the Condé Nast plant, resulting in yet another lucrative revenue stream. In its first year the plant's volume of business totalled $380,935; just eight years later this figure sky-rocketed to $3,450,255.[130]

Nast was one of the earliest American businessmen to understand the fundamentals of building a brand. He knew that nobody on his staff could be allowed to stand out – apart from himself – since it might dilute the strength of the *Vogue* name. This led to the increased use of the 'Vogue voice'.[131] Unless an article was commissioned by a famous author, all staff writers would be published with headlines like 'Vogue Says', keeping the tone of *Vogue* neutral and consistent. It also meant writers couldn't build personal followings that they could take with them if they left to work for a rival.

Nast's mission to establish *Vogue* as the official voice of luxury continued with his Vogue School and Vogue Directory. These were advertised in each issue, urging readers to call *Vogue* for advice and recommendations. Having a torrid affair with a Member of Parliament and need a discreet restaurant? Leave it to *Vogue*. Keen to get your hands on a new hat, but only stopping in Paris for one night on your journey to India? *Vogue* can secure your appointment with the best milliner. Lost your whole fortune in a gambling fiasco and desperate to marry your daughter to money? *Vogue* will take care of your invitations to the debutante season. Your darling blonde angels are old enough to go to nursery? Let *Vogue* suggest the right one.

There were some downsides to the ruthless advance of the *Vogue* name. A great number of fake 'Vogue' products appeared on the market, including Vogue ice cream, Vogue girdles and Vogue shoes, all of which Condé Nast Publications had to try to discredit in the magazine, since they couldn't copyright the word itself.[132] It was a nuisance and Nast continually had to write to his readers with yet another disclaimer: 'Thank you for your continued support, Madam, no, we do not sell candy now.'

Nast's success surely rankled with Hearst. It was around this time he developed what has since remained a primary tool in *Harper's Bazaar's* crusade against *Vogue*: poaching the best *Vogue*-trained staff. Over the years numerous invaluable photographers, editors, advertising managers, etc. have been lured over to Hearst, hypnotised by the millionaire's potential to grant huge wages. Some of the more opportunistic artists managed to take advantage of this by playing the two against each other to get better contracts. This made *Vogue's* blood boil.

Nast's success got Hearst riled enough to use his other publications to try to undermine his wily competitor. In September 1923 this segment ran in his newspapers:

VOGUE GIVES UP IDEA OF LONDON EDITION

Condé Nast, editor and owner of *Vogue*, has abandoned his attempt to establish *Vogue* in London, and has sold the English edition of *Vogue* to the publishing House of Hutchinson & Company.[133]

The story was completely made up and Nast's response was as weary and curt as so dirty a move deserves. He bought a full-page advert in the trade journal *Printers' Ink* the following week:

> This story, which appeared ONLY in the Hearst newspapers throughout the country, is absolutely false. I have not sold, and am not contemplating the sale of British *Vogue* to anyone. Condé Nast.[134]

Mind you, if he'd known the drama that awaited him in the London office, perhaps he would wish he *had* nuked the English edition and saved himself the headache.

CHAPTER 4

The 'Filthy' Editor

Sexual Subcultures

A New Woman for New Women

By the end of the war, women had begun to see themselves beyond their reproductive abilities and fashions were beginning to mirror the change in mindset. Looser silhouettes tiptoed on to the market and women were let out, sleek and sporty, ready to face the world and invent the flapper. Suffrage was finally granted in two stages in the UK, in 1918 and 1928. There was an incomprehensible number of war widows; women who now had to support themselves without a man. A landscape of death and devastation on this scale meant gender could no longer be relied upon to govern social norms.

Women had always been central to *Vogue*'s workforce, yet establishing the first official editor of British *Vogue* is tricky, due to records lost or damaged in the war. The majority of sources credit one of two main players: Dorothy Todd or Elspeth Champcommunal. Today's *Vogue* has bestowed the honourable title of first ever British editor on Champcommunal[135] (Champco to friends), while Dorothy Todd (Dody) is listed as the second.[136] However, Edna Woolman Chase of the American office makes no mention of Champco in her autobiography and treats Dody as the earliest editor.[137] These discrepancies are difficult to untangle: many other personal accounts are marred by decades of professional clashing and rivalry. It doesn't help that *Vogue* still did not have a full masthead.

It's worth starting with Elspeth Champcommunal, since she is officially recognised by *Vogue*. Champco was part of the artistic and bohemian Bloomsbury Set and was picked out by Nast and co. for her social connections. What the Americans hadn't realised was that the Bloomsbury Set, while fashionable, was by no means the spending aristocracy they'd meant to attract. Furthermore, Champco was a lively woman with a depth of fashion knowledge that baulked at taking orders from New York. Later she would become the head designer for Worth London and a founding member of the Incorporated Society of London Fashion Designers, a forerunner of today's British Fashion Council.

Some of the wilder details of Champco's life are bound up with contemporary suspicions of bisexuality. She never remarried after being left a widow and belonged to a liberal, sexually experimental group that thrived in the interwar years. Central to the rumours was her long relationship with a female editor with whom she often lived and travelled.

The suggestion that the first editor of British *Vogue* might have had lesbian inclinations is spicy enough, until the exploits of the second editor are aired. Appointed to the post of editor in 1922, and described as 'filthy' by Cecil Beaton, Dorothy Todd is one of *Vogue*'s most provocative figures. She was openly homosexual and lived with her long-term girlfriend at a time when female homosexuality was not even recognised by law. Oscar Wilde's infamous trial had brought the idea of male homosexuality into sharp focus some two decades earlier, but women were still considered to be physically unable to engage in truly 'inverted' behaviour.

Dody's sexual appetite directly affected *Vogue*. Her circle of artistic friends, many of whom belonged to a gay community, became regular contributors, so for a short while it seemed everybody involved with *Vogue* was part of a sexual subculture.

Oscar Wilde's niece Dolly was an early staffer, as well as a heroin addict in a long-term lesbian relationship.[138] Aldous Huxley, who is best remembered for penning the canonical *Brave New World*, spent years working for *Vogue* and had an open marriage with his wife. Raymond Mortimer CBE, the revered literary critic and homosexual, wrote a regular column; Marcel Boulestin, a food writer and the first ever celebrity chef spent the beginning of his career writing racy homosexual fiction; and Vita Sackville-West, sometime *Vogue* contributor, tested the limits of her own open marriage by embarking on regular trysts with both men *and* women.

Clearly there were already ideas circulating about what kind of a person you had to be to work at *Vogue*, although breaking out of the heteronormative mould was not the only clincher. It was, after all, still a fashion magazine, but even on the topic of fashion Dody had her own ideas. Already in her forties when she came to the attention of Condé Nast Publications, Dody was taken seriously enough to be summoned to New York to receive training directly from Edna Woolman Chase, in preparation for heading the London office. Nonetheless, Dody's version of *Vogue* would defy her American coaching.

It was the 1920s and the dust from WWI was settling. Keen to start afresh, the Western world was becoming a hotspot for intellectual activity. A new generation sprung up and with them came new ways of thinking about everything from architecture to interiors, science to philosophy. Modernism as a movement only had one rule: that all rules be broken.[139] Although *Vogue* under Woolman Chase maintained its conservative foothold, Crowninshield's *Vanity Fair* played a looser, more daring role in society by alighting on newly emerging cultural phenomenon and applying razor-sharp wit to the coverage. Bolder still was the editorial policy. In Crowninshield's first issue of March 1914 he promised: 'For women we intend to do something in a noble and missionary spirit, something which, so far as we can observe, has never been done for them by an American magazine. We mean to make frequent appeals of their intellects.'[140]

This revolutionary approach fascinated Dody. When she took hold of the reins of Brogue she began to take a page out of their book. Though the numerous fashion write-ups were created and sent over from the American office; cartoons, illustrations and the quippy tone of Dody's Brogue carry the unmistakeably kicky feel of *Vanity Fair*. Whether she acknowledged the debt to it or not, her magazine was in no way derivative. In one of her own editor's letters she wrote:

> *Vogue* has no intention of confining its pages to hats and frocks. In literature, the drama, art and architecture, the same spirit of change is seen at work, and to the intelligent observer the interplay of suggestion and influence between all these things is one of the fascinations of the study of the contemporary world.[141]

To look at Brogue of the early twenties is to see through the gaze of a forceful, adept and visionary editor, one who was not afraid to cross lines and push boundaries.

Dorothy Todd was born in London, the daughter of a flourishing property developer in Chelsea. Her father's personal life was as fruitful as his business: he fathered eight children with his first wife. Dody's mother, Ruthella, was the second; a younger, poisonous type.[142] When Dody's father died suddenly of a heart attack, her mother set about frittering away the enormous fortune, much of which was supposed to remain in trust to his ten children. Dody and her younger brother embarked on an unsafe and shambolic life, of being dragged around the gambling circuit as their mother succumbed to alcoholism. Dody was inquisitive, thoughtful and forceful; she once ran away from home and only returned on the caveat that she receive tutoring in Latin and Greek.[143] But along with the fluent French she picked up from her time at resorts, she also, regrettably, picked up some of her mother's worse habits and these would repeat in Dody's own history, for most of all she became used to enormous risks, not just in card games, but in life.[144]

A complicated childhood turned into a complicated adulthood. Dody's teenage years and twenties were overshadowed by the birth of her illegitimate daughter. Victorian ideals still dominated society, crushing women in an atmosphere of shame, repression and inexperience. Unsurprisingly, Dody acted as her daughter's 'aunt' and legal guardian, pretending to everyone, including her own daughter, that she was not the mother. The mystery of who fathered the child has never been solved and it would later be suggested that she'd been sexually abused.[145]

Nonetheless, Dody's daughter was well cared for, given an ample allowance and encouraged to enrol at university (in 1924 she was admitted to Oxford).[146] Despite their strained relationship, Dody's interest in her daughter's education was genuine. She exhibited this same interest with her many protégés, for Dody promoted learning for all young adults and careers for women in particular. Breathless entries in Cecil Beaton's diaries show how keenly the young photographer wanted to get her attention and how valuable he knew it would be.[147] Even Woolman Chase, who was no fan of Dody's, had to begrudgingly admit that her mentees always turned up trumps, noting that a great number of the young Englishmen Dody sponsored went on to great fame.[148] Well acquainted with the Bloomsbury

Set, Dody published Virginia Woolf; featured her sister, Vanessa Bell's interiors; and made her brother-in-law, Clive Bell, art critic. More importantly, she paid her glittering roster enough to live off, a privilege few artists or writers have ever enjoyed.

It didn't stop there. Dody sought to make celebrities of her colourful coterie, establishing their reputations by introducing bylines and using clever manipulations to cement their reputations. For instance, alongside the obligatory portraits of English aristocrats and diplomats' wives, Dody inserted images of her budding prodigies and their homes and gardens. This editorial arrangement elevated their status in the minds of readers. By shining a light on the developing cultural scene and throwing creative people together, she was directly responsible for encouraging artistic communities. In a sense, Dody belongs among the early twentieth-century patrons such as Gertrude Stein. However, her platform was *Vogue* and *Vogue* was always snubbed – a trivial, stylish, picture paper with impossible aspirations to the highbrow – which goes some way to explaining why Dody does not exist in posterity.

Vogue Flies the Gay Flag

Among Dody's comprehensive list of acolytes was Madge McHarg. In surviving photographs the rail-thin Australian émigré has the languorous look of a blonde ghost. McHarg was the seventh ever employee of Brogue and had begged her way into a job by sitting on the stairs three days in a row and ambushing the manager, reportedly entreating, 'you'll never have to see me again if I could just have four pounds a week – for I can't survive on three'.[149] Although she was living on a shoestring budget, McHarg was the daughter of a wealthy Melbourne trader who resented the lack of education she

was allowed as a girl. Her parents branded her impossible; seeing her
as a headstrong, spoiled girl who longed for a university education
not a finishing school. She hated her home country and instead of
making a good marriage she wanted a job. 'It was the usual thing,'
she said later, 'I ran away and had no qualifications at all.'[150]

But while she couldn't bear to have anything to do with conventional middle-class life, McHarg did everything she could to become
a worthy part of Brogue. She ran errands, fetched coffee, posted mail
and worked as a messenger from Monday to Saturday.[151] As Brogue
picked up momentum she began staying at the office well into the
night, surviving on just one poached egg on toast and a meringue
a day.[152] In her spare time she took evening classes to try to expand
her knowledge. When, after two years of this punishing routine,
she finally collapsed with jaundice, she was terrified. For the first
time she was unable to work to support herself. Descending into
total panic, her solution was to appeal to an old family friend, Ewart
Garland, sending him a telegram which read: 'COME AT ONCE
AND MARRY ME'.[153]

Despite ending up married – a condition she had always dreaded
– she would not allow this to grind her to a halt. She dealt with
Ewart as she had dealt with her parents: by giving him a hard time.
She would not wear a wedding band. She would not take his name.
She threatened him with immediate divorce if he dared impregnate
her.[154] And within a year she was already romantically involved with
Dody. After their affair ended, she made a point to always acknowledge her debt to Dody, of whom she said, 'I owe her everything.'[155]
She was not alone in this opinion. Dody was 'the absolute making
of Madge',[156] one writer noted. From lowly receptionist and runner
Dody elevated Madge through the ranks to take the post of fashion
editor. It was favouritism, but Dody had never been too hung up on
morality. The resulting Brogue that Madge and Dody triumphantly

worked on together for four short but glorious years is an avant-garde masterpiece.

The editorship evolved into a sort of partnership, sexual, as well as professional. Together, they developed a new idea, feeling that the magazine had to keep women up to date with thinking trends as well as clothing trends. For Dody, being fashionable was a case of being involved with culture and her *Vogue* was one of the earlier examples of women being given broader access to knowledge. Novelist Rebecca West credited them as superb editors, writing enthusiastically that they transformed *Vogue* from just another fashion publication to the very best of fashion publications, as well as an important guide to modernism and the arts.[157]

Alongside the usual fashion plates from Paris, Dody and Madge were the first to publish Man Ray's photographs, Edith Sitwell's poetry and they wrote about luminaries from Picasso to Churchill. To the careful reader, magazines from the Dody–Madge tenure reveal elements of a new gender fluidity. A stream of homosexual celebrities grace the issues, from ballet dancers to painters. Meanwhile the cartoons gently lampoon men with effeminate figures who routinely fail at heteronormative courtship.[158] One cartoon features an ageing millionaire who despised his relatives because they were young and, to exact a petty revenge, would send them inappropriate gifts. His great-niece is shown sitting in a tuxedo-style pyjama suit, puffing at cigars in a distinctly butch pose.

The elements of *Vogue* proper are still present. Aristocratic lineage is highlighted everywhere possible, in photos, features and breathlessly excited copy. And though some researchers have claimed that the Dody–Madge Brogue was actively anti-imperialist and anti-racist,[159] this will still seem questionable for a modern reader. One caption in the feature 'Seen on the Stage' uncomfortably accompanies a photo with the line: 'Frank Cochrane plays a Jew with splendid spirit. In the eighteenth century Jews were considered funny'.[160] The regular articles and adverts encouraging youth and slimness are diluted, but not eliminated entirely.

Though boundary-pushing, the magazine never succumbed to being *too* modern. Dody was always careful to address articles to the bright young things as well as Queen Victoria's generation. It was not an easy gap to bridge and sometimes the columns take funny turns trying to include both. Yet Dody's effort to address females in all age brackets shows a touching commitment to inclusivity and there are moments where Brogue tackles incendiary feminist subjects, such as illegitimacy.

During this heyday, even the controversial Dody got good press. She was still Rebecca West's 'fat little woman, full of genius',[161] the queen of *Vogue* who reigned over Bloomsbury.[162] Madge had also gone through a transformation. She soon became a vision in haute couture, forever dressed in silk and pearls. She succumbed to using her abandoned husband's pretty floral surname when Gertrude Stein commented her maiden name of McHarg was dreadful.[163] Their home was often the site of impromptu wild parties and the *Vogue* expense account was always in use at swanky restaurants. Dody and Madge captured the zeitgeist of the time, with their own lifestyle and in the pages of Brogue. That did not mean the skies were clear ahead.

Even among their most liberal peers they could seem a little scandalous. Virginia Woolf, at one of their parties, found herself proposing to publish Dody's memoirs.[164] She later adds that she must have been carried away, since the 'squalor' of Dody's private life which would make the project fascinating would also make it unpublishable.[165] As pioneers at the very centre of a new erotic and emotional ideal,[166] Dody and Madge were too far in to see the reluctance and judgement gathering on the outskirts. The discomfort, allure and repulsion which some of their associates felt provide some clue as to why all their friends disappeared when their high-wire act was cut short.

Back to 'Normal'

Whatever was going on in London was not going down well in New York. Condé Nast and Edna Woolman Chase had watched Brogue with suspicion and suddenly sprang into action. Woolman Chase claimed that Dody had twisted *Vogue* into something it was not and that as a result advertising was falling off by the pageful.[167] British publisher, Harry Yoxall, corroborates Woolman Chase's comment, quoting a whopping loss of £25,000 in the year of 1923.[168] However, this could be due to any number of myriad factors outside of Dody's editing. In 1926, Yoxall notes a rise in circulation was spoiled by the General Strike.[169] Nor did Dody merely let Brogue run into the ground. At the end of 1923 she halved the cover price in an attempt to remedy the situation and launched an editorial campaign with the tagline, 'Every page of Vogue shows you how to save money by spending it to advantage'.[170] Readership numbers did begin to climb again and shortly before she was fired, a survey found Brogue was in the top three magazines read by middle-class women.

Regardless, in September of 1926 the axe fell. Harry Yoxall, now business manager of Brogue, fired Dody on Condé Nast's instructions.[171] The day after, he fired Madge, whom he'd nick-named *'maîtresse en titre'*[172] ('chief official Mistress' in French). Livid, insulted, stricken, Dody threatened to sue for breach of contract but Nast, it turned out, was not above blackmail. Lording his knowledge of her relationship with Madge over her, he threatened to release damning details of her private life.[173] It was not a happy time for gay rights. Although in 1921 the Lord Chancellor of Great Britain opposed a bill that would have criminalised lesbianism,[174] later in the decade Radclyffe Hall's novel *The Well of Loneliness*, whose main character is a lesbian, was the target of a vicious campaign resulting in the book being banned under the Obscene Publications Act.[175] Dody and Madge's open-minded milieu accepted their relationship but the general outlook for equality was bleak. Dody was not willing to put Madge's or her daughter's future at risk by fighting with Nast and allowed herself to be silenced, though she did not go easily. Woolman Chase, ruminating on the events, commented, 'The lady [Dody] had a forceful personality and the sound of the wrench, when it came, reverberated from London to New York and back again'.[176]

Hereafter, the hypocrisy of the artistic and fashion world shows itself most unpleasantly. As Yoxall, the business manager, levied in his autobiography, 'No form of bitchery is beyond these charming creatures'.[177] Virginia Woolf bitterly abused Dody in her diaries, despite having profited directly through her generosity, describing her cruelly 'like a slug with a bleeding gash for a mouth'.[178] Other friends, acquaintances and outliers began to drop away and as days turned into months, Dody was unable to keep up appearances. Increasingly Madge would find her unconscious beside an empty bottle of whisky in a manner reminiscent of her mother's adventures. As Dody descended into alcoholism, Madge discovered she had been using her name to run up bills on a scale that was lunatic. Cornered by debtors, Madge made a terrified escape to France and spent years working to repay the sum. 'Once again I was homeless, penniless . . . only a few lovely and rather inappropriate clothes remained.'[179]

Though Madge eventually effected a comeback to *Vogue*, Dody never recovered. Prior to abandoning London completely in the late 1950s, she lived in a couple of messy rooms overrun with cats.[180] In old age she moved to Cambridge, alcoholic and very frail, she survived on a small government pension and handouts.[181] Despite this, Dody's spirit was not totally vanquished. Her grandson tells some pretty raucous stories regarding her sexual conquests.[182] Even at the very end of her life Dody managed to entice a young Italian woman away from her husband.[183] At the age of eighty-three Dody died, having survived longer than anyone expected. Her contribution to the British arts scene was invaluable and despite her personal failings, she does not deserve to have been 'erased as a blot on the otherwise immaculate history of Vogue.'[184]

This saga was only the beginning of Woolman Chase's woes caused by the London office, though in the aftermath of the firings she was given a short reprieve. Vogue had opened a French office in 1920 and Michel de Brunhoff, a competent relation of the Parisian editor, was induced to hop over to London and hold down the fort.[185] His assignment was to return the British edition back in line with Woolman Chase's 'Vogue formula',[186] mostly by printing duplicate content sent over from America. But there were other moments of insubordination surprising to Woolman Chase. Despite being appointed director of American Vogue, she still had to grapple with ingrained patriarchal views and the toughest of these professional trials seemed to occur in England.

When visiting the British office in the 1900s she found the publisher and advertising manager siding together against her and openly discussing what they saw as the meddling presence of a woman (she was seen as the 'Demon Housekeeper'[187]). They would routinely shut her out of meetings or dismiss her suggestions by claiming that she didn't understand their British audience. Yet as editor-in-chief and director of American Vogue she was technically their boss. After weeks of petty infighting she cabled Nast and insisted he appoint her director of British Vogue, because it would give her more authority to deal with the insubordination.[188] After that, the English team were legally obliged to include her at board meetings.

Their condescending attitude took a little longer to crack. It is testament to Woolman Chase's talents that the British publisher in question, originally so dismissive, came to look up to her. A decade after her death he still remembered her with a sense of awe, affirming: 'She was a brilliant editor, yet I was never able to analyse her brilliance. It seemed to come from instinct rather than knowledge'.[189] Unfortunately, just as the interim editor Michel de Brunhoff, Edna Woolman Chase and the British managers began to return the office to some semblance of order, new problems swarmed them like the plague.

CHAPTER 5

Obstacles Everywhere

The General Strike and the Great Depression

Hard Times in London

From today's perspective, the 1920s have acquired an electrifying allure. From the appearance of speakeasy-themed bars in East London and Brooklyn alike, to the 2013 Hollywood remake of Fitzgerald's epochal novel *The Great Gatsby*, the decade has become synonymous with flappers stumbling about in sequins, sporting sleek, chopped bobs; mobsters in spats selling bootleg liquor; Martini glasses jiggling to quick-beat jazz; showers of glitter in moodily lit clubs. All this glamour . . . and yet the truth of British *Vogue* in the 1920s is worse than prosaic, it's genuinely gloomy.

Brogue's London office proved a tense working environment. Not only had the mounting trouble with Dody and Madge Garland been coming to a head for some time, but there was no clear hierarchy, meaning the editor, business manager and advertising manager all had equal say in questions regarding the magazine.[190] To complicate things further, Edna Woolman Chase and Condé Nast frequently travelled overseas to reorganise, criticise and correct, a classic example of too many cooks in the kitchen. So when the orders were issued from New York to sack Dody, Harry Yoxall was deeply uncomfortable with the task. He wrote: 'Dismissing a colleague is never pleasant; dismissing an editor is grim. Particularly when you are scared of the lady.'[191]

Still more unluckily, this command came just as he was catching his breath following the General Strike of 1926, which lasted from 4 to 12 May. Of all the difficulties he faced in the 1920s, Yoxall thought the strike 'not so bad',[192] which, considering the entire nation's industry from transportation to food production was at a paralysing standstill, goes a long way to show the extent of what Yoxall's early career put him through. In any case, the resourceful Yoxall didn't miss any chances to promote his pretty fashion paper, political turmoil be damned. He'd sent the bulk of the mid-May *Vogue* issue ahead of time by railway freight, though he still wasn't sure the trains would be running well enough to distribute reliably. With this in mind, he took the precaution of having 7,000 copies delivered to the office, so that any member of staff with a car could sell them directly to newsagents.[193] He would start his day by picking up anyone who lived along the route from his house to *Vogue* HQ, then distribute parcels (as many as would fit in each vehicle) and assign each person to an area of London or the Home Counties.[194] In the afternoon there would be emergency meetings with their trade association, then back to the office to tally that day's sales.[195] He'd spend the evenings trying to get hold of old friends who might have access to a bus or – if his keenest prayers were answered – a locomotive and who might then be able to help transport *Vogue* deeper into the provinces.[196]

The General Strike was really a dispute between the British government and trade unions, but it affected the publishing industry when the printers of the *Daily Mail* refused to produce an issue criticising a trade unionist.[197] With papers not going to press and no way of getting copies across the country without transport anyway, the media fell silent. In the days before the internet this left people completely disconnected. Yoxall, while flogging his wares at Penge station, was surprised to get an order of twenty-six copies of *Vogue* when the usual order was four. He asked the bookstall manager if he was sure he'd be able to sell them, to which the bookstall manager replied, 'Lor' bless you, they'll read anything now they haven't got the newspapers.'[198] The government, in an attempt to bridge the gap in the news cycle, conceived and launched the *British Gazette* in just a couple of days.[199] It hoped to use this poor excuse for journalism to control the message reaching the public. Yoxall dealt with this latest development with his usual aplomb: 'I used this propaganda sheet very suitably, for blackmail purposes. I picked up copies at the old *Morning Post* building where it was printed, carried them around in my car, and refused to sell them to newsagents unless they took an equal quantity of *Vogue*.'[200]

Although the strike only lasted nine days, returning everything to its previous order took months. At least one issue of *Vogue*, meticulously put together, had to be discarded because of printers and missed deadlines.[201] Advertising and circulation had declined, just as they'd been expecting an improvement. After the departure of Dody, Yoxall was effectively in charge of editing British *Vogue* as well, along with all his other impossible duties and even had to take over writing reviews when a handful of journalists walked out.[202]

This one-man-band situation lasted at least six gruelling months, after which an interim editor (the French Michel de Brunhoff) appeared and Yoxall could return to agonising over his – and his American bosses' – main problem: increasing circulation. His dedication to the job is astounding. Throughout spring and autumn he would take five-day tours across the country, from Yorkshire's industrial towns to Sherwood Forest, from Birmingham to grim outposts of Manchester, canvassing for sales with every single newsagent he could find. *Vogue* did not have the money to hire travelling salesmen for this back-breaking task, nor did Yoxall trust anyone else with the precarious business. The days were long, starting around 5 a.m. and finishing only after 8 p.m.[203] In one week his diary showed he'd driven some 400 miles and made 129 stops.[204] On Saturdays, he would try to catch up on office admin.[205] He kept this up well into the 1930s.

Yoxall's experience roving around the greying, subdued island, bartering with working-class shop-owners is worlds apart from the perceived life of a *Vogue* employee. And had he been a lady editor rather than the business manager, it might have turned out quite differently. The British imprint of *Vogue* was still a source of anxiety for Woolman Chase and the Dody debacle had made her even more domineering. She needed a well-behaved English ambassador. The woman she hired was drafted into *Vogue* in 1926, but her name does not appear on all mastheads until 1929, suggesting that she was probably shadowing Woolman Chase and learning the ropes in New York, as was customary for foreign editors. Woolman Chase was also spending long periods of time at the British office, trying to help weather the storm.[206]

The ornamental appellation Alison Violet de Froideville seems just perfect for an editor of *Vogue*, but it ill-suited the pragmatic woman behind it. Its Frenchified feel and aristocratic intonations were inherited from her father, though Alison was a girl raised in strained circumstances, winning a scholarship to Oxford which she couldn't afford to take up and who ultimately took a secretarial course in lieu of a full education. Her true origins were as modestly middle class as Edna Woolman Chase's and Condé Nast's. As such, her married name of 'Settle' seems more appropriate. Yet once settled, she was unsettled soon enough. Her barrister husband contracted tuberculosis and died in 1925, leaving Settle with two young children to support. During his illness she had already become the main breadwinner and had built up a solid reputation as a newspaper journalist.

Working on papers required a keen eye and a lot of get-up-and-go, especially since female journalists were still something of a novelty.[207] When Alison Settle officially became the editor of British *Vogue*, a different set of behaviours were expected of her, to be fulfilled with the same zeal and commitment of Woolman Chase in New York. Much of British *Vogue* was ready-made. The covers were sent over from the office in the States. Most of the written content featured stories identical to the American edition: a blend of English aristocrats and American movie stars. The best fashion illustration and photography – still a new phenomenon – was emerging from their Paris studio and supplying all magazines under Condé Nast Publications. Little in the British edition was homegrown. What *Vogue* needed Settle to do was represent the brand.

The diaries she kept during the second half of her tenure are chock-a-block with names, meetings, travel plans and shows, with little or no indication of her own feelings. It reads like an endless, mind-numbing merry-go-round, her editorial role mostly requiring her to dine whatever fashionable artist or writer was in the city that day. Much about how *Vogue* micro-managed Settle's life can be seen in extracts from her journal. In December 1930, for example, she was required to journey to France for a business trip, despite being in recovery from a recent operation. Her notes reveal an endless string of social engagements, jumping in and out of Rolls-Royces and first-class train carriages while drinking champagne cocktails and trying to numb herself with pills. The pain becomes so intense that she writes no medication helped and at times she was on the verge of blacking out between dress shows and sports clubs.[208] The only result of this intense personal agony was a fluffy article titled

'The Chic Woman's Day on the Riviera', which omitted any record of physical discomfort but included a photo of guests at Lady Dunn's villa on Cap Ferrat.[209]

Woolman Chase also pressured Settle to maintain close relationships with fashion industry insiders and attend frequent parties. She was told it was her 'duty' to become good friends with Helena Rubinstein, because she took out double-page adverts for her beauty brand.[210] When Woolman Chase found out Settle lived in Hampstead with her family and came to work by tube, she put her foot down here too. In one of her more draconian moments, Woolman Chase said Hampstead was essentially vulgar and Settle was forbidden from living there.[211] Settle went on to elaborate in a later interview that Woolman Chase insisted she live in a flat with a uniformed porter and a lift,[212] but when Settle moved to a flat she hated in Mayfair to make Woolman Chase happy, on her next visit to London Woolman Chase found this flat wasn't good enough either and ordered her to move yet again. In her own private accounts, as she prepared to leave her children behind in Hampstead, she wrote with uncharacteristic anguish of how she couldn't bear to leave her home, where her husband had died, her children had been born and where she'd been so happy.[213]

Like a member of the royal family, Settle had to cultivate her public persona and become a legitimate figurehead for the thousands of readers who devoured *Vogue* magazine. She had to be a convincing face for the investment of advertising money as well as an encyclopedia of the best in everything, seeing as it was *Vogue*'s job to inform the entitled readership. Although she respected Woolman Chase, she clearly struggled with the *Vogue* strictures and did occasionally lash out at the publication. Once she wrote, 'HOW LITTLE OUR AMERICAN BOSSES cared for the written word'[214] and years later, she reflected that *Vogue* was so snobby about money and status, it was more elitist than all British society magazines combined.[215] It annoyed her no end that Condé Nast and Edna Woolman Chase were indifferent to publishing literary prodigies like Virginia Woolf, but objected to minor changes in layout.[216] She would write to her daughter after leaving *Vogue*, stating that working for *The Observer* gave her a cleaner conscience, since the pursuit of new clothes and beauty seemed empty and futile. The demands of the ever-expanding colossus that was Condé Nast the company ground her down. When Settle left under a cloud in the mid-1930s, Edna Woolman Chase was fed up. Not trusting any more Englishwomen with the task, she sent over an experienced editor from her American office, Elizabeth Penrose, to head up Brogue.

The *Vogue* vice grip was experienced differently by business manager Harry Yoxall and editor Alison Settle. His was the impossible problem of explaining England's awful post-war economy to obliviously rich Americans. Hers was a stifling existence in a gilded cage. Either way, *Vogue* had them both.

Worse Times in New York

Meanwhile, the thirties in the American office were darkened by two blows that nearly brought *Vogue* to its knees: the Great Depression and the loss of sparky mentee Carmel Snow. These separate events had knock-on effects that would be felt for decades. The late 1920s and early 1930s were characterised by severe unemployment and economic instability, both in Britain and across Europe, a situation which eventually deepened into the global crisis now known as the Great Depression. The United States was also hit, but there was one key difference: they hadn't been expecting it. Edna Woolman Chase, ensconced in her elegant New York office, wrote disdainfully about

England's 'attitude of acquiescence',[217] claiming that 'If this happened to us we would not just lie on the floor, moaning and groaning, like the British: we would get up and DEAL with it'.[218] An awkward comment, since Condé Nast Publications *and* Condé Nast the man were hit with unspeakable damages in the Depression, while British *Vogue* began to recover and make a profit (albeit from sales of patterns not the magazine).[219] By 1933 they were truly prospering, something that must have been hard for the Americans considering what they were going through.

The historic facts are known to many. On Black Tuesday, 29 October 1929, the market lost $14 billion in a day, nearly five times more than the federal budget for a year. After the initial crash, a wave of suicides broke out in New York's financial district. Clerks in hotels started asking if guests wanted rooms for sleeping or jumping.[220] As the news spread a panicked public ran to drain their accounts of any savings, resulting in a total collapse of the banking system. In 1929, Condé Nast was in his mid-fifties and was listed in the *Social Register*, known by sight at the Ritz in London and in the salons of Paris. The 1920s for American *Vogue* had been record-breaking. The company earnings rose from $241,410 in 1923 to $1,425,076 in 1928.[221] In the time he had owned *Vogue* the circulation had risen by 121,930.[222] It also carried the most advertising pages of any magazine on the market. In 1928 *Vogue* had a total of 159,028 pages, while *Harper's Bazaar* only had 83,454.[223] In just the four years between 1924–8 the combined revenue of Condé Nast Publications increased a staggering 213 per cent.[224] It was a hell of a lot to lose.

Although Nast had never been a big speculator, he had been seduced by some Wall Street wizards and when the value of all his assets began plummeting, he realised he'd overstretched himself.[225] It was too late. Nast was forced to repeatedly seek loans to try to save his sinking ship and, unbelievable as it must have seemed to those who knew him, the signs were clear. The man was on the verge of bankruptcy. Ever pragmatic, Nast quietly went back to the office. According to a colleague: 'he just abandoned the *dolce vita* and returned to work.'[226] As soon as word got out, the vultures began to hover. All kinds of predatory capitalists gathered to see if they could rustle up the funds for a buyout.

Luckily, the changing fortunes of the British issue meant suddenly they were in a position to partially bail out the American arm. Yoxall would later boast that ever since then the British branch 'has never failed to show fine figures – in its accounts as well as in its beauty pages'.[227] When further funds were needed and no investors could be found in the USA, Nast had to turn to the UK for hope again. Just before his creditors ate him alive he was rescued by Lord Camrose, an English press baron. Leaving Nast with editorial control, Lord Camrose silently became the biggest shareholder, a fact kept secret, even on Fleet Street, in case it affected *Vogue*'s reputation. Although Camrose was cordial and eventually made a profit from this venture, he disdained the extravagance of American magazines.[228] The British press, though editorially inferior, made fat margins that converted to hard cash.[229] For Lord Camrose that was what counted. Terms invented later such as 'profitless prosperity' and 'deficient publishing' went drastically against Nast's personal outlook of 'you have to spend money to earn money', but nonetheless adequately sum up the fate of Nast's beloved company in this sorry chapter.[230]

The lightning had struck – but the thunder was still to come. Back in 1921, Edna Woolman Chase had hired Carmel Snow, a young Irish ingénue, to help her out as the company shot to new heights practically week on week. Snow had a sense of fun and a sense of fashion; a huge, clannish, dancing, drinking Irish family; and a cartload of ambition. As Woolman Chase's special favourite, she brought Snow into important meetings, trained her in both writing and styling, coached her on how to conduct meetings and how to write business letters.[231] Nobody was in any doubt that Snow was being groomed to take over when Woolman Chase retired and Condé Nast – who had been urging Woolman Chase to consider the issue of succession for some time – was more than pleased with this *Vogue*-bred beginner. But in 1929, one of Snow's beloved brothers, Tom White, landed himself a job as the general manager of the Hearst publishing organisation (still owners of rival *Harper's Bazaar*) and a red flag was raised in Nast's mind. He mentioned it to Woolman Chase and suggested to Snow that she sign a contract with *Vogue*.[232] Snow was outraged by the proposition and the matter was dropped. By now, Snow held the highest position in the American office – that of American editor. Although Woolman Chase was editor-in-chief, she was often abroad troubleshooting with the Parisian and London branches and so, to all intents and purposes, Snow ran the American edition. Along with all the other *Vogue*-ettes, Snow had pitched herself against *Harper's Bazaar* and, like everybody else, tried her best to outwit them. Nobody would have expected she was capable of switching sides.

Yet in 1932, in the black valley of the Great Depression, events took another unexpected turn. Nast had just begun to discuss a lifeline from Lord Camrose and was travelling to Europe to finalise the details. The day before he left he visited Carmel Snow in hospital, where she had just delivered her fourth baby. A few days later, Snow sent a message to Woolman Chase urging her to stop by the hospital immediately. Fearing something had happened to her right-hand woman or the newborn, Woolman Chase rushed over in a worry.[233] Mother and child were doing well, unlike Woolman Chase when Snow told her she was leaving to go to *Harper's Bazaar*. This act of betrayal upturned the American office once again, broke Nast's heart and hit pause on Woolman Chase's retirement plans. American

Vogue was in financial trouble already and now had to contend with the loss of its most important editorial staff member after Woolman Chase. Not only had Snow gone, but she took her entire department with her, as well as all the contacts and expertise carefully amassed over a decade at Woolman Chase's side. The intensity of Woolman Chase's distress at the defection is glaringly obvious in a reply she sent to Carmel Snow who had invited her for dinner after the lapse of several years:

> I wish I could accept, but the old relationship that existed between us was so made up of our long years of work and play together that when you threw that all aside in order to build up the property of the man who had been our meanest rival, you killed in my heart an affection and a faith that nothing but your own words could have ever destroyed.[234]

Since Woolman Chase couldn't bear to leave Nast to muddle through the nightmare alone, she put off her retirement for another twenty years and determined to see *Vogue* through the rough patch, come hell or high water.

CHAPTER 6

Frog

Launching the French Edition in the Fashion Capital

A Family Affair

Oh, the little *Parisienne*! How easy it is to imagine her. Sailor stripes and jaunty beret. The black bob popularised by Coco Chanel. That effortless French street style we catch glimpses of on the broad boulevards, once piloted by designers like Poiret and Patou. The *parisienne* is a cultural icon and she sits on fashion's historic throne. France.

As a fashion publishing magnate, Condé Nast wanted to align himself with its legacy. And as a man hellbent on acquiring assets, he knew gaining a foothold in Paris would be a strategic move, giving *Vogue* a new authority in the eyes of readers in Britain and America. A Parisian office would further consolidate their title-property rights, spread the name of *Vogue* and, crucially, allow staff to nurture relationships with leading designers on their own turf. Access to the seasonal shows was essential and having a list of trustworthy native speakers on Nast's payroll would be a huge help. Negotiating with designers was seldom easy and if blacklisted, *Vogue* risked having no content. A French version would also give

Vogue advantage over *Harper's Bazaar*. Further, Nast was keen to retain the Parisian fashion illustrators. A highly skilled, highly in-demand subset of artists, they were vital to the success of any fashion magazine and Nast didn't want to share the best ones with *Harper's*. He wanted to invade this new capital, harness the power of the *parisienne* ideal and control the influence French design had over stylish women worldwide. He wanted to establish a monopoly. The quicker the better.

With the fiasco of Brogue still fresh in her mind (the showdown with Dody yet to come, but the magazine set-up was a headache), Edna Woolman Chase heaved a sigh of exasperation when she heard Nast was expanding further.[235] She knew the greater part of the workload would be hers to shoulder. What she hadn't accounted for was the ingenuity of the French, who persuaded Nast to buy more magazines than he bargained for.

During WWI, Paris, like much of Europe, suffered a number of setbacks across many industries, including fashion. This meant that although an old reverence for French culture was still prevalent, New York design was thriving. America had the added benefit of a healthy economy and all the advantages of the machine age; already it was cultivating a mass market for clothing. If Paris wanted to stay in the game they had to keep control of haute couture and the couturiers worked hard to corner their niche. Paul Poiret was the first dressmaker to declare himself an artist, a radical move at the time, since designers were considered on a level with craftsmen or skilled tradesmen. To promote this angle Poiret teamed up with a well-known French publisher, Lucien Vogel, to create a hefty, exquisitely drawn, expensive magazine: *Gazette du Bon Ton*. The stunning journal was full of garments, intended to convince readers that fashion was more than mere fabric.

Vogel managed to persuade a group of draughtsmen to work for him, promising them a share of the profits if the magazine did well.[236] They were eight foppish boys of good families who had studied and grown up together . . . and they would become the first generation of truly accomplished fashion illustrators in Paris since before WWI.[237] They remained devoted to Vogel, who continued to mentor them for the rest of their careers. Nast got his hands on them by buying a controlling stake in *Gazette*, blocking Hearst again. This meant that when the war ended and American stock was high on the Continent, the best illustrators were at *Vogue*'s disposal thanks to Nast's association with Vogel. The time was ripe to launch a French edition of *Vogue*.

Appearing in 1920, it was nicknamed 'Frog' by the Americans to match the British Brogue. Even though they were in Paris surrounded by the best illustrators and designers, Woolman Chase, critical as ever, felt that the early efforts were messy and misguided, not quite up to scratch with the glossy manual she was putting out in NYC.[238] Though the real conflict at the start of French *Vogue* had little to do with the content.

Having so advantageously allied himself with Condé Nast, Vogel was keen to foist yet another title upon the American millionaire. For some years, Vogel and his wife Cossette had been editing a fashion supplement aimed at the middle class, *L'Illustration des Modes*. Woolman Chase wanted to poach Cossette Vogel and hire her as the first editor-in-chief of French *Vogue*[239], the well-connected, experienced Cossette was perfect, but she loved *L'Illustration des Modes*. She went so far as to travel to New York to pressure Nast into purchasing her supplement and ultimately succeeded in bulldozing Nast and Woolman Chase into complying with her plans.[240] Nast bought *L'Illustration*, renamed it *Jardin des Modes* and it continued to cater successfully to the mid-income readers that *Vogue* considered itself above. In the end, Cossette Vogel accepted the post as first editor-in-chief of French *Vogue*, running it alongside the Vogel–Nast magazines, with help from members of her family.

Cossette Vogel's supplement steadily made money for Nast which French *Vogue* would proceed to lose. The standard *Vogue* model, which relied on advertising, was not much use in France since dressmakers preferred to advertise their wares directly. They would pick a socialite or aristocrat who was well known in the chichi circles of Paris and turn her into their muse.[241] This way designers could ensure their clothes were being seen at the right events, while the fashion ambassadors could be extremely well dressed for a discount.

During the twenties, when revenue was flowing from other magazines, the great losses sustained by French *Vogue* seemed irrelevant. But as the Vogels got busier and busier working for Nast's other French interests, Cossette could no longer manage all her duties and another editor-in-chief had to be found for French *Vogue*. They summoned Michel de Brunhoff back across the Channel to replace her in 1929.[242]

Editors, Artists, Photographers, Models

For an early picture of Frog, we must defer to Bettina Ballard, an American staffer sent to France in 1935. Raised in California, Ballard had studied in Paris and acquired a fluency in French that made her stand out. Since Woolman Chase wanted to recall some staff from Paris but didn't want to leave too broad a gap in her ranks, she shipped over the only bilingual candidate from the USA – choosing to overlook the fact that Ballard was young and had only been at *Vogue* about a year.[243] During the glory days it had become customary for staff to swap jobs or hop from one country to another. This was partly because *Vogue* was keen to accommodate its prize photographers, illustrators and editors, and partly because it saved them from having to train up new staff. These measures also discouraged senior and junior staff alike from defecting to *Harper's Bazaar*.

Ballard experienced something of a culture shock at French *Vogue*. Instead of the camaraderie she'd witnessed at the American headquarters, the Paris office yielded no friendships and had 'none of the warm Condé Nast family feeling'.[244] Interwar France was beset with economic uncertainties and political allegiances swung from left to right, making for a downbeat atmosphere. The café society which had flourished in the 1920s waned in the 1930s, as the Great Depression awoke everyone from *les années folles*.[245] It also deterred the students and tourists who had joyfully crowded the city from spending freely.[246]

Then there were matters of a more local nature. For the French there was their way of life which they took very seriously. Ballard notes that although her colleagues were perfectly polite, no one so much as asked her a thing about herself.[247] Mustering up the courage to invite one of the editors to eat with her one day, the reply came, 'I always lunch at home. We do not go to restaurants for lunch in France.'[248] A few months later, when she let slip to her manager that she ate her lunches at a workman's café, he was visibly shaken.[249] It was assumed all Parisians kept a live-in cook.

There were other minor mistakes which conspired to make Ballard feel an outsider. On arriving in an unfashionable ensemble on her first day of work she realised she could have done nothing worse to alienate her achingly chic co-workers.[250] Once a formidable French lady informed her that it was inappropriate to socialise with men unless they were lovers.[251] Society was so cliquey that the only invitations she received were from designers who'd already fallen out with everyone else at *Vogue* and wanted to bend her to their will. The net result was Ballard felt lonely right to her bones.[252]

But despite their differences, the staffers meant no harm and as Ballard settled in she was able to observe the habits of another *Vogue* and its people. Although after the elegant New York office Ballard felt the badly lit, dilapidated Parisian one, despite being on the Champs-Élysées, didn't match up.

The main room belonged to Michel de Brunhoff, the editor-in-chief. Bright-eyed and plump, de Brunhoff dressed in Savile Row tweeds and puffed a pipe, a hangover from his days in Britain.[253] Warm and charming, he had a natural gift for managing the capricious behaviour of his illustrators and photographers. He was extremely popular not just among his own, but throughout the whole industry. Part of what made de Brunhoff fun to work with was his liveliness. He had trained for the stage, but according to Woolman Chase he couldn't memorise a single line.[254] Nonetheless, his penchant for comedy routines and mimicry remained strong and employees could frequently find him and one of his dearest artists, Christian 'Bébé' Bérard, hamming it up in the office. They would do impersonations of their favourite designers or cast Bérard's little Maltese terrier, Jasmin, in the starring role of some silly drama, dressing her in the most outrageous designer hat available.[255] When amusing a crowd of colleagues without Bérard, de Brunhoff enacted silent films, playing all the roles himself and shivering the whole time to replicate the flickering of a bad-quality screening.[256]

The second room in the building officially belonged to American *Vogue*, who had their own separate staff creating and sending pages to the USA with the help of a French editor. These English speakers seldom interacted with their Gallic counterparts. It was the third room that housed the shining wonder of French *Vogue*, Michel de

Brunhoff's right hand and one of the rarest pearls of Condé Nast Publications.

Duchesse Solange d'Ayen had been discovered in the late 1920s and turned into a fashion editor. Her peerage came from her husband, whose family were one of the oldest in France and whose château was built by King Louis XIV. A delicate woman, Duchesse d'Ayen provoked as much delight and devotion as de Brunhoff. Woolman Chase, whose praise was generally thin on the ground, had her as 'charming'.[257] Bettina Ballard called her 'exciting' and 'enchanting'.[258] Condé Nast probably hit close to the mark when he said, 'Everyone I see who knows her, gives her the most extravagant praise for her charming personality and her intelligence. Much of this may be due to the fact that she is pretty and a duchess!'[259]

The final of the four rooms was presided over by the manager, Iva Patcévitch, who had married a British *Vogue* fashion editor. They made another cuttingly graceful pair until his wife quit the magazine when she contracted typhoid. Only Patcévitch's secretary was an outlier. An unpleasant, portly Frenchwoman, described as having a particularly sour smell and funereal air, her moody clopping through the halls as she turned off lights to scrimp on bills actually ended up boosting office morale – an active dislike of her created solidarity among everyone else.[260]

As usual, Edna Woolman Chase was not impressed by foreign working practices and the Parisian delegation suffered her interference just as everyone else had to. Their timetable made no sense to her. The French editors wouldn't return from lunch until at least 4 p.m. and would only truly get stuck in at around 5 p.m.[261] De Brunhoff was notorious for staying until the small hours, coaxing drawings out of some illustrator or sketching through endless pages on his own desk. He had a tortuous way of editing: he could only get his ideas out and down via a pencil and would constantly cover huge layout sheets with plans of what would go in the next issue, drafting and redrafting as everyone chattered incessantly. He relished an environment of deep confusion, intensified by having loads of people milling around, debating heatedly over pictures and words, waving paper about.[262] De Brunhoff's late-night sessions were fuelled by taking a suggestion from an editor and turning it into a 'big visual production'[263] on the spot. None of this suited the meticulous Woolman Chase. Throughout the twenties she had been greatly occupied with the British and French offices, which she was constantly trying to bring in line with her American model. And while Woolman Chase liked Paris better than she liked London, her struggles against Parisian procedure were even more futile than her efforts in the UK. She would insist on scheduled editorial meetings, forcing de Brunhoff to 'write things down in the cramped little spaces of a plan sheet with an unhappy, stubborn defiance on his face'.[264] But before even one issue was fully finished these careful ideas would fall apart and the scatty midnight meetings would be resumed.

Another French custom which drove Woolman Chase mad was their reverence towards designers. In her opinion the staff overvalued ateliers and were too attentive to the whims of precocious couturiers. The tantrums of Chanel, the threats of Mainbocher, the impossible paranoia of Vionnet, these were expected, and even respected, in Paris. Woolman Chase in New York, however, felt pandering to these artistic temperaments was getting in the way of her employees doing their jobs. The purpose of fashion magazines has generally been to report on fashion, not to criticise it, and *Vogue* in particular always went to extraordinary lengths to support the industry. Her view was: 'In the end we cease to be editors and are just shoved about by all these conflicting interests and our entire life is spent in trying to reconcile other people's wishes. I am rebelling definitely against this . . . I intend to edit this magazine for the best interest of the reader.'[265]

It was true that finessing designers took up a lot of time at French *Vogue*. Overly sensitive, they hated having their models placed on a page facing another designer's. They also objected to having outfits included in editorial which they weren't ready to show to the public. They were extremely wary of having their work copied and mass-produced by buyers. Some had ongoing feuds with certain photographers, whom they didn't want anywhere near their clothes. If the designers were unhappy enough, *Vogue* editors could expect to be banned from shows or locked out of *maisons* by intimidating managers.

The designers alarmed de Brunhoff, who preferred to leave them to Duchesse d'Ayen or some other editor. His own efforts were concentrated on another group of difficult personalities: the artists. De Brunhoff managed to sweet-talk celebrated creators like Dalí, Vertès and Cocteau into contributing – a real win for a fashion journal. He also mentored hopeful illustrators in a manner similar to the way Dorothy Todd had promoted budding writers in London, but the talent which gathered around his doors was considerably wilder, weirder and trickier to manage than anyone Dody had had to deal with. André Durst was supposed to become a photographic marvel but was interrupted by WWII and eventually killed himself drinking whisky. An even bigger handful was the flamboyant, openly homosexual Bérard. Although his work was lively and beautiful when he was showing off, drawing on a tablecloth in an upmarket restaurant in front of admirers, it was agony getting him to produce anything relevant. Woolman Chase had another gripe: his sketches weren't realistic enough; women couldn't order clothes by looking at the pictures. On the other hand, she was too scared to fire him in case *Harper's Bazaar* snapped him up. In the end her competitive streak won out and Bérard was kept on.

The Duchesse d'Ayen used to describe her relationship with Bérard

as a sort of twisted love affair in which she would berate him and beg
him to produce results.[266] Bettina Ballard would spend days trying to
hunt him down to get the necessary drawings for their next deadline,
searching all over the city including his flat where he barely stayed,
the brothels in which he would sometimes hide, his beloved bistro,
theatre rehearsals and the boudoirs of famous harlots, where he could
occasionally be found trimming feathers for a fancy-dress ball.[267] His
style was to roll into the office at around 6 p.m. where de Brunhoff
would gently murmur into his ear, egging him on to do just a little
more, just a *little* more, while lighting Bérard's cigarettes and subtly
changing the model's pose.[268]

Bérard drew simultaneously with both hands and sweated pro-
fusely on to the pages (he would cover up drops of perspiration
by incorporating them into the painting, turning them into flower
buds or butterflies) and wipe his paintbrush in his own beard,
which was also full of spaghetti and little bugs.[269] Occasionally
he would pass out at parties during an opium high, though his
excesses extended to food and alcohol too, especially rich French
fare. On comedowns he would break into suicidal weeping fits
during which he would ride round and round in a taxi, disgusted with his own behaviour.[270] When his end came, many at
Vogue believed French society had a hand in it. On the one side
they adored him as a talent, on the other they judged him for
squandering this talent on commercial work with magazines. This
conflict tore him apart. Woolman Chase advanced an alternative
theory for his death, stating with black humour, that: 'Along with
the opium and liquor he'd go on bread binges . . . thrusting it down
his throat like a ravenous animal.'[271]

It did not end there. Photographers were prima donnas and mannequins caused endless trouble with the immensity of their egos. The
only difference between these two breeds of *Vogue* creatures and the

artists was that the former tended to remain locked up in the studio, not roaming freely through the streets.

The studio in Paris was exceptionally well equipped and everyone was very proud of it.[272] It was a vital link in the chain of the Condé Nast authority because it meant that the staff of Vogue could pool their contacts among dressmakers, milliners and managers to get their hands on the newest collections as quickly as possible. Once they had convinced boutiques to loan them items they could be quickly taken to the studio and photographed by the finest photographers available. Finally, the images would be edited and redistributed to whichever publications they were most suited to (including the American and British editions). This meant Vogue was providing the most up-to-date styles to their readers internationally due to the quick turnaround and had the most material to choose from by virtue of their strong relationships with the couture houses. The shadow of Condé Nast Publications was long and it fell across most of fashionable France.

The studio was tucked at the top of the Champs-Élysées building and presided over by the tiny, gold-toothed Madame Dilé.[273] During collection season the editors would be working at night photographing gowns, sensible suits and heapings of jewels. This had to be done in the evenings, after buyers had seen them and before they were needed back in salons to show clients the next morning. Things were still informal enough then for Vogue to borrow luxury wares without security; Ballard remembers casually dropping off bags of diamonds with a sleepy concierge at Cartier at 2 a.m.[274]

The comedies and tragedies played out at the studio dwarfed the productions of de Brunhoff and the white Maltese terrier back in the office. Ballard, who loved studio work, described how the models created an atmosphere of suspicion, rivalry and lethargy.[275] The air smelled like a gym, since deodorant hadn't yet been popularised and a horrible tension reigned . . . until someone's temper exploded.[276]

Several famous mannequins, most of them Russian or Swedish, emerged from French *Vogue*, their reputations made by photographers like Horst. Lude was the most well known – and the most terrifying. A Russian exile in Paris, she adored Horst and would smile for Madame Dilé, but otherwise she ruled the roost with a stony stare.[277] If she was forced into a dress she didn't want to pose in she would ruin the picture on purpose.[278] She went to extraordinary lengths to achieve perfection, going so far as to have part of her breasts and thighs cut away. The surgery went badly wrong and she could no longer wear low-cut pieces.[279]

Another superstar mannequin of Horst's was the Swedish Lisa Fonssagrives. When she wanted to wear something she would bat her eyelids and hold the editor's hand to her face, staring into their eyes pleadingly.[280] She erupted into a jealous fury only once, when she thought Horst was paying too much attention in a sitting to Inga Lindgren, another Swede, who had dashingly landed in Paris via parachute.[281] In 1938, Madame Muthe excited everyone by walking into the office out of the blue, cradling a stunning blonde newborn in her arms.[282] De Brunhoff burst into Ballard's rooms gabbling to come and see the 'Virgin Mary' and 'baby Jesus'. A few months later this infant lost his appeal by wetting himself copiously on a sample of Lanvin's evening wear.[283] Terrible things were to happen to some of these ravishing girls at the hands of the Gestapo during WWII.

Before WWII broke out, the mood at French *Vogue* was one of fun. Photographers were a nightmare, but kept everyone on their toes. Beaton was forever improvising, creating backdrops that could be by turn amusing or epic. He photographed models next to life-size sketches of the outfits they were wearing and juxtaposed haute couture with piles of rubble. Titled Frenchwomen, occasionally coaxed into posing by Duchesse d'Ayen, had the awkward tendency of walking out.[284] This uncertainty thrilled everyone and a sense of magic enveloped de Brunhoff, Ballard and the Duchesse d'Ayen, the trio who would stay throughout the night with a retoucher and a printer.[285] Eventually they would descend into an intimate friendliness that defied French convention, fostered over rushed twilight dinners and sleepy sunrise coffees. They were so busy conjuring beauty that they had not noticed the storm gathering in the countries around them.

CHAPTER 7

Fashion Is Indestructible

WWII

The War Is Announced

In the summer of 1939, Condé Nast tried to persuade his British managing director, Harry Yoxall, to move to New York.[286] He was keen to have this shrewd-minded ally at his side. As an Englishman, Yoxall didn't want to desert his compatriots in their hour of need; but as a father, he couldn't miss the opportunity of moving his children to safety in case the threatening war broke out in earnest. In the end he comfortably installed his family in the States before persuading Nast to let him return home. He sailed back to Europe the day after Germany invaded Poland on 1 September 1939.[287] Britain and France joined the fray just a couple of days later.

For the British this was especially grim. The country was scarred by reminders of the last war, by strikes and lingering poverty, as well as exhausted by the squabbling of their politicians. The incumbent editor, Elizabeth Penrose, wrote presciently to Woolman Chase five whole months before the declaration of war, reporting: 'Life in these parts is pretty hectic and there is scarcely time to do the absolute essentials . . . Even as I write this Hitler is screaming on the radio.'[288]

When the Germans made their move, Penrose urged management to send home any foreign staff for safety, including herself (Penrose was American-born). She then spent a sunny weekend in the countryside, just before catching her passage back to America, and there she heard the prime minister make his 'Britain is at war' speech over the radio.[289] Immediately after that she heard her first air-raid siren. She'd secured her return to the US not a moment too soon.

Harry Yoxall, uncontested hero and guardian angel of British *Vogue*, also believed WWII was inevitable months before the outbreak and he wanted to be prepared. He sat down and wrote precise individual instructions to every member of staff on what to do in case of emergency, addressing these in sealed envelopes.[290] He also removed the most recent monthly ledgers, office records, master cutouts for *Vogue* patterns and films of the cutting charts, storing them all safely in the cellar of his Richmond home.[291] He even had a war issue of *Vogue* made up and sent to the printers in advance.[292]

On 3 September 1939, Bettina Ballard received news of the war from her Paris bed where she was nursing a cold.[293] She listened to the declarations from the British prime minister and French president over the radio with inappropriate excitement. Despite the uncertainty, change was electric in the air. With the benefit of hindsight, the way the fashion world responded to the news seems baffling and astonishingly naïve. For the most part nobody had expected a war, especially not the Parisians who seemed to believe the Germans wouldn't dare attack their army. This egotism did not dissolve with mobilisation. Couture collections largely went on as normal and visiting *Vogue* staff, including Woolman Chase and Horst, attended the shows before making their leisurely way to a group holiday in Geneva.[294] Most of the staff of French *Vogue* were vacationing too – it was only later that the information sunk in. Tourists fought tooth and nail to win passage home and while Woolman Chase had an early ticket and made away in time, other American *Vogue* employees camped in makeshift quarters and bartered for places on boats.[295] Then transport stopped. Shop windows were papered over. Houses were shuttered. Men everywhere dragged their military uniforms out from under the mothballs. Many abandoned the city to hunker down in the country . . .

. . . And then they returned. The stars of café society were bored stiff without the gaiety of Paris. Soon, cosy little dinners by candle-light were popularised. Maxim's restaurant was reinvented as a sort of speakeasy, packed to the rafters with patrons again. From the moment Woolman Chase arrived back in New York she sent memos with questions about how the couturiers were dealing with war conditions and requests for stories on what the smart set wore to air-raid shelters.[296] The main fashion news was that wearing white accessories was suddenly 'in' because they made one glow seductively during a blackout. The activity Ballard describes reads unnervingly like a story of children playing war. Her output was full of gossipy memos, about luxury private shelters built by celebrities, descriptions of elegant travellers suffering on slow trains and the chic air-raid costumes designed by Edward Molyneux. She even documented how Parisians stopped wearing hats for a couple of weeks, until Madame Suzy the milliner rushed back to create a special wartime number.[297]

The difference in attitude between Britain and France is glaring. While the London staff wrote: 'We . . . feel the real pinch and fear of the war',[298] the society reporter in Paris said: 'Here we are, living at the Ritz, and keeping Versailles open for the weekends.'[299] Other accounts continue the absurd frivolity. Hermès made exqui-site leather cases for gas masks. Rumours were spread that women weren't in uniform because nobody could decide on the design.[300] Men trickled back into the city on various kinds of trumped-up leave, though *Vogue* staffers tried to take their leave during the collections so they could help out at the magazine when most needed. Ballard dismissed all of this as the 'sit-down war' and by December vanished to the Alps on a skiing holiday.[301] The winter collections went on as normal, with only a few couturiers absent, mostly those who felt they were likely to be directly targeted by Nazis. The familiar French cynicism reigned and everyone was bored to sobs, until the Germans moved in, easy as anything, in 1940.

British Stoicism During the Blitz

Now that there was officially a war on, managing director Harry Yoxall's experience would not differ so vastly from the editor's. Especially since they were sharing an office. Yoxall would no longer be careening across the valleys and hillocks of England, towing boxes of magazines. The editor would no longer be dabbing her lipstick in the powder room of Claridge's, following a luncheon with Cecil Beaton or Elizabeth Arden. *Vogue*'s London headquarters was blasted to bits, though as Yoxall comments, everyone's was.[302] A particularly terrible fire-raid took place in London in 1941. Yoxall had been on patrol duty elsewhere until 6.30 a.m. but as he got home, the company secretary called. Hearing there'd been bombings, he went all the way to the city to check on his workplace – and it did not look good.[303] Yoxall got as close as he could to the fires in Fleet Street. Ducking down lanes and alleys to avoid flying manhole covers (they were getting shot through the air with the impact of the explosions and hitting firemen with such force they broke bones), he made it to *Vogue*'s edifice with gritted teeth.[304]

There he found floors had collapsed, the walls bulged. He left the simmering remains to seek out the wardens of *Vogue* HQ, thankfully uninjured, who told him the sprinklers inside had been keeping their papers safe until an unexpected second volley had ripped through the water mains.[305] They had lost not just bricks and mortar, but 450,000 patterns and 400,000 magazines.[306] A priceless archive, produced over decades. They'd also lost all the ledgers except the most recent ones removed by Yoxall, together with the list of their subscribers.

The resourceful Yoxall rounded up some factory staff and sent them to his house in Richmond, where the equipment and cutting charts were stored, with orders to set up a work station in his basement to enable the production of small batches of *Vogue* patterns.[307] Business was business. The only other salvageable piece of *Vogue* property, found sad and squashed under some hot rubble, was Ginger the tomcat, official *Vogue* mouser.[308] Everybody was very pleased to dig Ginger out of the remains, but the feline himself must have felt this incident put him at risk beyond his professional obligations. Following the trauma he defected to a nearby milk shop and refused to visit the magazine again.

The attack on Britain had barely been raging three weeks when British *Vogue* needed another editor. Elizabeth Penrose had gone home. Others had joined volunteering organisations or were conscripted. Audrey Withers became editor when one after another her colleagues disappeared until she was asked to take up the post because, as Yoxall pointed out, there was no one left.[309] Withers was in her mid-thirties when this mighty task landed on her shoulders and had been an employee for nearly a decade. Once again, *Vogue* had stumbled upon a perfect leader, cool-headed and ingenious, to sail them through a tempest.

Brought up in the English countryside, Withers was part of a bookish household. Her parents cultivated their daughter's intellectual tastes rather than extravagant ones. A committed letter writer and retired doctor, her father corresponded with the likes of A. E. Housman and later in life Withers would recall the family spring-cleaning rituals, in which every one of the 3,000 books in their library would be dusted.[310] After boarding school and a degree in PPE at Oxford, she moved to London and found herself a job in a bookshop, while harbouring dreams of working in publishing.[311] Matters did not progress smoothly. The city she'd come to was the one crippled by WWI in the midst of the slump and Withers was made redundant time and time again. Months of fruitless searching for employment wore her down – she would compare the pain of unemployment to the death of a loved one.[312] Her luck finally turned when she answered an ad for a subeditor role on *Vogue* with a wage of £3 a week.

On 1 December 1940, the American edition published an article titled 'British Vogue Weathers the Storm'. The piece is credited to Withers and paints such a nuanced and poignant portrait of the British experience that it still hits home. From her light and elegant opening sentence: 'Bringing out a luxury magazine in a *Blitzkrieg* is rather like dressing for dinner in the jungle',[313] to the ominous sub-headings such as: 'The Problem of Time-Bombs', Withers covers a great deal of ground. We learn that models were hard to find because their husbands or fiancés on the frontline would urge them to evacuate to the countryside. We read that in the countryside desensitised villagers, many disfigured by shrapnel wounds, spent their Sundays lying on their backs in the fields watching hundreds of German planes passing overhead – it was their only entertainment. She describes London buildings constantly bursting into flames and how each department at *Vogue* had to keep a suitcase ready by their desk. These were not for spare clothes or a toothbrush, but for essential documents – for art directors the layouts, for editors the copy – which they would grab, pack up and flee into the street with as soon as signals sounded, tottering it along to wherever would be deemed 'safe'. There, the suitcase would be cracked open, so that not a second of working time was lost.

It's hard to imagine the matronly Audrey Withers, in blazer and low-heeled brogues, marching her skeleton staff down to their air-raid shelter. And yet, they adapted to life in the middle of open warfare. The scramble to get down to the cellar after sirens sounded took ages; until Withers got a new system in place. Roof-spotters were employed to alert them moments before guns would open fire, meaning the *Vogue* troupe wouldn't waste time abandoning their desks too early. By the end Withers was so complacent that she would stay in her office, simply popping on her gas mask and letting the deafening shells drop around her, blowing the glass out of the windows as she kept writing.

Being in the basement was no excuse to stop working. Having scuttled down the six flights of stone stairs carrying everything from notepaper to raw photographs, shovels to sandwiches, the staff would settle on fold-out chairs and start dictating letters. Secretaries would hammer away on typewriters balanced dangerously on their knees. Even fashion shoots would take place underground. At night, all *Vogue* material would be put to bed, carried down to the shelter in a laundry basket. The action-packed programme involved nonstop noise and movement; bombs hurtling down, while debris bounced upwards from the impact, making entire streets tremble. Every so often a house would crumble into nothing. The staff were naturally depleted. Some had died, some had disappeared. Several had been injured by flying bits of glass or explosives.

The famous British 'keep calm and carry on' attitude shines through. Withers' article is flanked with photos that are both comical and heartbreaking. One shows Harry Yoxall, neatly attired in a suit and posing mid-phone conversation in his grandiose office, his desk and floor littered with thick slabs of glass from bombed windows.[314] Another image shows the staff with their chairs pulled into a circle like schoolchildren, holding an editorial meeting with a pickaxe beside them, ready to dig their way out in case the air-raid shelter caved in.[315] They were constantly frustrated by a shortage of gas (the kettle wouldn't always boil and they missed having their tea) and foiled in their travel plans (every day the commute would be disrupted, meaning that journeys of thirty minutes might go on for hours and involve strings of changes, to say nothing of the fact that they might as easily be killed en route to work as get there alive).

One of Withers' problems was finding enough material to put in the magazine and, surprising as it seems, a couple of pretty fashion editors in heels and hats would be sent roaming through the ruins of London looking for luxury items to photograph. Shopkeepers were consistently hit by bombs, losing their windows as soon as they got put in, along with any displays and often their stock. Withers outlines how innovative dressmakers would find new ways of showing their merchandise. Some used darkened windows, some reinforced the panels with wood and put smaller items for display in each new square. John Lewis reopened with almost nothing to sell after being completely gutted. Many independent designers transplanted to rural areas and continued churning out garments in the back rooms of cottages and stately homes.

If gathering content was a literal minefield, so was finding the people to arrange it and the resources to complete it. The photographic studio had been both flooded and burned. There was not enough energy to keep the lights on or to dry the prints and few of the staff had any idea of how to develop film roll, since most photographers had been packed off to fight. Same happened with artists – even the women. One regular used to sit on the stairs for safety, knocking out drawings in between her long hours training to become a nurse, only to be called up for service. And after all of this there was the battle at the printers and engravers; delays in transport, post and distribution; the chronic dislocation of businesses and the collapse of their powerful network of contacts. The magazine carried a little disclaimer during the war years: 'The war is taxing the nation's transportation facilities to the limit, and there will undoubtedly be delays in the delivery of your copies of Vogue. We regret the inconvenience to you, but this is a matter entirely beyond our control.'[316] Each issue was a deathly struggle between the determination of Audrey Withers and the forces of destiny. Withers tended to win.

Exactly what motivated everyone in this herculean effort is another question entirely. Harry Yoxall, by now managing director, claimed he was overly conscientious by nature.[317] He also tended to downplay the gravity of situations. His famous nonchalance endured throughout WWII. He observed dismissively that bomb stories had become boring, although he does bother to describe the Great Fire of Richmond in 1940, during which there were at least twenty-seven major fires in the borough in one night.[318] The trembling earth beneath them, the molten explosives raining out of the darkness . . . none of this stopped Yoxall from climbing through a hatch on to his roof and trying to put out the blaze on his own property, all while making jokes at his wife's expense. Recently returned from America, she still changed into evening dress for dinner and kept spilling water down her cleavage every time she handed Yoxall freshly filled buckets to douse the flames with.[319]

The courage and manic hard work of Audrey Withers and her staff were in keeping with the overall national mood. The British public were caught in a kind of noble fever, obsessed with ideals of being productive and invincible. Everybody wanted to do their bit and the staff must have felt that continuing to produce Vogue was their way of contributing to the effort.

But personal circumstances aside, they also couldn't escape the

influence of politics. The problem of rationing had affected the publishing industry immediately; papers were limited to 60 per cent of
their pre-war production.[320] This huge change forced publications
to slash their page numbers and cram information into tiny spaces.
Art departments needed to rethink design, while editors readdressed
word count. Withers was not afraid of radical decisions. Since paper
was now a high-value commodity, even scarcer than sugar, she
pulped the *Vogue* archive to keep them going – resulting in further
losses of records and historical material. Rationing became so severe
that a subscriber had to die before a new one could sign on.

Austerity also affected fashion itself. The Utility Clothing Scheme
was introduced at the end of 1941 to reduce waste and decrease
the use of raw materials such as wool and leather. Less fabric saw a
lighter, freer silhouette emerge, which Withers found invigorating.
She claimed the scheme did an enormous service for British fashion,
which she felt benefitted from the forced simplicity.[321] Other regulations, such as a ban on heels over two inches high, meant dressing
showily soon became a mark of bad taste. Dark colours were encouraged, as they represented mourning and were low maintenance.

British *Vogue* was not just on the receiving end of new restrictions.
The Ministry of Information had been set up within hours of the
outbreak of war to monitor and manage public opinion, domestic
propaganda and censorship. Initially they were hampered by a lack
of leadership, but when Brendan Bracken was appointed Minister
of Information in 1941, things turned around. Bracken, a personal
friend of Winston Churchill and a prominent newspaper publisher,
was quick to identify the importance of women's magazines in
shaping the nation's outlook. This becomes doubly important when
one remembers that the nation *was* women, since the men were
off fighting. Fashion papers and other ladies' press acquired a new
importance.

Vogue did not escape Bracken's attention, so Withers and editors from other popular media were invited to briefings when information on subjects ranging from health, to food, to clothing needed to be put across. Withers was among those summoned to help in a government campaign for shorter hair.[322] With women taking up factory work, hair was being caught in machinery and there was a surge in scalping incidents. Would *Vogue* be able to make short hair chic? Withers thought they could, so they ran a piece showing film actresses and a prominent TV presenter with neatly trimmed heads, proving that stars and working women alike could sport cropped hairdos.[323]

Although there was a distinct slant towards the practical, women were still pressured to look good. Maintaining one's looks was a way to give Hitler the finger by proving the people weren't beaten, as well as giving the boys overseas something to fight for. Red lipstick was a fast favourite and came to symbolise a solidarity among women literally 'putting on a brave face'. Although many used beetroots to stain their lips because of shortages, famous brands released new shades with wartime names to tempt their customers: Helena Rubinstein's 'Regimental Red', Elizabeth Arden's 'Victory Red'. The message of 'beauty is your duty'[324] was touted in British *Vogue* from the early 1940s. In 1942 American *Vogue* published a letter from a soldier who wrote, 'To look unattractive these days is downright morale-breaking and should be considered treason'.[325]

The first cover of British *Vogue* after the declaration of war in September 1939 featured a gold royal coat of arms, with the lettering and background in the red, white and navy of the Union Jack. In this issue, *Vogue* promised to be 'practical and useful' by helping their audience economise 'in dress and personal grooming, household management, cooking and gardening'.[326] It points out that this follows the government's wish that business ought to carry on where possible. And, it noted, it would still be *Vogue*. In their own words: 'charming and civilized, a tonic to the spirit – more indispensable than ever.'[327]

As the war wore on, deprivations only grew. It was increasingly difficult for both *Vogue* and the government to say 'keep your chin up' to the suffering millions. By 1942, the idea of 'beauty is your duty' had morphed from a courageous effort to a bedraggled state of just-get-by. 'Make Do and Mend' had arrived. The powers in parliament were hoping this increased focus on domestic tasks and the creation of new chores would keep the disheartened populace busy. Several *Vogue* pattern book covers reference the Make Do and Mend movement, promoting frugality amid harsh rationing. An illustration in March 1942 shows no models, featuring instead the instruments used to assemble clothing.[328] *Vogue*'s intention is obviously to glorify sewing tools, presenting them to readers as noble, worthy and fierce – a woman's natural weapon in war.

In a May 1942 issue, a feature titled 'General Economy Issues his Orders of the Day'[329] was published, following the adventures of a cartoony soldier character, the 'General', who wears fabric ends and a folded newspaper hat to symbolise the 'Economy' in his name. Among his orders are: 'Saving every page of every paper for re-pulping. Using every scrap of mending thread . . . Knowing that our strength depends on our thrift.'[330] A 1943 cover shows a photograph of an elegant woman with a hat seductively pulled down over her eyes.[331] The text advertises coupons alongside style advice.

In these fine-minded actions *Vogue* led by example. Apart from pulping their own archive, fashion photographer turned official war photographer Cecil Beaton sacrificed an immense portfolio of works for pulping. In an article called 'The Stuff of Vogue' a collage of his old photographs is published – great beauties, society darlings, even royals – all of which he was destroying for the war effort.[332]

Somewhere on the horizon there was the promise of new hope, the possibility that they would go on to become pages on which a future *Vogue* might be printed. Now the physical magazine would have as short a lifetime as the fashions it featured.

What we now call 'recycling' was, in the 1940s, known as 'salvaging', implying a hardship and redemption appropriate for war. The high morals suited *Vogue* as much as anything else – their job was, and still is, to present fetishised items. These could be handbags and hats, or these could be values such as honour, love and loyalty. Anything can be given the glossy treatment. Through this approach Withers was able to promote cheap outfits accommodating textile restrictions, low-budget living and quick fixes for household problems – all in the name of the nation. Never before had *Vogue* been able to promote spending a little rather than a lot.

Saving French *Vogue* from the Nazis

Across the Channel, the Nazi occupation of France had revived the German's long-held desire to supplant Paris as the centre of fashion. During WWI they had plagiarised French fashion magazines, publishing them in Vienna and distributing them in Europe, hoping the readers wouldn't notice they now featured subpar German design in place of Parisian couture. Their other big idea was to relocate couture business by simply lifting all of the designers, as well as their employees, suppliers, tradesmen, etc. and physically moving them to Berlin. Luckily, French couture, represented by Lucien Lelong, managed to hold the Germans off by arguing quite logically that the industry would be disrupted if transferred.[333]

While they eased off the ateliers, the pressure on publishing, however, remained intense. The Nazis saw the media as a way to proliferate their propaganda to womenfolk. Newly launched enemy magazines penned smug articles about fashion's bright future in Greater Germany, claiming the Parisian legacy had been squashed.[334] Soon they were limiting the number of French fashion magazines allowed to operate. Their handling of the press was cold and systematic, calculated to permeate civilian minds. For Michel de Brunhoff and the French *Vogue* cadre it was time to show everyone what they were made of.

Safe in New York, Condé Nast had the foresight to send de Brunhoff a telegram. It ran: 'We are about to be cut off from each other. I know you will have to make vital decisions. This is to tell you that I approve in advance every decision that you will make in the name of Condé Nast Publications.'[335] During the mass exodus from Paris as the Germans invaded in 1939, society columnist Johnnie McMullin reported: 'Biarritz at this moment is a unique sight in the world today . . . *All* the rich people of Europe are here.'[336] But as McMullin gushed about the fleeing aristocracy, Tommy Kernan, an American who had recently taken over the manager role in France, quietly slipped away. He was fleeing the city with the *Vogue* ledgers and the liquid cash of Les Éditions Condé Nast.[337]

During the night, to ensure the documents' safety, he slept in a field with the cash underneath him. He was aiming for Bordeaux, on the outskirts of which an abandoned château had been hired ahead of impending disaster.[338] Approximately forty people connected with *Vogue* used the place as a refuge until they could return to their homes in Paris or abroad.[339] De Brunhoff with his wife and three children were there, as were the Vogels, for whom concern was great. Lucien Vogel has been an outspoken campaigner against Hitler. After a long and frantic night spent urging them to run for their lives, the Vogels made their escape just before the Nazis showed up at the castle gates.

The Nazis had come to take over the château, wanting to use it for themselves. Using his most charming manners de Brunhoff managed to persuade them to move on by emphasising the lack of furniture at the castle, which meant they'd have to sleep on straw palettes.[340] It was his first big coup because the Nazis left everyone alive. When de Brunhoff returned to Paris, the Germans hauled him in to talk magazines. They were preparing to shut most of them, leaving only a couple of the luxury journals and a few mass-market titles. Both de Brunhoff's babies – French *Vogue* and *Jardin des Modes* – were on a list that saved them from being discontinued.[341] His joy did not last: the Germans wanted these publications to enter a pool of regulated papers which meant de Brunhoff's editorial choices would be forcefully dictated to him. Instead of claiming the control Nast had authorised in his telegram, de Brunhoff told the enemy officers that he couldn't legally assume responsibility on behalf of the proprietors in America.

The Germans kept pestering de Brunhoff, showing up at least another three times to try and encourage him to relaunch *Vogue*, going so far as to bribe him with a share of the profits or a juicy salary.[342] They recognised de Brunhoff's editing experience and his long friendships with many couturiers as skills they couldn't replace. In the end, de Brunhoff checked himself into a hospital with fake symptoms to avoid their increasing harassment. He would laugh later that the Nazis had often leaned on a false wall in his office on their visits, but never discovered the salvaged *Vogue* paperwork he'd secreted there.[343] Tommy Kernan was holding up with equal determination. When he returned from the mission to Bordeaux to their headquarters on the Champs-Élysées, he found the rooms had been raided, the safe blown open, the desks turned upside down.[344] Presumably the Germans had been looking for the missing files which Kernan and de Brunhoff were hiding. Though this wily pair succeeded in concealing *Vogue* records, the high-tech photographic studio had been seized. The Germans were using *Vogue* equipment to shoot propaganda, and Kernan wasn't allowed in.[345]

French *Vogue* was owned by an American corporation but published in France as a separate French entity. This fiddly business structure was both a blessing and a curse. Kernan figured the Germans didn't care whether they were stealing an American or a French paper – it was all wartime plunder to them – but if he could stop them taking control of French *Vogue* by making use of this confusing detail, then he would. He was concerned the next German tactic would be to claim the magazine was abandoned property and start reprinting it themselves. Kernan and de Brunhoff conferred and decided the best thing to do was to try and restart the magazine, or at least pretend to do so.[346] This would halt the charge of abandonment and keep at least some of their former employees from starving.

Kernan went to apply to the propaganda office for permission to resume printing, only to find himself faced with Lieutenant Maier, a failed photographer whom Kernan had turned away from *Vogue*'s door many times.[347] It was an awkward encounter, with Maier thoroughly enjoying the reversal of power. Kernan was given an endless list of rules to follow, which included providing full biographical information on any staff that he intended to re-employ in case they had Jewish relations.[348] Kernan dragged this bureaucracy out as long as possible, waiting for the Germans to lose interest. When the topic had cooled, Kernan and de Brunhoff made another move, liquidating all remaining assets of Les Éditions Condé Nast and lobbying to have an administrator appointed to them. Amid these machinations, they managed to have the company placed under the protection of the French court.[349] For the remainder of the occupation, when the Nazis came sniffing around Michel de Brunhoff would shake his head regretfully and declare the organisation was under the Tribunal of Commerce's administration. Kernan and de Brunhoff understood fully that if the Nazis got their hands on French *Vogue* it would spell the end of *Vogue* everywhere, tarnishing the magazine's name irretrievably in the eyes of the free world and resulting in a slow death for the corporation. Their mission was to save the whole of Condé Nast Publications and guarantee its future.

Death of Condé Nast and the End of the War

The United States was having an easier go of it. The war seemed a faraway thing, removed from their world and a touch distasteful. But the staffers of American *Vogue* producing the magazine faced other horrors, for there were worrying events occurring closer to home.

The double whammy of Carmel Snow's betrayal and his plunge towards financial ruin had completely rattled Condé Nast. Despondent and overwhelmed, he began to lose his touch. Had he been a younger man these incidents might have stoked his fire, but in his declining age it was probably the reason he succumbed to ongoing cardiac pains in 1942 – smack in the middle of WWII. Before dying he penned a rambling last letter to his beloved editor-in-chief, Edna Woolman Chase. A regrettable schism had slowly opened up between them, dissolving a partnership that had been brokered in a more cordial and hopeful era. Nonetheless, Nast's final words are moving: 'Edna, we have been a great team. I believe I have been a wide-awake and intelligent publisher, but I am the first to admit to myself and acknowledge to the world, that, without you I could never have built *Vogue*.'[350]

Unknowingly, he was writing to Woolman Chase on his deathbed. For some thirty-three years they had laboured obsessively together, feeding each other's aspirations and insanities. A visitor to the offices

once expressed a lively interest in the relationship between Nast and
Woolman Chase, convinced they had to be romantically entangled
to be that close. The sarcastic reply from one staffer implied they
were so in love they even had a child which they doted on.[351] The
child was *Vogue*. Condé Nast the man might have died quietly in
the middle of a global conflict, but Condé Nast the company was a
fine legacy indeed. Whatever people's criticism, *Vogue* had been fed,
fattened, nurtured, shepherded and shielded from harm by a line-up
of brave protectors. The heart-warming comradery of *Vogue*'s wartime staffers and her second father, Nast, are like rays of sunlight.

Even the *Vogue* photographers were doing important work in
the name of service. British-born *Vogue* favourite Cecil Beaton was
hired as a war photographer, largely to drum up American support
for the allied nations by producing works of devastated foreign
countries. He continued to work for *Vogue*, producing London-based
imagery of new ruins for them. The architectural splendour of the
English capital was peeled back by aerial bombardment. But even in
unhappy scenes Beaton saw glamour and theatrics. The aftermath of
one bombing had him extolling that 'quite remarkably spectacular
Piranesi effects of ruin are achieved'.[352]

In one legendary shoot he posed a model in a slim suit, her back
towards the camera. She is surrounded by piles of rubble heaped
taller than her, a mess of bricks and snapped beams. There is only a
remaining pair of archways left standing and the model is looking up
at a plaque hung between them. The plaque marks a spot previously
destroyed in the Great Fire of London, proving that the city had
risen from the ground before and hinting it would do so again after
the Blitz. The message of hope is overlaid with the blatant message
of the photograph's title: 'Fashion is Indestructible'.[353]

Even more vital were model-turned-photographer Lee Miller's
contributions, published in both American and British *Vogue*. Lee

Miller's unlikely career began in Paris, where she was a muse to the surrealists and Man Ray's mistress. She had been featured in *Vogue* numerous times and so was on familiar terms with all the European editors. When the war started, Miller decided to concentrate on photography, feeling passionately that she wanted to be involved. The result is a portfolio of the most searing war imagery of any era we know. Dissecting the material Miller shot during WWII is too mammoth a task, but among her wartime assignments were photographic series from Nazi concentration camps Buchenwald and Dachau, many of the shots showing the dying or the dead. She was another of the unique deities that hurtled in and out of the *Vogue* universe like a comet.

Miller won much admiration from her editors, especially the British editor Audrey Withers. Withers understood that while it was all very well to publish the standard messages about morale, Miller brought *Vogue* 'right into the heart of the conflict'.[354] Determined to have a clear account delivered to readers, Miller insisted she write the articles to accompany her photographs. Women in Britain had few ways of getting their news or hearing truthful reports on how the war was progressing in other countries. With Miller, *Vogue*'s content crossed from clothes into current affairs.

There was also the all-important aspect that Miller was a woman and back then war correspondents were all men. Miller used uniquely female reference points in her writing to engage a female reader, such as comparing military equipment to corsets. She was an exhilarating personality and Withers winced to cut a single word of her writing, though she often had to due to paper rationing. It was thanks to Miller's insights that Withers could call her luxury journal 'The Intelligent Woman's Guide to much more than fashion'.[355] She would never forget who gave her magazine depth and tried to accommodate the star reporter long after, although Miller left the permanent staff in

1949. Though she did occasionally still contribute at Withers' request, Miller's husband eventually wrote to the editor begging her to stop sending commissions – he claimed working upset Miller too much.[356]

By 1944 the British were flagging. And though American *Vogue* were still publishing articles about their experience, a piece written by Lesley Blanch, a British *Vogue* editor, shows London's exhaustion. 'We don't live so much as manage,' she pens. 'We all look pretty tired. As pretty as we know how, and make-up and hairdressers are not denied us, but it's quite a struggle, being as tired and under-vitaminized as we are. The greyish, rather dragged look is due to nervous strain'.[357] Withers kept her team going as best she could, for she was the editor of a luxury magazine who might spend all day talking about rare diamonds, then go home and mop her own floor. She was notoriously frugal. It was public transport over taxis, sandwiches at the desk over swanky dinners on expense accounts. For a while she was a staunch Labour voter (she was amongst the few left-leaning editors in *Vogue*'s history) and in her eighties, long after retirement, she still had enough political conviction to volunteer for the Social Democratic Party. Withers was so stoic that even Dior couldn't sweep her off her feet, she disapproved of his style because it was impossible to wear on a bus. Later, in 1954, she would be rewarded for her part in WWII, by being appointed an OBE.

When the war came to its end in 1945 one envisions an atmosphere of pure celebration, parties, parades. But the cover of *Vogue* is oddly quiet. It is a painting of a blue, almost cloudless sky with 'VOGUE' spelled out at the top in white lettering. Not one person, not one landmark. But it wasn't without meaning. The empty heavens emphasised clear blue overhead – no planes, no missiles, no time bombs – an ending to the bombardment. The discretion with which the British staff wrapped up the war was typical of Withers, the ultimate poster-woman for duty. When asked years later where she had been on VE Day, she replied, 'Was it a week day? If it was, I was in the office.'[358]

Their neighbours in France had also tired of their ordeal. When Bettina Ballard came back to Paris in December 1944 after serving in the Red Cross, she found Michel de Brunhoff and his wilting team in the new year, holed up in the tiny headquarters of *Jardin des Modes*. The atmosphere was ominous, the whole place had a sense of dread and desolation.[359] Ballard felt that de Brunhoff had aged decades in the mere four years since she'd seen him. He was hunched, his hair white, his heart broken. His teenage son had been hunted down and brutally murdered by the Gestapo. De Brunhoff never recovered from the senseless loss.

The Duchesse d'Ayen had also faced unimaginable hardship. Her husband was arrested for his well-known pro-allied feelings, after which the Duchesse herself was arrested. She spent months in solitary confinement in Fresnes prison, where occasionally she would face day-long interrogations. To keep herself from going mad she danced in her cramped cell and composed imaginary articles reporting on prison fashion or beauty behind bars. She succumbed to malnutrition and by the time she came out was so bloated and covered in sores her daughter barely recognised her.[360]

From the time of her release, Duchesse d'Ayen tried to keep up with her husband's location, following rumours to prisons and concentration camps in France and Germany. The last time she saw him she was waiting in a big crowd of other wives and mothers, having heard that captives were being moved through a certain town square. Eventually the men appeared, stumbling two by two, surrounded by guards. As she ran towards them a German soldier pushed her over and knocked the package she had brought for her husband out of her hands. In the crush of it she still managed to spot his face and hear his voice as he cried, 'My little Sol, here I am!'[361] Then he was gone. He died the day before his concentration camp was liberated. Their teenage son, like de Brunhoff's, had also been killed. Duchesse d'Ayen never went back to *Vogue*.

The staff of French *Vogue* were shell-shocked by what they'd been through. It is testament to Michel de Brunhoff's leadership and courage that nobody gave up on Frog. Even the American office was taken aback by his desire to restart the edition as soon as possible; but de Brunhoff was adamant.[362] He was determined to turn the page. In November 1944, Edna Woolman Chase, de Brunhoff and two representative couturiers did a two-way broadcast. Woolman Chase's emotions were high:

> To me, personally, it was a deeply moving event. I trembled as I stood at the microphone waiting to hear for the first time in four years the voices of Michel and Lucien Lelong . . . then came Michel's voice.
>
> 'Hello Edna, my heart is beating fast.'
> So was mine.[363]

The first issue after the liberation of Paris was released in January 1945, thanks again to the iron determination of de Brunhoff. Not only had he been religiously creating bound volumes recording couture fashion every six months during the war, meaning there was a record of trend evolution (many couturiers had remained in Paris and continued selling their collections twice a year as usual), but he also personally procured the supplies. Public transport and cycling were the only way of travelling after the liberation, so de Brunhoff struggled through the thick snow on a bike to the printer's,[364] and haggled for ink from friends on the black market.[365]

Woolman Chase wrote that his reward was a beautiful magazine with tons of advertising, received with open arms.[366] There was a lot for de Brunhoff to be relieved about: for France, the loathsome war was over; Paris was French again; his remaining family would be safe; his friends were coming home; his loyal staff would receive their dues; many of his artists, photographers, writers and editors would pour back into the city to revive the magic and art of clothes again. He would stay at French *Vogue* for nearly another decade, able to celebrate the fashion industry he'd had such a major part in saving.

CHAPTER 8

The Powerful Years

Vogue Gets Bigger, Richer and More Sophisticated

'New Look'; New Vogue; New Ways of Life

No fashion collection has ever marked the beginning of a moment more clearly than Christian Dior's 'New Look' did in the mid-twentieth century. His debut show, which took place on 12 February 1947, would set the tone for the next ten years. From the gloom and gravity of yet another world war, Dior rescued women everywhere from the drab and utilitarian, from the rationing and funerals, from the ruins of newly fallen cities. Inspired by the beloved Granville garden of his childhood he turned skirts into huge, flouncing ball-gowns like upturned bouquets. Waists were cinched wasp-thin, busts were shapely, shoulders contoured, hips were padded out like spreading petals.

This frivolity was exactly what women needed after what they'd been through. Dior created the collection to bring joy, and he succeeded. Fashionable folk from both sides of the Atlantic went into frenzies over the new style. It was devilish. It was demure. It was heartbreakingly delicious! And it was the catalyst for change that inspired the ultra-feminine fifties. A Vogue editor present at the first showing hailed Dior's efforts as a complete revolution.[367] It wasn't just a question of rich ladies buying frocks, the 'New Look' was recognised by butchers and taxi drivers, it entered modern vocabulary and brokered Christian Dior's personal stardom. At one point, he earned more than all the other Parisian couturiers put together.

This breath of fresh clean air washed right through *Vogue*, triggering other changes, though not always happy ones. At the close of WWII, the formidable Edna Woolman Chase was in her late sixties and many of her former colleagues were dead, retired, married, missing in action or had simply moved on. Particularly difficult for her was the loss of Condé Nast himself. And just as she had been planning a long-awaited getaway with her beloved husband, he became unwell and died in 1950.[368] He didn't live to cross the threshold of the new home they had been building. From here on, it becomes evident that the immortal Woolman Chase, grande dame of *Vogue*, was finally declining. Of her husband's death she wrote with a deep melancholy:

> It would perhaps be natural to think that a woman so engrossed in a career as I have always been, indulging in so much activity, surrounded by so many fellow workers, would miss a husband less than a woman whose entire interest centered in her home, but that is not so. For twenty-nine years Dick was the strong, unchanging factor in my life on whom I counted. I don't mean that we never had disagreements – we had battles royal – but we belonged to each other . . . It is a sad thing to be a woman, for we survive and survival can be lonely.[369]

In the final pages of her autobiography, she discusses how growing old in real life differed starkly from the glamorous old age she portrayed in *Vogue*. She laments fashion democratising to a point of unsustainability and that the expert craftmanship she had valued was disappearing.[370] Although these complaints may seem typical of someone as they get older, that doesn't make them invalid. Designers *were* licensing (and compromising) their designs to make more profit. Manufacturing cheaper textiles *was* on the rise. Consumers *did* start buying more and caring about quality less. Still, Woolman Chase stayed on, only retiring from her post as editor-in-chief in 1952 by which time she was seventy-five and even then she retained her position on the board. She had spent fifty-six years at *Vogue* in total, thirty-eight as editor-in-chief. Longer than anyone else in the whole history of *Vogue* to this day. She had gone from a teenager addressing envelopes to chairman of the biggest fashion publishing company in the world. Who could possibly replace her?

After the loss of Carmel Snow to rival *Harper's Bazaar*, Woolman Chase had had to begin from scratch in her search for a successor – and her new heir-elect was Jessica Daves, a fashion merchandising editor who'd joined back in 1933. After the debacle with Snow, Daves was the prudent choice. Snow had brimmed with personality, bite and verve, a chaotic irresistible character who became famous for never eating, favouring a three-Martini lunch. Daves was her polar opposite: a plump, conscientious, diligent worker-bee who stayed at the office late every night. Daves, who had been brought up in a strict Southern household and was the granddaughter of Methodist ministers, carried the same sense of responsibility and unerring duty that Woolman Chase's Quaker upbringing had instilled in her. She may not have been a fashionista at heart, but she could be counted on. When Daves ascended to the editorship, *Vogue* was a global behemoth, quite literally a fashion bible. It was also prosperous, turning millions in revenue. It was Daves' job to try and keep it there.

Luckily Daves was surrounded by an exceedingly strong team. In Condé Nast's place as president was the charismatic Iva Patcévitch and in Dr Agha's place as art director was newcomer Alexander Liberman. Unsurprisingly the 1950s issues look different, though this might be as much to do with changes in style as staff restructuring. There is no period of *Vogue* which oozes glamour like the mid-century covers. Each frontispiece alters the pose of the model and typography of 'Vogue', a visually exciting effect which sadly gets replaced by samey headshots in the 1960s through the 1970s.

The figures on 1950s covers point their slender feet from under voluminous skirts, dripping in diamonds and sinking manicured fingers into glossy fur mufflers. Classic elegance is key. Wasp waists, bejewelled turbans, pillbox hats with netted veils and dainty white-gloved hands are everywhere. In editorials and on covers alike men wear tuxedos. Occasionally a baby or a puppy completes a blushing portrait of domesticity. None of these models pout or glower in the manner we now consider standard. Many of them smile, whether seductively, shyly or with genuine happiness. This gives the impression that they're real people, not unattainable mannequins. These models made you feel like you could become one of them if you had the right outfit.

The credit for these covers must go to the art director, Alexander Liberman, even though he had the advantage of working with some of the most wonderful photographers in fashion history. He discovered Irving Penn and his dramatic monochromes. He continued commissioning Cecil Beaton and his muted fairy-tale scenes, as well as working with Horst P. Horst's cinematic-style stills and Erwin Blumenfeld's soft, sepia close-ups. No wonder these editions are often hailed as cornerstones in the golden age of magazine publishing. But although colour photography was a developing technology and an important tool of *Vogue*, the most famous photographers tended to stick to gentler palettes. Blumenfeld explained that early colour photography was so keen to prove it could capture all shades that the result was often a tacky over-saturation. What the famous *Vogue* photographers produced was more concerned with artistic merit than it was with Kodak innovations.

Liberman's ideas sprang from his Russian roots, where a vocation as an artist was valued higher than it was in the West. Yes, in his career he'd been enticed by the thought of a stable income and so had landed in the commercial realm of fashion publishing. His nascent attraction to art was dramatically renewed in the 1940s, when he began reading about modern art, examining the theories of Kandinsky and others. According to his stepdaughter he came to believe there was a sacred dimension to fine art that was beyond photography and graphics.[371] She suggests that he began to look down on his work at *Vogue*, confessing to her that he saw himself as a true artist and this made him feel superior to magazines.[372] All this might have meant nothing if he hadn't been encouraged by a friend to go and photograph the studio of Georges Braque while on holiday in France. Liberman leaped at the chance and enjoyed the project so much that he began to dedicate his time to visiting other artists' studios, photographing and interviewing the likes of Cézanne and Monet.

This private hobby, originally intended for his own satisfaction, bled into *Vogue*. In 1952, Irving Penn convinced him to publish some of these essays in the magazine and the 'Artist in his Studio' feature became a regular, each one an in-depth look at the habits and life of modern masters.[373] They published pieces on luminaries such as Chagall in 1955 and Picasso in 1956. Yet even before this series appeared, art had begun creeping on to the pages. In 1951, Liberman had conceived an editorial shoot by Cecil Beaton in which models wore versions of Dior's 'New Look' ripped off by local American dressmakers and posed in front of Jackson Pollock canvases. This not only introduced a new way of using art as a commercial prop, but it connected the world of fashion to the hallowed ground of fine art.

No matter how stunning the frocks, the era was marked by a growth of mass production which threatened to eradicate craft and the personal touch. *Vogue*'s Americana issue of 1947 praises the textile industry of the USA which had produced more than 1 trillion garments in the previous year,[374] but in practice ready-to-wear had its great opponents at *Vogue*, where couture was king. The Americana issue might have boasted about American industry, but the brand's image (and therefore its income) came from presenting the most luxurious of luxuries to the richest and the most beautiful. If fashion was democratised, how could they continue selling exclusivity? Yet there were prêt-à-porter champions on the *Vogue* payroll, not least Jessica Daves. Keen to see the circumstances as an opportunity, she treated *Vogue* as a means to educate public taste,[375] believing strongly that taste was something democratic which could be both taught and learned for the benefit of all, not just the elite.[376]

Daves wanted to make fashion accessible, as the title of the feature 'More Taste Than Money' shows. The content treats taste as the highest power in fashion. One column even opens with the line, 'you need an eye for what's new and good, and the inclination to wear it. And you won't find either of these by looking in your purse'.[377] By promoting style over price she stood up for ready-to-wear. But as their apparently superior taste became part of *Vogue*'s ammunition, it was increasingly treated by Liberman as the latest must-have in editorial pages. The intention was to provoke a new social insecurity about whether one had taste or not. This helped shift copies; nobody would want to be tasteless.

Art had become the nucleus of New York society, with crowds gathering around charismatic dealers and institutions like the Museum of Modern Art. In 1945, a whole *Vogue* issue was dedicated to MoMA.[378]

With Paris destroyed, the post-war art scene had decamped to New York. Wealthy Americans were attracted to spend on private collections, while the reputation of artists overlooked in Europe, such as Dalí, were consolidated. Fashion could command more authority if it was considered highbrow. Art would be more visible if it was fashionable. And artists increasingly took commercial work previously considered beneath them, with Dalí producing no less than three *Vogue* covers in the 1940s. Cultivating taste, developing an eye for style, acquiring a cultured mind . . . these were the new values by which *Vogue* would define the upper echelons of society. Now everybody could afford to buy clothes, but very few could afford art.

There were other, less subtle clues that betray how much influence the fashion media had begun to wield, with the 'New Look' still at the core of many changes. Since Dior's seminal show made front-page headlines, journalists worldwide paid more attention to fashion. Courses for fashion writing proliferated and in 1952 Parsons School of Design in partnership with New York University (NYU) began offering a BSc in fashion.[379] Press numbers covering the couture collections snowballed: in 1949 over 300 international writers were covering the Paris shows; by 1957 there were 500, plus some 800 buyers.[380] Cheaper air travel facilitated more frequent trips, while really successful commentators achieved new heights. Former British *Vogue* editor Alison Settle had her columns syndicated, as did Eugenia Sheppard, famed fashion arbiter whose witticisms made her name across NYC. The USA had developed a robust economy by the mid-1950s; Americans had serious spending power and they were keen to express it by indulging in luxury. Once again, they were the primary customers of Parisian couture, restabilising the ateliers by promoting French design in American media. They also supported the upsurge of new fashion hubs like Italy, which was experiencing its own economic boom and, thanks to the exposure provided by

American publicity, were able to establish their own cohort of internationally recognised designers such as Simonetta and Pucci.

Differences began to emerge between fashion magazine and newspaper coverage. Magazines struggled to remain impartial and fell
prey to advertisers' demands for positive reviews. Newspapers were
able to publish critical commentary. Along with the industry's new
prestige and the formalisation of fashion journalism came a shift
in tone. The *Vogue* voice told women exactly what to wear for what
occasion and how, which accessories would be perfect for what. 'Sep-
arates' were becoming increasingly popular as part of an emerging
casual-wear market. Since these were a novelty, magazines felt the
need to teach women how to mix and match combinations into full
outfits. Providing how-tos, wardrobe planning and rulebooks on
what to pack for holidays, from yachting to skiing, quickly became
a must.

The conversation about colour now entered the sphere of clothing.
In 1949, three consecutive *Vogue* frontispieces boasted a rainbow
palette and 'Color in your Life' was used as a tagline on a front cover
in late April.[381] Contemporary designers felt women had no clue how
to dress themselves and a contributor to a trade journal goes so far
as to beg department stores to hire colourists to advise women which
tones flattered them.[382] *Vogue*'s glut of tutorials was either fulfilling
a desperate common need or was adopting society's new dictatorial
attitude to femininity. Women were facing new pressures to be
socially successful, well arranged and, most of all, obedient.

For all the sophistication and splendour of the pictures in *Vogue*,
the content has definite patriarchal undertones, complete with casual
references to domestic violence. One uncomfortable piece suggests
questions such as 'are you a snob?' and 'have you stopped beating
your wife yet?'[383] turn up in polite dinner party conversation. A 1956
issue includes an article on what makes women memorable, beauty

or charm? If you were born with neither your only hope was to dress well.[384] In a section aimed at men, we're firmly told that pretty women are the best, since nobody wants an unattractive mate. Sexiness, however, was vulgar and too much beauty was showy and in bad taste.[385]

Vogue propagated these ideas, but how guilty they are is difficult to judge. Did they tap into warped social values to sell their product? Yes. Did they realise they were doing it? Probably not. After all, there are times when even men are given strict directives in *Vogue*. A considerable chunk of coverage is dedicated to diet plans, including recipes and tips on calorie counting, a pressure men do not escape. One piece details a new contraption which looks like a fold-out bed with a motor that men could take to the office and lose weight just by lying down on it. Many advertisers promoted weight loss, with products like high-tech bathroom scales. In late spring 1954, an article discussed the benefit of a summer figure (a precursor to the beach body), which could be enhanced by buying structured bathing suits to hold in any bulges, something like the Spanx of today.[386]

As much as women were expected to live up to the Stepford wife ideal, the pages of *Vogue* reflect a general desire to live a beautiful life and betray very American anxieties about failure. The new habit of travel meant pages and pages discussing beach vacations, country house parties, cruises. You could find the right attire to wear for a helicopter ride over the skyscrapers of NYC. Or for swanning through a French château, guidebook in hand. Sports were popular, especially golf and tennis. So were resorts or visits to friends' estates, but all required carefully coded dressing (if you were inspecting your host's greenhouse, Bermuda-length shorts would be the appropriate costume). To complement these themes are the many adverts for tourist agencies and designer luggage. Nor were these high-class diversions for the young and adventurous only. One of *Vogue*'s most singular inventions, Mrs Exeter, travelled quite as much as anybody else.

First appearing in 1948, Mrs Exeter was a product of the marketing department, conceived to give comprehensive advice to older readers. Although from its early days *Vogue* had written rather patronising pieces aimed at ageing ladies, Mrs Exeter was a radical invention that finally acknowledged the importance of women over the age of thirty: their spending power, their position in society, their increased longevity and vitality. It was also one of the first times ageing was discussed candidly, showing that although women's bodies change over time it was still possible to stay stylish. Mrs Exeter's pieces are missing a byline and are written in the third person, as though they were written about the exploits of a real person. In one issue she is described as a woman of a certain age,[387] in another she is a heroine of fifty-odd.[388] These pieces are a pleasant surprise, for Mrs Exeter is prudent and likeable. By giving her a distinct personality, *Vogue* shows that social skills and cultural capital are assets to a woman and that her identity didn't have to hinge on a husband (never mentioned) or her net worth. She encourages budgeting, but not denying herself; discusses the styles of her youth, providing nostalgic fashion snapshots; in some places she promotes prêt-à-porter. Before, the vocabulary might have snootily recommended 'covering' or 'concealing' 'difficult areas'; with Mrs Exeter the angle was that her tastes had merely *evolved*, her inclinations becoming naturally more elegant.

Mrs Exeter was so popular that she got a spin-off in British *Vogue*, although the two Mrs Exeters had different voices. *Harper's Bazaar* followed suit, introducing a similar column titled 'At my age', though this was more censorious, printing lists prohibiting unsuitable garments rather than extending helpful tips. Mrs Exeter lasted as long as Jessica Daves, who as a practical person, and originally from the marketing department, probably had no small part in creating her. There were many forces at *Vogue* and sometimes they pushed in different directions. Jessica Daves wished for equality in fashion, so she fought for style over money, fashion as functional and Mrs Exeter as a symbol against ageism. Art director Alexander Liberman was for luxury and style as elitist tools, fashion as art and women as one-dimensional beauty templates. These opposing philosophies did not, however, make American *Vogue* confusing and inconsistent. Instead, they turned it into a curiously beautiful and wide-ranging publication.

Vogue readers were expected to live a life of leisure. But to those who worked at *Vogue* the idea was laughable. The frenzied new motion of fashion brought new responsibilities and required the staff to keep their nose to the grind day and night. In 1951, *Life* magazine published an article titled 'Bettina's Busy Day', detailing the schedule of American *Vogue*'s fashion editor Bettina Ballard during Paris Fashion Week. By 8 a.m. she would be holding a morning conference in her hotel room. At 9.15 a.m. she had to be at a Balenciaga show, bedecked in a Balenciaga suit. At 10.15 a.m. she was at a Schiaparelli show, wearing a Schiaparelli coat to cover up the Balenciaga underneath. Then a full change of clothes – switching the Balenciaga suit for a black Dior one – and she was taking her seat at the Dior opening. The car that drove her from show to show held the clothes she would have to slip in and out of to avoid offending each designer and she'd often change uncomfortably in the back while they careened through traffic. Nowadays magazines can borrow clothes and send them to different countries to photograph, but in 1951 the only way editors could get pictures was by holding night studio sessions. This meant at midnight Bettina Ballard and photographer John Rawlings were only just getting started directing models on set. At 2 a.m. Ballard would be picking through a plate of chips, still wearing all her pearls and scrutinising the photos they'd just taken, before deciding which ones to mail back to headquarters. Only then could she go to bed, to repeat it all again the next day.

Even while working to this strict timetable Bettina Ballard was considered creative rather than practical. Executive editor Mildred Morton (described as having 'the coldest, cruellest heart imaginable'[389]), who managed the relationship between advertisers and editorial, was always watching in case Ballard compromised the business side of *Vogue* by not honouring hard-won deals between brands and magazine. Ballard and editor-in-chief Jessica Daves didn't get along either; Ballard felt that she should have been awarded the editorship. In general, Daves received a fair amount of criticism for being too homely. A so-called friend compared her face to a baked apple,[390] another editor said, 'everything about her was unappealing'.[391] At Liberman's Christmas parties Daves was laughed at because she munched canapés awkwardly, chewing until her hat slid forward and the veil she wore was dunked into tuna filling or liver pâté.[392]

Worse in the eyes of the *Vogue*-ettes, was that she advocated prêt-à-porter, even writing an extremely technical book called *Ready-Made Miracle: The American Story of Fashion for the Millions*. Even in this dry text her support seeps through; she calls business leaders 'heroes' who'd brokered a much-needed change in the volatile apparel industry.[393] This approach must have disgusted the cognoscenti like Ballard and Liberman, who believed fashion was the stuff of dreams, not numbers. *Vogue* remained a snobbish place to work. Junior staff were still drawn from the daughters of the wealthy and salaries were so low they were referred to as 'pin money'.[394] One office joke claimed one junior said to another, 'I'll have to get a real job now. Daddy can't afford to send me to *Vogue* anymore'. There were also masses of leggy blondes who passed through the premises, only to go straight out again with a ring on their finger. For many of the daughters or divorcees of the rich, *Vogue* was a rite of passage. The bored heiresses, the uninspired models, the ex-wives of statesmen, sportsmen, playboys and Hollywood actors, with their alimony cheques and divorce settlements secured, all glided in and out of *Vogue*. It was their natural perch; they did not know where else to go in between husbands and holidays.

Daves didn't fit the mould. A middle-class working woman through and through, it's sometimes surprising in view of all these divisions that she managed to keep a steady grip on *Vogue* throughout the 1950s. But a new era dawned and as chance would have it exotic editor superstar Diana Vreeland quit her job at *Harper's Bazaar*. At *Vogue*, art director Alex Liberman sat up. He declared that *Vogue* needed help with its fashion sections, claimed Daves had no creativity and dismissed her as nothing but a manager.[395] Daves' name was changed from editor-in-chief to editorial advisor on the masthead – a token title always given to EICs who were on their way out – and the last year she served was 1964. Getting rid of Daves was one of the first moves Liberman made as he gained more control at the company, though to understand this better it's important to meet *Vogue*'s new owners.

New Owners: The Newhouses

Condé Nast Publications was bought for $5 million in 1959 by Samuel Irving Newhouse Sr, who built the Advance Publications media empire from scratch. Legend has it that his clothes-crazy wife, Mitzi, had looked up from her reading one morning and said, 'Darling, don't forget to buy me *Vogue* today.' Newhouse Sr, misunderstanding, acquired the company when she'd just wanted the latest issue of the magazine.[396] Newhouse Sr was the eldest of eight children born to

Jewish immigrants in New York City. Forced to step up to the head of the household aged thirteen due to his father's bad health, he left school and started working to help sustain his family, waiting all the while for opportunity to strike.

It came in the form of an ailing local newspaper which fell into his boss's hands and his employer, recognising the young man's spirit of enterprise, took a chance and placed the newspaper under his control. If he turned it around, he would be given an owner-ship stake. Quickly realising that a lax approach to advertising was the newspaper's problem, Newhouse Sr returned the periodical to profitability in record time and, realising his formula could work elsewhere, started investing in other loss-making publications. His modus operandi was: find a bargain-priced daily in a growing com-munity, procure it, then acquire the second most important. Next, he would shut down one of the papers, thereby establishing a monopoly which allowed him to set advertising rates as high as he pleased. Bil-lionaire investor Warren Buffett called this strategy an unregulated tollbooth.[397] Yet this system, repeated over and over again, earned Newhouse Sr one of America's great and glittering fortunes.

His son, Samuel Irving Newhouse Jr, known as Si, was born and raised in completely different circumstances to his father and was well accustomed to luxury. Unlike his prosaic father, Si Newhouse displayed a greater interest in the arts from early adulthood. Unfor-tunately for Si Newhouse, he had trouble escaping Newhouse Sr's shadow. A somewhat withdrawn boy, he dropped out of college and settled in Manhattan. A failed marriage and three children later saw Si Newhouse at middle age holed up in a bachelor pad, drifting between positions at his father's various papers. It was when he washed up on the bright shores of Condé Nast Publications that he realised where he belonged.

Si Newhouse slid quietly into the *Vogue* offices, asserting his ownership during the tenure of Jessica Daves. Although he was originally horrified at the idea of taking a 'tacky' official job title, he was eventually persuaded by Liberman and became the publisher of US *Vogue* in 1964 – the same year Daves was erased.[398] It would be easy to put the glory and the blame of every *Vogue* victory and every blunder up until his death in 2017 at the door of Si Newhouse. But *Vogue*, especially the new *Vogue* backed by the overflowing Newhouse coffers, had bottomless funds, prestige and glamour . . . and a limited number of job vacancies. Unsurprisingly, this was a recipe for some pretty brutal in-fighting among the senior staff and some deft puppeteering of Si Newhouse by those bold enough to try it.

Just before Condé Nast died, he dictated a letter to his right-hand man Iva Patcévitch, naming him the next president of the company. Patcévitch was a White Russian who had served in the Tsar's army before escaping to America. He was erudite and fine-boned, a gifted athlete, financial wizard, beautiful piano player, Marlene Dietrich's lover and Nast's personal confidant. (That is not to say he didn't have some of that foolish extravagance that comes so naturally to fashion folk: the majority of his life he carried a gold swizzle stick from Cartier in his pocket to remove excess bubbles from his champagne.[399]) It was Patcévitch that secured the sale of *Vogue* to the Newhouses – a decision he would come to bitterly regret when he was later ousted by them. In other monumental decisions he allowed himself to be unduly swayed by the other behind-the-scenes titan: Liberman.

It was Liberman who conspired to fire Jessica Daves, Liberman who pushed to hire Diana Vreeland as her replacement and Liberman who was soon to be responsible for booting her again when she no longer suited. Vreeland had a reputation as a wild and exciting editor and Liberman was very much taken with her for a time. When remembering Jessica Daves leaving American *Vogue* and Diana

Vreeland arriving, Liberman claimed the Newhouses had wanted
him to take over as editor from Daves, but he said he declined
because men should be managers, not getting involved with fashion.[400] Instead, he was made editorial director, a new title that gave
him omnipotent control over all the magazines at Condé Nast. The
memo sent around announcing Vreeland's appointment said she
would be working closely with Liberman. Remembering this years
later, Liberman commented wryly, 'They wanted me controlling her.
But Vreeland was uncontrollable.'[401]

The Newhouse family can also be credited with reviving one of Condé
Nast's favourite company protocols: to expand, expand, expand. As
much as Nast had loved scooping up ailing periodicals and launching
Vogue and her various offshoots across seas, so, it seemed, did the
Newhouses. Their first foray into foreign lands occurred almost imme-
diately, with a plan to launch *Vogue* Australia.

Australia had long been subject to English trends which made their
way from Europe despite the distance. Largely populated by descend-
ants of the British and Irish, Australia had always looked towards
the rainy UK for style tips. Inhabitants of this young territory had to
grapple with its wild nature, as yet undeveloped infrastructure and
tropical climate, which all necessitated practical working clothes. But
by the late 1950s Australia was becoming more sophisticated and was
supported by a fairly robust economy. Aussies were travelling, being
exposed to different lifestyles and buying beautiful merchandise
abroad. This sounded good to the Newhouses, especially since the
only competitor was a magazine called *Flair*.[402] There wasn't much
chance for any local publication anyway; they would be up against
Vogue's blue-blood connections, top-of-the-range equipment and
gold-standard photography. By now *Vogue* was very far ahead in
the game.

To aid them, the Newhouses drafted in Bernard Leser, a German-born Jew who had escaped the Nazis and went on to become a gregarious shoe salesman in the Antipodes. His career in textiles and footwear licensing brought him into contact with Reggie Williams, then chairman and managing director of Condé Nast UK, who was impressed by Leser's energy, if not experience. When Leser was on business in London he was approached to help start a new branch of the magazine, a proposal he heartily accepted. *Vogue* Australia was first launched as a division of the British company in 1959. The supplement appeared three times a year and sales were significant enough to greenlight a full *Vogue* Australia edition. With the help of spunky editor Sheila Scotter they grew the luxury magazine to a record circulation in excess of 60,000. Leser would later launch and grow an Australian *Vogue Living* with similar success.[403]

The first cover of *Vogue* Australia was photographed by Norman Parkinson: a headshot of a dazzling blonde with a sedate, gentle expression. The soft-focus image gave the cover a delicious golden glow that feels appropriate for the hot, beachy continent. The post-war obsession with colour filters through, even here, with the caption reading: 'SPRING RADIANCE. Colours, Clothes, Cosmetics'. For the early success of *Vogue* Australia, credit has to go to Bernard Leser. He pioneered it, fought for advertising with stubborn local businesses and advocated Australia as an exciting market rather than a boring backwater. For proof of Leser's influence, nothing is more indicative than the illustrious path he paved for himself. So successful was his Australian pilot that he was appointed the first non-British managing director of Condé Nast UK in 1976 and later, the first non-American president of the whole of Condé Nast Publications in the USA in 1987.

Vogue's next international move was less driven by a singular personality and appeared instead as a natural by-product of economic, historic and cultural factors.

When, you might ask, did 'Made in Italy' become bywords for style? Post-WWII a remarkable period of creativity imbued the nation, touching architecture, art, cinema, photography and, of course, *alta moda* (high fashion). Spawning until roughly the 1970s, Italy drove on to the scene by providing deliberately unfussy luxury and popularising sportswear. French couture was prescriptive and hard to put on, while Spain was suffering severe economic deprivation. Italy too was in rubble, but it saw a chance to rebuild its own fortunes by aligning with the booming USA, something Spain, as a Communist country, couldn't do. Soon, American movie stars became ambassadors for Italian chic, while American tourists lined the pockets of locals from Capri to Perugia. A surging textile industry was stoked by American dollars. The Italians felt they deserved this injection of cash: it was, after all, the American forces that had broken apart their previous regime and monitored their election after the war.

From the Piedmont region, small merchants like Loro Piana started exporting their finely spun wools. Textile mills were revived, from the Milanese cotton industry to the Lombardian and Tuscan silk tradition. The fast-moving lines of manufacture that ran like arteries through the Dolomites and the Venetian Lagoon, the Berici Hills to the feet of the Po Valley, all under the governance of La Serenissima – the old name for Venice – were jump-started. Soon they began to distinguish themselves through product innovation and the development of synthetic fibres. Promoted as an alternative to Paris and the Riviera, Italy was suddenly on screens with Audrey Hepburn's *Roman Holiday*, and later *La Dolce Vita* and *It Started in Naples*.

This generated a smart, slick, sporty crop of Italian designers, many of whom had aristocratic bloodlines, noses for publicity, agile minds and sharp tongues. Their calling card was superlative yarn and simplicity of cut. Germana Marucelli was born into a Florentine family of craftsmen and popularised light tunics named after friars and bishops. Other prominent designers included Irene Galitzine, a princess who liked sandals,[404] Simonetta Colonna and Emilio Pucci with his vibrant kaleidoscopic fabrics. This first stock paved the ground for many future generations of Italian designers: Prada, Gucci, Fendi, Ferragamo, Missoni, Valentino, Versace. As the global gaze fell on Italy, so Condé Nast Publications began to think. Why not a native *Vogue* for this new market?

As the Italian market was already busy with magazines, the Newhouses decided to break in slowly. A partnership was sought out with another paper and in 1961, when it launched, the product was called *Novità* to prevent any damage to the *Vogue* name if it flopped. In 1965 it was rechristened *Vogue + Novità* and only in 1966 did it become *Vogue Italia*. As with many of the sister publications, including British *Vogue* and *Vogue Paris*, *Vogue Italia* had multiple editors who saw it through the embryonic stages, sent over from the New York office. It would be decades until *Vogue Italia* came into its own and scared the higher-ups considerably by making a name for itself as a radical dissident.

CHAPTER 9

Youthquake

Scandal in Paris, Swinging Sixties in London

Racism in Post-war France

At *Vogue Paris* Michel de Brunhoff remained the editor until the mid-1950s, making him another lifer at Condé Nast Publications. Despite his advancing age, de Brunhoff's editing sense, his instinctive finger on the pulse of fashion, never wavered. He even played a part in the creation of Christian Dior.

Dior had run a modest art gallery in Paris which had gone bankrupt in the Depression of 1929. Not sure how to make a living, he produced some sketches and took them to de Brunhoff, who didn't think they were good enough to use in *Vogue*, but made Dior's crucial introduction to various couture contacts. He understood intuitively that Dior belonged in design. One such introduction resulted in a job that provided much of Dior's training in fashion. De Brunhoff later discovered Yves Saint Laurent, introducing him to Dior and thereby launching his career too.

But times had changed and French *Vogue* was no longer on the fashion frontlines for Condé Nast. Previously, it produced all the fashion pages for British and American *Vogue*, now, American editors would come to Paris and produce the pages themselves. De Brunhoff did not object, on the contrary, he seemed glad to give up the responsibility.[405] He avoided necessary conversations on ready-to-wear, which he was opposed to. He was also keen for his daughters to work with him and take his place afterwards, which was technically against Condé Nast's company rules, which discouraged nepotism. There's no doubt his enthusiasm was waning. The company owed him a great debt for saving French *Vogue* from the Nazis, but they still needed an editor for right now. A co-worker remembers walking into his office in the mid-1950s, just before his retirement, and seeing his normally overflowing desk completely empty.[406] Like Edna Woolman Chase, he would die just a few years after leaving *Vogue*.

The woman who succeeded him in 1954 was very much in keeping with *Vogue*'s surprising abundance of war heroes. Edmonde Charles-Roux was from a diplomatic family and had grown up among the intellectual elite of various European capitals. However, her nationalistic feeling was strong enough to see her join up as a nurse at nineteen, when the war broke out. She was wounded first in a hospital bombing, while saving soldiers from the blaze, and wounded a second time after becoming a member of the Resistance. Returning to her native Marseille, decorated with military honours, she found that the high-society milieu of her parents frowned upon a woman who'd been on the frontline. Ostracised for her overly liberal views she decided to start over and left for Paris. On her way to the capital she met a wealthy shipowner about to invest in *Elle*. The magazine was new, one of the many launched to fill a gap in the market left by the press that the Germans had forced shut. After two years cutting her teeth at *Elle* she moved to French *Vogue* in 1948.

Six years was a short amount of time to go from ingénue to editor of a *Vogue* edition, but Charles-Roux made an impression. Once at the helm there was a sharp shift in perspective. Unlike de Brunhoff, who was enchanted by buoyancy and creativity, Charles-Roux could not see fashion as an art form. To her it was an agent of social change and crucial to reviving France's export economy after the war. In the pages of French *Vogue* prêt-à-porter clothes were placed beside pop art. Big names would sit alongside young and inexperienced writers and photographers. She pushed hard to make luxury accessible and her sound moral compass was her mainstay throughout the editorship. However, the Newhouses were wary of her politics.

In 1966, Charles-Roux planned to feature the African-American model Donyale Luna on the front cover. The Newhouse family in New York heard about this and sent Alexander Liberman to talk her out of it. Liberman was closely connected to Charles-Roux. Her brothers had been to the same school as him, their families had been part of the same highbrow circles when Liberman lived in Paris and the snobbish Liberman loved the fact that she was from a noted lineage. Up until her firing, Liberman's stepdaughter claims he referred to Charles-Roux as 'one of his two or three closest chums'.[407] Still, the dispatch he was there to deliver was a difficult one: the Newhouses didn't want a black cover girl in case it put off conservative advertisers in France. Though the details are hard to confirm, it seems this was an act of racist censorship. But Charles-Roux wasn't moved by Liberman's persuasions; she wanted Luna on the cover.[408] She refused to budge and so she was fired, a decision she unceremoniously heard only when she went to the accounts department to pick up her paycheque and was informed it would be her final one. Though Donyale Luna never made that cover of French *Vogue*, she was the first ever black model to have a cover on British *Vogue*.

Edmonde Charles-Roux was the sort of editor we would prize now, a 'queenly figure'[409] imbued with integrity. Nor was fashion her be-all and end-all; she was a serious writer whose first novel was published a few months after her removal from *Vogue* and went on to win the highest literary honours in France. It was Liberman who suffered losing this remarkable woman from his life and her subsequent fame would affect him deeply. His stepdaughter analysed: 'Edmonde stood for everything in European society that Alex could have achieved and either could not or cared not to attain: rigorous intellectual discipline, true intellectual achievement.'[410]

Although Liberman would spend his later years trying to reconcile his conflicting desires, the episode with Charles-Roux exemplified his more distasteful side. And although Alexander Liberman was one of the sharpest art directors *Vogue* ever had, he is also remembered as being the envoy willing to do the dirty work of Condé Nast's directors at any cost.

Editing in Post-war Britain

Wandering through one of London's art galleries in the 1950s, the National Portrait Gallery perhaps, or the Royal Academy, you might have espied two ladies doubled up with laughter, openly jeering at the portraits. Audrey Withers and Bettina Ballard used to sneak out of the *Vogue* offices during Ballard's snatched visits across the Atlantic and make fun of the pompous faces on the walls.[411] Attired in couture suits, immaculately accessorised and with dashes of lipstick, nobody would have expected such conduct from two elegant representatives of the glossy media. Ballard, who loved to drag out visits because the company would put her up at Claridge's and foot the bill for lunch appointments at Le Caprice, was fully aware of the posturing superficiality of her world.[412]

Withers never criticised the ridiculous aspects of her job or showed any resentment at the hypocrisy, even in the fifties when the British were suffering the hangover from WWII. The pages of *Vogue* might have resumed writing about stockings and petticoats, but post-war rationing meant women still couldn't get their hands on them. Many were still wearing the boxy suits of the 1940s, while everywhere else in the world girls were spinning down streets in Dior's new skirts. Utility clothing schemes had democratised fashion to an extent but now that the war was over, the class war raged again. Couture sparkled far out of reach, available only to the beautiful people, while ready-to-wear in the UK faced problems. In one popular anecdote a buyer bumps into a clothes manufacturer and asks, 'How's business?' The manufacturer duly replies, 'Difficult. Suddenly they want both sleeves the same length.'[413]

Peace resumed, *Vogue*'s offices filled up to the rafters once again with former models and rich men's daughters. One journalist from Fleet Street recalls seeing these editors invade a designer's salon 'armed with the tall, rolled up umbrellas which were a great fashion accessory then . . . very intimidating to lesser mortals'.[414] Meanwhile Withers proudly published works by literary stars from Kingsley Amis to Dylan Thomas, releasing literature written by the middle class next to prohibitively expensive garb available only to the upper classes. By 1960, Withers wanted to retire and travel. She had by now held the post of editor for twenty years. She had stayed just long enough to witness seismic change as the self-conscious, self-congratulatory status quo turned into the smiling, toe-tapping teenage spirit embodied by Twiggy.

The Swinging Sixties arrived like a strike of lightning. Suddenly, gangsters and pop singers mixed with socialites and film stars. Severe-looking dames in gloves were swapped out for baby-faced models like Jean Shrimpton and Pattie Boyd; household names, not nameless clothes horses. Fashion photography was dominated by the working-class dropout David Bailey, and Lord Snowdon (Antony Armstrong-Jones), the Queen's brother-in-law. From different ends of the social spectrum, both were devoted to *Vogue*. Setting them side by side showed that the old regime was crumbling. Status no longer mattered, only style did.

A great deal was going on at Brogue. Firstly, there was trouble over stocks and shares. The secret that Lord Camrose had bought Condé Nast Publications in the 1930s broke when Camrose sold his company, Amalgamated Press, to the Mirror Group in 1959.[415] The president of Condé Nast, Iva Patcévitch, had hustled to find someone in America to buy out *Vogue* and its sister magazines before they became the uneasy property of a UK tabloid. It was this tussle between London and New York that the Newhouses silenced by buying the company and becoming the overlords.

Following Audrey Withers' departure, her successor, Ailsa Garland, was drafted in at the very start of the decade, 1960 itself. Her primary experience was as woman's editor on newspapers. Her insights are particularly unique in what they reveal about journalism, then a male-dominated field that was barely beginning to recognise the female reader's needs. By the time Garland took over, Brogue had achieved autonomy from the American edition and no longer had content sent over from the States. This was no small achievement – for almost half a century British *Vogue* had been carefully regulated by eagle-eyed seniors in New York. For Garland, leaving newspapers for *Vogue* was one of the hardest decisions of her life, not that she was a novice on magazines. She had actually cut her teeth at Condé Nast; her first job as a journo was on *Vogue Book of British Exports*. This subsidiary publication was started by managing director Harry Yoxall, in an effort to boost income during the war. Released quarterly, it was a trade journal intended to promote British exports to a global network of buyers, bringing welcome advertising revenue to Brogue's coffers.

In her youth, Garland had been part of the small team whose job it was to present this more down-to-earth version of *Vogue* for an international audience. Their office was just above the main premises at 37 Golden Square and the atmosphere was extremely formal. All the fashion editors wore hats, even when sitting at their desks, and kept their veils on while working at typewriters.[416] But intimidating though the environment was, Garland picked up an understanding of how important it was to dress correctly for *Vogue*, along with an encyclopedic knowledge of the rag trade.

When she finally took the plunge to return to British *Vogue* as editor, she found herself at a new address in Hanover Square. The organisation adopted an open-plan arrangement when they moved to this imposing structure, now part of the Mayfair Conservation Area. The editor's office was a square space with glass walls that didn't quite reach the ceiling.[417] The result unnerved Garland. She couldn't so much as fix her lipstick or pull up a stocking without being watched.[418] She couldn't avoid anybody or interview people in private. Her voice carried enough for it to be inconvenient: once she ordered her secretary to summon a staff member to tell them off, only to find the woman in question had overheard her and pulled a quick sickie.[419] 'I do not feel happy in a goldfish bowl,' she wrote in her memoirs.[420]

The surroundings were different to a life on the dailies and her assignment was different too. On newspapers an editor's job was to inform and entertain. Garland described the brief for *Vogue* as involving: 'considerations of advertising, acceptance by the trade as an authority, maintenance of the Vogue image, the ability to lead'.[421] The items within the pages were there to beautify women and the editor who oversaw these pages had to uphold the brand. Now keeper of the flame, Garland had to find solutions to the problems of the sixties, the most pressing of which was a new one on her tongue.[422] It was called budgets.

When courting Garland, the president of the company, Iva Patcévitch, had asked her why she thought *Vogue* could afford her. Under such a line of attack, Garland had been forced to argue she wasn't after a high salary; what she wanted was a challenging position. She was prepared to take a pay cut to be offered the role of editrix at *Vogue*. Crafty businessmen have always known how to get employees to dig their own graves. Garland was therefore alerted to the delicate matter of finances at the British edition. It wasn't so much that they didn't make money, more a preliminary caution due to Europe's unstable economies. Still, the budgets had her by the throat. She described them as a 'formidable affair' with every item from photostat paper to postage stamps being counted and estimated to produce a projected figure, to then be compared to the final cost at the end of every month.[423] There was a business manager, Lily Davies, who handled everything from bookings, to travel arrangements, to managing the tempers that came with the talent. Her most important duty, however, was keeping everyone tightly strapped into their budgets.

It was a hectic job being the editor before the internet. The first order of the day was reading through the mail, answering invitations, passing fashion news on to the fashion room.[424] Appointments had to be cross-checked with a secretary, who cross-checked them with other secretaries. Briefings for the shoots came next. A head of department would wheel in her picks with the help of junior staff, arrange them on the rail and proceed to show them to varying exclamations from 'Marvellous!' to 'Can't stand that'.[425] A key consideration was whether the manufacturer of the clothes paid for advertising. If they did, their pieces went in. If they didn't, they'd think twice. Copy-editors would take on the text, scribble, cross out, rearrange and edit. Fashion editors would hotly debate which photographer, studio or location to use and where props would come from.[426] Ideas would be bandied about, the photographer might suggest something complicated, like a shoot on the busy Portobello Road with models surrounded by every breed of dog. Somebody might have a puppy at home, somebody might volunteer their neighbour's pet. It was always a case of pitching in.

Next the editor would go to the art department to look at layouts, weighing up space with budgets and advertisers always in mind – giving more room to one brand might offend another.[427] Back to her private office – no longer the glass box – where several staff would by now be forming an orderly queue to speak to Garland on a variety of topics including promotions, beauty, ads, typos, events, colours, sick leave or lunch plans.[428] Garland's own lunch was taken in the outside world, but only if accompanied by the chairman or managing director of a big-name firm.[429]

Back again, this time to look at the next issue but one, with all the heads of department, brainstorming ideas and allocating tasks. A romance issue might mean pink lingerie, trips abroad in secluded coves, fashion stories with lovers.[430] The business manager would then go away to book photographers, models, make-up artists.[431] Lists would be made of fees, as well as lists of contacts whom they might be able to pull in for some very *Vogue* favour. Schedules were written up and handed round. Since they were working on no less than three issues at a time, all this organisation was crucial. Famous contributors needed to be cosseted, so they felt appreciated by the firm and would go back out into the world and say, 'The Editor? Oh, she's a charming creature!' to all their important friends.[432]

One thing is abundantly clear: to keep the job you needed high energy levels. Little clues to the intense pressure of this life stand out like red flags all over Garland's autobiography. After every day in Paris seeing the collections she would 'fall into bed'.[433] At the end of the week she'd lose her voice from nerves or tiredness.[434]

Garland concedes the job was 'full, exhausting', yet it obviously did have its fun moments. She once accompanied her team to do a story in Barbados, taking along her five-year-old son as playmate for the daughter of the photographer's assistant. The island was so impressed by the *Vogue* cavalry that a special calypso was composed in their honour by a steel band, and one verse of the lyrics ran: 'Fashions you read of from far away / Advice to women to brighten their day / All the thought of Miss Garland, the heart of the scheme / For a sample of this, read Vogue magazine.'[435]

Youth in Full Swing

By the mid-sixties, the social landscape of London had been upturned. The era that brought rock 'n' roll, miniskirts, the space age and mods was in full play. The baby boomers were out in force and they were into beehives, The Beatles, dropping acid and leather catsuits. Glamour and privilege were no longer worthy currencies. As if he set out to prove this, a twenty-something reporter for the *Evening Standard* (later disgraced Conservative MP), Jonathan Aitken, conducted a series of interviews with some 200 subjects that were defining a scene in some new way. The result of this anthropological document is a book titled *The Young Meteors* (1967), which spotlights personalities in fields as varied as photography, music, politics, art, television and even gambling and prostitution. The collection shows a new elite emerging from the heart of London's East End which blatantly celebrated creativity over birthright.

Photographers like David Bailey no longer had to pay their dues for half a lifetime to find conventional success. The young suddenly had money of their own and even women could earn some – and occasionally did. A new cohort of designers sprung up around the

King's Road in Chelsea, Jean Muir and Mary Quant among them. Who represented society also shifted. The previous dominion of noble lineages disappeared, engulfed in the tidal wave of youth that swept the island. This was the first teenage generation free from conscription and free to enjoy life's spoils. The number of births in the United Kingdom had spiked after WWII in 1947, when there were an estimated 880,000 newborns (for comparison, the Office for National Statistics records just under 580,000 births in 1941).[436] The millions of adolescents that were the result of this boom were the country's future.

When Ailsa Garland stepped into her role she understood the importance of age. In an attempt to cater to the daughters of *Vogue* readers, Audrey Withers had introduced the feature 'Young Idea' in the early 1950s, though it was Garland who developed it into a regular section. In its early days, youth was identified as somewhere between seventeen and twenty-five and formal debutante-style gowns with matching gloves were the order of the day.[437] When Garland took over, her opinion was the pages were still too 'debby' and not at all fitting to the moment.[438] There had been hardly any firms making clothes suitable for younger girls and most wore simplified versions of their mothers' wardrobes. In the 1960s, as this began to change, Garland's *Vogue* rushed to cover the news. Soon, 'Young Idea' was transformed into a triumphant calling card for innovations in British design.

The photography in this section clashed with the rest of the magazine; it was dynamic, action driven and natural in gesture. The publication still had to feature haughty grandeur in the fashion stories, providing static and solemn portraits where the models looked thirty even if they were twenty. This was because the bulk of the readers still belonged to the older generation and alienating them before getting their children properly on side would have been foolish. Instead, *Vogue* planned to cater to both groups by subtly dividing the content, that way it could gradually seduce a new generation that would eventually supplant their parents in paid subscriptions.

In the 1950s, photographers had had major issues taking pictures of ready-to-wear. John French, who had been David Bailey's mentor, used to stuff empty toilet rolls down belts at the back of a garment to try and give them shape. That wasn't his only trick: he carried clothes pegs to pin back oversized jackets.[439] His ingenuity was tested when faced with ill-fitting, off-the-peg items, but it was the models who had to exercise the most patience. Exposures took a long time and they had to try to sustain a pose in their awkwardly tightened get-up or else be tied to a pole to help them stay still. This improved in the 1960s, with the evolution of design and camera. An impish David Bailey could run circles round his muses while snapping away.

The photographer Norman Parkinson was among the first to treat models like people instead of frozen mannequins, allowing them to have facial expressions. He was also the first to take pictures of girls while smoking or eating. Getting his models moving was forward-thinking, but the mature readers found it improper. He paved the way for fresh blood like Tony Armstrong-Jones (later Lord Snowdon), who produced shoot after shoot with the models slipping on banana skins or pitching out of windows.[440] His work is a wilderness of the frenetic and kinetic. So crazy was Armstrong-Jones about movement, that legend has it if you referred to one of his sessions as 'sittings' he would make the girls run.[441]

Then there was David Bailey, who brokered his reputation by landing a huge job for *Vogue* all the way in New York, where he went accompanied by one of the grander editors, Lady Rendlesham. The fashion story they covered was published in 1962 with the title 'Young Idea Goes West' and showed his muse (and flame), Jean

Shrimpton, slouching through the gritty backstreets of Manhattan. They had been thrilled to go so far from home; back then it was unheard of for working-class youth to travel anywhere, let alone cross continents. Decades later he shrugged off the experience coolly in an interview, saying it was so cold the camera stuck in his hands and that Lady Rendlesham cried nonstop.[442]

The cohort of British designers who came to the fore in the sixties were badly needed. Just as David Bailey and Lord Snowdon had bumped up the reputation of British *Vogue* by being their first breakthrough artists, so landmark brands like Mary Quant, Jean Muir and Biba redeemed British style. Geometrically patterned tunics and miniskirts, along with an array of playful items like go-go boots and metallic hot pants, gave sixties fashion the feel of a child's dressing-up box. It was the Brits' first proper attempt at ready-to-wear and they kept it simple.

Tania Mallet, a model who later became a Bond girl in *Goldfinger*, chronicled the sharp shift in attitudes. When she started modelling in her late teens young models were extremely unusual. She poignantly describes her inexperience visiting Vogue House for the first time, trudging through the rain wearing old trousers and arriving dripping wet, her hair plastered to her face.[443] She stumbled into a room with a number of sophisticated faces who'd all been modelling in the fifties, their hair in perfect beehives: real-life imitations of fashion plates. Feeling sheepish and out of place, Mallet slunk into a corner feeling she'd made a fool of herself, but a funny-looking photographer poked his head round the door and, to her enormous surprise, picked Mallet for the job.[444] She embodied the adorable naïveté of a child – just who this new world wanted to speak for.

In 1965, a 'Young Idea' page covered the opening of the 21 shop, one of the leading boutiques promoting emerging British designers such as Ossie Clark, and Foale and Tuffin. The models were shot in dynamic poses next to young men. These boys were a select group of 'Young Meteors' and included Kenneth Tynan, who'd been appointed *The Observer*'s drama critic at the tender age of twenty-eight, fashion photographer Terence Donovan and Vidal Sassoon. By traversing their areas of expertise and moonlighting as male models for a *Vogue* spread, they exemplified another stereotype of the sixties: the creative crossover. Another groundbreaking notion, the Chelsea set and Carnaby Street crowd often worked in interchangeable roles. Never before had people dared stray from what was perceived as their rightful place, yet this too was changing. Barbara Hulanicki, founder of the legendary store Biba, had been *Nova*'s fashion editor as well as *Vogue*'s fashion illustrator, taking on jobs as she felt drawn to them.

By now, 'Young Idea' had fourteen pages to fill. The art department was also becoming more daring. The British *Vogue* covers from the 1960s are far more experimental than the American counterpart, illustrating a new sought-after blend of highbrow and lowbrow. The tone inside also evolved to mirror a lightness and playfulness. It no longer dispensed orders as it had in the war years. Instead, the text asked questions: 'Couture Clothes, are they worth the money?'[445] It's not a daring query by today's standards, but never before had magazines given up their position of authority and opened up conversations.

Taking pleasure in consumption was no longer a taboo either and catchy slogans such as 'What makes Britain wear so well' and 'Buy nothing until you buy Vogue' captured the zeitgeist. Even *Vogue*'s trendiest competitors could not compete with the glossy periodical rampant with support for British design, alive with primary colours and cutting-edge suggestions. Behind the printed pages many brilliant interns and trainees were coming up through the Vogue Talent Contest or being given chances on shoots and running assignments. For now, a heartening meritocracy reigned.

Questions of Class

In the end, Garland was not cut out for life at Condé Nast. The complicated web of the *Vogue* world was suffocating, impossible to untangle. Exhausted beyond repair just four years after starting, she left in 1964 and returned to newspapers. Her replacement, Beatrix Miller, was made of sterner stuff. Bordering on the intellectual, Miller's background was in journalism, though her early years included a stint as a secretary on the Nuremberg Trials for MI6. Miller had an interesting path into glossies, starting with a junior post at *Queen*, an avant-garde English magazine, which she left in 1956 to take a copywriting job at American *Vogue*.

When *Queen* was bought by Sir Jocelyn Stevens in 1957, a publisher and newspaper executive (and Poppy and Cara Delevingne's grandfather), as a birthday present to himself, he was dead set on enticing Miller back and famously called her in the middle of the night to say, 'You don't know who I am, but I am ringing to offer you the job of editor of *Queen*.' Miller replied, 'It's 4.00 am. You're mad,' and hung up.[446] When she did accept the post, she became part of its transformation into an eccentric anthology that brokered its status with the Chelsea set and made *Queen* journalists popular figures in their own right. So popular in fact, that *Vogue* wanted them. In 1963 editor Marit Allen moved, then in 1964 Beatrix Miller was poached by Condé Nast too.

British *Vogue* was grand for English magazines, yet nothing compared to American ones. It was New York that had the big budgets, super-organised work flow and the numbers to run like an industrial operation. Miller had a headmistressy manner and was capable of canning a whole issue if she was unhappy when she saw it. However, the Brogue regime wasn't onerous: staff trickled in closer to 10 a.m.

than 9 a.m., took the pleasure of three-course lunches in cafés where they would while away hours chattering and by 6 p.m. everyone had peeled off home, including Miller who exited at 5.30 p.m. sharp in her Jaguar.

Grace Coddington – who went on to become creative director at American *Vogue* – joined in 1968, when her previous career in modelling was coming to an end. Vogue House was still at the illustrious address of 1 Hanover Square, but Coddington found it underwhelming on the inside. The lobby was a forgettable wood-panelled space; while upstairs was a muddle of messy open-plan rooms. The furniture looked like it had been dragged in from a skip; the floor was done in cork, tired and stained. Coddington recorded her first impression as: 'The lift doors parted – and what a disappoint-ment it was!'[447] There were still a lot of well-born, well-connected women at the magazine, even if they were in junior positions. One of Coddington's assistants was a 'girl of independent means' who dyed her hair magenta, drove her Mercedes almost as fast as Beatrix Miller drove her Jag and ended up marrying a polo player.[448] There is something thrilling about these dashing *Vogue*-ettes of the early seventies recklessly burning rubber in their sports cars.

Miller had arrived in magazines at the crossover moment; just as class barriers were being knocked down. She was intelligent and original enough to embrace this. Although she liked writers properly trained and never accepted half-rate copy, she was also supportive of aspiring writers and made sure a great deal of hopefuls made it in through the door. Marina Warner, now Dame Marina Warner, critic, novelist, journalist and the first female president of the Royal Society of Literature, was hired as a fresh-faced graduate on Miller's instinct. Among Miller's other main drives was the Vogue Talent Contest. She recruited from the shortlisters and winners liberally, encouraging them to pitch to her and allowing their imaginations a degree of editorial freedom. When novice Sandy Boler wrote in to complain about *Vogue* still being elitist, Miller gave her a regular feature called 'More Dash Than Cash'.

There is a perfect, beautifully irreverent spread during the Miller era, poking fun at British etiquette from Nancy Mitford's book *Noblesse Oblige* (1956). One of Mitford's rules was that a lady ought never to wear imitation jewels, colourful underwear or diamonds until after breakfast,[449] so they pictured model Cathee Dahmen performing all three sins, with one shot showing her brushing her teeth while wearing a huge faux rhinestone choker which does nothing to hide the fact that she's also topless. Meanwhile a fuzzy close-up of a model with a mane of marmalade hair went to print with the caption: '"dyed is vulgar!" *Is it?* / "Never wear clashing reds" *Why not?*'[450]

Even more daring is model Gala Mitchell tearing through Hyde Park with a Victorian-style baby pram wearing gold silk dungarees, orange tights and yellow heels. It was 1971, and yet surrounding her in the candid shot are the immaculately dressed nannies of the rich, in full uniform that included white caps and aprons over plain dresses, their hair pinned back. They were taking out the heirs of Chelsea and Kensington for a morning walk. It's hard to believe that in the seventies domestic staff were still employed in such numbers, let alone given identical maid outfits. Miller's subheading ran: '"Is it in bad taste to dress extravagantly or showily when mingling with people who are all plainly dressed" *Is bad taste a bad thing?*'[451]

Challenging the remnants of England's prescriptive, class-based society showed that fashion could be used, subverted and played with to make readers think more broadly about the world they were living in. Then again, Miller loved shooting on location in gardens, because this felt properly English to her. She was motherly (Coddington remembers fainting on a trip, after which Miller started carrying sweets in her handbag to bring up her blood sugar levels if it happened again[452]); and she could be decadent, with her obligatory lunchtime negroni and dinner parties featuring Elizabeth Taylor, Richard Burton, Princess Margaret and Paul and Linda McCartney.[453] When she retired, it was at the end of a successful stewardship from 1964 to 1984. It would be a very, very long time before British *Vogue* questioned social norms again.

CHAPTER 10

Expensive Entertainment

Backstabbing and Big Business

Diana Vreeland's Fantasy World

Up in the Central Andes of Peru, at an altitude of some 20,000 feet, a peculiar little group was clustered. The longest mountain chain in the world and the second tallest range, it is composed of plateaus carpeted in green moss, peaks so high they dissolve into inky-blue shadows and glassy lagoons created by thawing glaciers. The entire panorama is brushed white by rolling clouds. It seems unlikely that one would find British photographer John Cowan here, capturing an editorial for American *Vogue*. Yet there he was, in the late 1960s, trying to immortalise the gleeful prancing of some models wearing mink. Also joining him for this frostbitten adventure were celebrated hairdresser Ara Gallant and fashion editor Babs Simpson, who had a severe case of vertigo.[454]

Cowan had been planning a lavish spread in which the snow-clotted mountain range, gloomy verdure and Inca ruins would come together to make it look as though the models themselves – in myriad outfits of suede, mufflers, weskits and dirndls as well as a plethora

of fur from chinchilla to lynx – were lifting off and floating through
the cloud-swept landscape. The helicopter pilot who had deposited
them there had warned them of a 5 p.m. cutoff point; if they stayed
any later they would have to be rescued.[455] But the curfew came and
went, the pilot left and night descended. Eventually, the group had
to scale down the mountain, the models still in stilettos, until they
found a cave and managed to light a fire.[456] They spent the night in
there, huddled together in the furs. They woke up the next day to
be greeted by a furious Peruvian army and encircling their hideout
were tracks left by mountain lions.[457] They were swiftly deported.

This spread made it to the printer and was published in American
Vogue's October issue of 1968,[458] though there were endless other
'expensive glitches'[459] – courtesy of the latest editor-in-chief Diana
Vreeland – which wouldn't see the light of day. The surreal, Dalí-
esque Peru adventure was by no means a one-off. Vreeland once
sent David Bailey all the way to India to photograph white tigers
then never ran the images. Another series with model Penelope
Tree was rejected by Vreeland due to her complaint there was 'no
languor in the lips'.[460] Reshoots were frequently on the agenda. So
were tantrums. Exotic locations, while scintillating, required months
upon months of preparation. Visas had to be approved by the State
Department. To clear customs the staff had to put together a carnet of
every single item on the trip, down to the tiniest accessories, ensuring
everything that left the country came back.[461] On one trip in Iran, one
editor recalls spending her evenings untangling hundreds of antique
French curtain tassels they were using for an 'ornamental look'.[462] On
another occasion Vreeland suddenly decided a huge hat needed to
be at a photoshoot taking place in the Himalayas. To join the team
who had already left for Asia, the hat, in its hatbox, had to be carted
up a mountain by car, jeep, camel and finally by donkey, to reach the
remote spot. Irons, ironing boards and sewing paraphernalia had to

go wherever the clothes did. These expensive clothes often needed mending and altering on the spot.

Creating one of Vreeland's 'looks' was arduous. Fabric swatches had to be sent for, delivered, chosen, sent back; clothes were then commissioned, modified, discarded, re-ordered; hairdressers, make-up artists, models, editors, assistants, stylists, photographers had to be trialled, hired, fired. Each step had to be committed to Polaroid, so everybody on the team could track the changes.[463] The development bills for the camera film alone were insane. And, of course, it's Vreeland who holds the record for the most expensive photoshoot in history. In autumn 1966, 'The Great Fur Caravan' appeared in the magazine, taking up a whopping twenty-six pages.[464] The team – which included a seven-foot-and-something tall sumo wrestler – spent five weeks in Japan, where they hauled fifteen trunks of garments up snow-covered mountains. Posing in tall ermine boots, white ermine coifs, mittens of Empress chinchilla and Russian lynx, the era is noticeably pre-PETA. Shot by the legendary Richard Avedon, overseen by fashion editor Polly Mellen and starring supermodel Veruschka, the editorial is rumoured to have cost $1 million. That's roughly $7.5 million in today's money.

'The Great Fur Caravan' is described as a 'fashion adventure' and the team behind it a 'cast of characters'.[465] It was also common at the time to call a photoshoot a 'story'. The vocabulary goes some way to explain how *Vogue* under Vreeland thought of fashion. Having been born at the turn of the century, Vreeland spoke wistfully of the spectacular clothes worn by the grandes dames of Paris in the early 1900s. With her youth in the Roaring Twenties and her direct experience of the changes wrought by both wars, Vreeland was a front-row witness to astonishing shifts in fashion. Positioning herself as the last remaining true aesthete and something of a fashion scholar, she brought fantasy and history together in *Vogue*'s pages.

Vreeland eschewed the recipes and household tips then common to women's magazines, believing the romanticism of Russia and China was more important. She understood what ephemeral qualities change our lives and it was this instinct that brought the magic in, balancing what made her appear difficult, of questionable sanity. The problem with Vreeland's dreams was that they always came with a very real price tag. Who would ultimately pay?

Alex Liberman's Adventures in Brown-nosing

Born in 1903 to a socialite and a stockbroker, Vreeland made the gossip columns as a debutante. Despite a lack of conventional beauty (her mother called her 'my ugly little monster'), she made a high-profile match with a handsome banker who moved the family to London, where her fledgling eccentricities took hold. She painted her skin stark white, with thick lines of unblended rouge on her cheeks. She learned the rumba instead of nursing her infants. She ran a lingerie shop where Wallis Simpson was reported to be a customer. Upon returning to New York she was spotted dancing on the St Regis hotel rooftop by Carmel Snow, editor-in-chief of *Harper's Bazaar* and offered a job on the strength of her outfit. The Vreelands lived in reckless extravagance and never had any money, so in a bid to stave off financial horrors she took the job. She would spend twenty-six years under Snow, who speedily promoted her through the ranks to fashion editor.

For a while, Vreeland ran a column called 'Why Don't You . . .', providing extravagantly insane advice such as 'Why Don't You . . . wear violet velvet mittens with everything?'[466] or 'Why Don't You . . . use a gigantic shell instead of a bucket to ice your champagne?'[467] Her fashion editor's eye produced the photoshoots which placed

VOGUE

VOGUE—A DEBUTANTE

The cover of *Vogue*'s first ever issue, released across America on the 17th of December 1892, priced at 10 cents and featuring a pretty debutante.

Above: *Vogue*'s most formidable editor-in-chief, Edna Woolman Chase. At one point she was the editor of American, British, French and German *Vogue* at the same time, and is still the longest serving editor in the magazine's history, having held the post for thirty-eight years.

Right: Condé Montrose Nast, *Vogue*'s second owner and publishing tycoon, who launched the magazine overseas.

Right: Bettina Ballard, Fashion Editor, working on photo sessions overnight during the Paris collections.

Below: 'Fashion is Indestructible' by Cecil Beaton. Shot amid the ruins of the Blitz in London.

Spring Ball Gowns by Cecil Beaton. Showing a co-existence of fashion and art, the model wears a pale blue dress with ostrich feathers pictured in front of a Jackson Pollock painting.

Autocratic editor-in-chief Diana Vreeland, shown in her apartment, the 'Garden in Hell'.

Cover for Colombe Pringle's ground-breaking issue of *Vogue Paris* in December/January 1994, featuring Nelson Mandela as guest editor.

Left: Colombe Pringle, editor-in-chief of *Vogue Paris* 1987–1994, known for her trailblazing Christmas issues.

Below: Liz Tilberis and Anna Wintour at Donna Karan in 1994. Pitched against each other in the media and polar opposites in looks, both had been editor-in-chief at British *Vogue*.

November 2017 cover of British *Vogue*, guest edited by Meghan Markle.

Emmanuelle Alt, current editor-in-chief of *Vogue Paris*, with Edward Enninful, current editor-in-chief of British *Vogue*.

Harper's Bazaar at the cutting edge of fashion, even if *Vogue* was still the staple. A colleague from *Bazaar* remembers that during WWII shoe rationing she was responsible for popularising ballet slippers, thus netting one of those insane American fortunes for the manufacturer, Capezio.[468] A friendship with Jackie Kennedy resulted in the First Lady consulting her on what to wear for her husband's inauguration. She injected the whole industry with a heady artifice that transported women into dream worlds. But her genius made her too unpredictable to leave unsupervised. Carmel Snow kept her on a tight leash and when she retired the promotion went over Vreeland's head to Snow's niece. This snub was too much for Vreeland, who effected a swift exit from *Harper's*. Liberman claimed her for *Vogue*, hoping the new owners would be impressed.

Diana Vreeland called 1962 'the year of the jet, the Pill'.[469] Although the sixties were born in London, they were Vreeland's moment. She was stimulated by the new faces, the changes and came up with the term 'Youthquake'.[470] Visual excess continued to dominate her life. Her living room, known as 'Garden in Hell', was Chinese red from carpet to curtains, cluttered with oriental divans, snuffboxes, books and cushions in more shades of red. She kept a maid to dress her, clean the inside of her handbags and iron her five-dollar bills.[471] She was famous for her bombastic one-liners including: 'The bikini is the most important thing since the atomic bomb!'[472] 'Pink is the navy blue of India!'[473] 'A little bad taste is like a nice splash of paprika!'[474] Best of all was her cryptic command to a photographer: 'Find me the gypsy Queen who bathes in milk and has the most beautiful skin in the world!'

A wanton atmosphere invaded the *Vogue* offices. Vreeland's assistant describes a rogue Great Dane biting a chunk out of an evening gown on a shoot.[475] Studios complained that models were too stoned to stand. A swimwear editorial got pulled because the model had track marks from injecting heroin all over her arms.[476] Models were 'throwing temper tantrums, stealing fur coats'.[477] One visiting designer insisted on reading everyone's palm before showing anyone his clothes.[478] In the documentary *Diana Vreeland: The Eye Has to Travel* (2011), a fashion insider declares, 'She was the most expensive thing . . . the Newhouses ever had. She cost a *fortune!*'[479]

For many years there had been a close friendship between Iva Patcévitch, president of Condé Nast, and Alexander Liberman, the art director. Both were White Russians who'd lived in Paris. It was Patcévitch who promoted Liberman, making him the youngest art director in New York. And it was this close friendship of twenty-seven years which Liberman casually discarded in order to become Si Newhouse's favourite when the company changed hands. When the new owner, who clashed with Patcévitch, asked Liberman whether Patcévitch was doing a good job, Liberman did nothing to defend the man who'd secured his own future all those years ago. Once Patcévitch was out of the way, Liberman was free to cosy up to Si Newhouse. A former Condé Nast employee says:

> Liberman found a shy, somewhat under-exposed guy named Si Junior and took him under his wing . . . He exposed him to a different world. Nobody had ever spent a lot of time with Si or showed any great interest in him. So Si's attitude about Alex was not only that he was a talented human being but that he was somebody who took an interest in *me*, somebody who spent time with *me*.[480]

The spell he cast over Si Newhouse allowed Liberman to become the dominant voice at Condé Nast for the next quarter of a century. Talented though he was, Liberman couldn't have maintained his position without his cunning, coldness and calculating mind. Always immaculate, he used the phrase 'dear friend'[481] before delivering a cutting insult. Nicknamed the 'Silver Fox'[482] in later years, Liberman seemed willing to go to any lengths to stay at the top of *Vogue*, not only controlling the staff, but even compromising himself. He was willing to accrue debt, constantly borrowing from the bank and his friends to maintain his *Vogue*-appropriate lifestyle. He expected the same of other employees (it's difficult to decide who is more at fault here – *Vogue* for not paying its staff properly or Liberman for believing the staff weren't dedicated unless they were prepared to amass hefty debts in the name of employment). Lord Snowdon commented, 'He was as arduous a self-promoter as you can meet, very slippery, like an eel, always wheeling and dealing for himself.'[483] Even Si Newhouse, who spent four faithful decades by Liberman's side, was forced to admit there was much self-interest in his character.[484]

Liberman's friendship with Si Newhouse served him well. When Newhouse was named chairman of Condé Nast in the mid-1960s he raised Liberman's salary to half a million dollars (this became a full million per annum in 1980).[485] On weekends, Si Newhouse would take Liberman as his unofficial advisor to galleries to sweep up de Koonings and Rauschenbergs. Even from these artistic expeditions Liberman profited – Newhouse bought a number of Liberman's own artworks too.

But as much as Liberman was happy to syphon off Newhouse funds for his own enjoyment, he disapproved of Vreeland's similar sycophantic efforts. For all Vreeland's love of ephemera and mystique, there was also a blood-deep attachment to money. She knew her place well enough to make her own play at seducing the Newhouses, becoming a fixture at Mitzi Newhouse's parties. A colleague recalls after runway shows Vreeland would rush over to Mitzi, virtually throw herself on the woman, and proceed to shower her with compliments.[486]

Vreeland was the autocratic editor from hell long before Anna Wintour. *The Devil Wears Prada*, a thinly veiled portrayal on Wintour by a former intern, was preceded by *Funny Face*, the musical with Audrey Hepburn, where the magazine editor character is based on Vreeland. Her regime at American *Vogue* was exhausting and unconstructive, calibrated to set people against each other. She issued her first orders from the bath and swept into the office at midday, burning a fog of incense thick enough to choke the secretaries. For lunch she had a peanut butter sandwich with half a bowl of melted ice cream, after which a nurse would arrive to give her a vitamin shot.[487] From Jessica Daves, Vreeland had inherited an office that ran like clockwork. Under Vreeland, this distorted into an ugly circus. Staffer Grace Mirabella compared her system to a Roman gladiatorial contest:

> Vreeland's run-throughs often were like feeding lambs to a lion. . . . There were many tears, many casualties. More than one editor threatened to throw herself out of a window after a run-through with Vreeland. Secretaries quit left and right. . . . Editors jostled for favor with Vreeland and tried to bury each other in the process. I'd hear screams all the time from the closet.[488]

With everybody tripping over themselves to try to get in Vreeland's good books and sabotaging each other in the process, things spiralled quickly. Liberman had just about managed to hold his tongue while Vreeland was at the height of her popularity in the 1960s. But as the decade closed, he saw an opportunity. Increasingly, women needed practical, sombre clothes that mirrored the economic downturn. Vreeland did not respond to this new landscape, preferring to still offer purple raincoats, vinyl blouses, and body stockings, instead of catering to women's practical needs. They responded by cancelling subscriptions. In the first three months of 1971, sales of advertising space dropped nearly 40 per cent.[489] Mirabella concedes that advertising had fallen across the whole industry in response to a general recession but when Liberman and Si Newhouse 'looked at the numbers, they saw Vreeland's face.'[490] One can sympathise with Liberman's frustrations on the topic of Diana Vreeland. In one of his many remonstrations with her to be more sensible budget-wise, she shocked him by replying, 'Alex, after all, this is only entertainment.' Of course to Si Newhouse, whose family had built a modern American empire, this was deeply perturbing. To them *Vogue* was not entertainment, it was business.[491] When Vreeland was finally fired in 1971, she demanded Liberman give her some explanation or take responsibility. This showdown led to the last of her famous bons mots coined at *Vogue*: 'We've all known many White Russians, and we've known a few Red Russians. But Alex, you're the only yellow Russian I've ever known.'[492]

Grace Mirabella's Beige Years

Inheriting Diana Vreeland's throne was not going to be easy. Almost a lifetime in the industry had earned her some colourful nicknames that illustrate the semi-religious fervour she inspired. Sacred Monster. High Priestess of Fashion. Empress. Oracle. The conclave secrecy with which the successor was chosen made the final choice even more surprising. Liberman had alighted on Grace Mirabella, a pragmatic, golden-haired 40-year-old with an easy modern American style.

The fashion world was deeply unimpressed. To insiders, Mirabella was too vanilla. Andy Warhol scathingly said she'd been hired because '*Vogue* wanted to go middle class'.[493] A colleague publicly

called her a 'nine-to-five girl' in *Newsweek*.[494] Other sharp tongues
at *Vogue* nicknamed her 'the secretary'.[495] Gianni Bulgari paid her
a visit to discuss how the 'vulgarization' of *Vogue* would affect his
advertising. A slew of famous photographers, designers and her own
colleagues at *Vogue* passed through Mirabella's offices to grill her on
her intentions and to gawk at the offensive *normality* of the creature.
The message from fashion was clear: Mirabella wasn't worthy.

Nobody, either then or now, seems to give Mirabella much credit
for not having crumbled under this pressure. A *Vogue* lifer, Mirabella had been on the staff since her early twenties and grafted all
the way up to becoming Vreeland's second-in-command. Nobody
was closer to the action, or spoke Vreeland more fluently. 'I was
Vreeland's shadow, her alter ego . . . I did not love the image Vreeland felt she had to present to the world . . . But I loved, I absolutely
adored, with what I can only describe as the passion of a schoolgirl
crush, Vreeland the woman' Mirabella wrote in her autobiography.[496]
When Vreeland's reign ended and Condé Nast Publications called,
Mirabella was on a shoot in California. This situation must have
been deeply painful and was made worse by the fact that Vreeland
was kept on for an extra six months as consulting editor. Vreeland
herself was completely heartbroken. Mirabella candidly admits to
her own cowardice, stating she couldn't bring herself to clear the air
with Vreeland and instead avoided her completely.[497]

The many naysayers were right about one thing with Mirabella:
she did mean change. Mirabella, whose specialism was sportswear,
was roughly thirty years younger than Vreeland. Her finger was on
the pulse of the 1970s and she was well placed to cater to the 'New
Woman'. All the big topics of the decade: feminism, political upheaval
incited by Watergate, outbreaks of protests against the Vietnam War
and for gay rights, the economic downturn and the oil crisis . . . these
were all on Mirabella's radar. She may not have known every consti-

tutional detail, but she knew what women wanted to wear at a picket line or on their first day of college. In fashion history, the 1970s have a bad reputation. With the economic crash the length of skirts fell, so at the beginning of the decade the midiskirt replaced the mini at the Parisian shows. In America the midi was considered overly conservative and ageing. Absurdly, this battle made its way into geopolitics and the Democrats against Nixon became unexpected advocates of the mini, seeing it as a symbol of American freedom, while the midi was shunned as a tool of dictatorial Europe.

The controversy over hemlines led to the women of the mid-seventies to skirt the issue entirely and adopt trousers en masse. The second wave of feminism meant many were disparaging of trends and began to see fashion as a tool of oppression. Countercultures such as drug psychedelia and the sexual revolution became widespread and were absorbed into consumer society. Blue jeans, once a staple of the working man, became fashion statements with the birth of designer denim brands. The influence of music from punk, to glam rock, to hip-hop, the increased visibility of black Americans in film and the arrival of street style meant that fashion was no longer trickling down from the Parisian couture houses, but bubbling up from places like the Bronx.

Mirabella might not have been the one to introduce street style to *Vogue*, but she was the right woman to render a curated *Vogue*-version of these themes. The daughter of an alcohol importer in Newark, she'd had to put up with endless snubs from her patrician colleagues in the 1950s and 1960s, but the 1970s probably felt like her time. As a high achiever who remained unmarried until later in life, she could sympathise with other women who were trying to forge their own path. Vreeland had been well born and felt comfortable with people from a similar background. Even her models, such as Veruschka and Penelope Tree, were descended from either money or nobility. Mirabella wanted to be the first to champion people of real merit in American *Vogue*. New kinds of famous faces, like political activist Gloria Steinem, appeared in the pages while kittenish child-girls like Twiggy disappeared. Mirabella was also to be the first American editor to put a black model on the cover.

In another brave stride *Vogue* expanded to include politics, health and wellbeing. The articles span from sincere takedowns of senators,[498] to updates in medicine promoting the benefits of vitamin E.[499] There are reports on the cutting-edge development of the pap smear to detect early signs of cervical cancer.[500] These topics had seldom, if ever, made their way into women's magazines before. The tone, instead of being giddy or glossing over 'unladylike' facts, is serious without being solemn. Brains were the new sexy, wellness was the new sexy, and grown women with opinions were very, very sexy.

For the wholesome all-American ideal this *Vogue* represented, there was quite a lot of sex in general. Adverts are nothing short of raunchy. Ads for cigarettes discuss length and size, for lipstick tout wetness and moistness, and for holidays hint at wilderness and heat. The images show male bodies, frolicking females and saucy smiles. These are clearly responses to the sexual liberation. Mirabella herself was tentative about the amount of sex creeping into the pages and blamed Liberman and his interest in *Playboy* and *Penthouse* for taking it a little too far on occasion.[501] Where possible, she wanted the sex element to liberate women, not cross over into satisfying the male gaze.

Fashion also got an overhaul. Gone were the go-go boots and sequinned false eyelashes. Gone were stiff haircuts, gone was make-up as a mask. Mirabella's *Vogue* is deliciously classy. Tall, bouncy blondes sashay across the pages, light cigarettes in purposeful motion, seductively pour themselves wine and adjust earrings in their own boudoirs. They cut across beautiful rooms with powerful strides, drive fast cars, hair whipping in the wind. On beaches they lounge with their friends not their husbands and often slightly older women appear with younger ones, both looking extremely put together and professional, giving age a new dignity. At last women are doing it for themselves – and succeeding elegantly.

When it came to models, Mirabella was after the healthy, smiling, all-American ideal. The clothes are glamorous, but clearly allow for movement. In the 1950s and even the 1960s, a great deal of fashion depended on having a man around to do up the zip of your dress or a maid to adjust your finery. For a long time, it was surprisingly complicated for a woman to dress herself. In the 1970s, finally all women, from teenagers throwing on jeans for school, to typists off to their day job, and even to the pampered heiresses with their fat cheque books, could be entirely in control. This marked a fundamental change to women's lives. The stylish, practical clothes, heavy emphasis on American designers over the traditional European houses and candid new voice catapulted *Vogue* to new heights. Although readers in the Bible Belt who were offended by the quantity of sex, cancelled subscriptions, it barely mattered, for Mirabella's magazine broke records.[502] During her tenure circulation tripled from around 400,000 to 1.3 million, with the corresponding increase in gross revenues rising from $9.1 million to $26.9 million.[503]

This outward success in no way meant life behind the scenes was any easier. By the 1980s, Mirabella admits to a burgeoning disillusionment. As the fashion industry had begun to attract ever-increasing numbers of press and media, so fashion shows had to accommodate larger and larger audiences. The intimate presentations of yesteryear became the bombastic runways of today. A small audience can be shown clothes up close to appreciate design, but the vast crowds which were now drawn to catwalk shows had to be entertained.

Brands responded by adding music, lights and, not least, by vamping up the clothes. Mirabella hated the carnivalesque turn and held a particular vendetta against Christian Lacroix whom she appears to largely blame for the movement.[504] The opulent, impractical clothes he produced stood against everything she had pioneered. Consumers too had changed: 'I was used to being around people who *did* something . . . these people were out of style in the 1980s. A "new aristocracy" had been born of investment bankers and their skinny wives,' she wrote.[505]

Along with this feeling of disconnect regarding the new trends, came a distancing between Mirabella and Liberman. They had been close collaborators for some twenty years, but Mirabella was becoming a disaffected subject. Presumably it didn't help that Liberman was omnipresent at *Vogue*. When Mirabella was given the editorship, it was with the proviso that she work 'under the overall guidance of Mr. Liberman, Editorial Director of Condé Nast', just as had happened with Vreeland.[506] Once again he had final say on everything, as well as who got hired and fired, meaning Mirabella was often stuck with a team whose vision didn't align with hers. It began to rankle her that, although *Vogue* was a magazine made mostly by women for women, it was the men on the business side who made all the decisions and who earned good wages, while the women in editorial roles drew a pittance. It didn't help that Si Newhouse never consulted her but exclusively conferred with Liberman. She was growing weary of being dismissed, belittled and ignored.

When Mirabella had wanted to run a story on breast cancer, Liberman had replied: '*Vogue* readers are more interested in fashion than breast cancer';[507] Mirabella's cutting riposte: 'I've been a woman longer than you, and they're interested in both';[508] when she wanted to cover the pro-choice movement, Liberman said 'nobody cares';[509] and when she pitched a piece on women's evolving place in society, his response was: 'You don't need to do another story about working women. Women are cheap labour and always will be.'[510]

In her mid-forties, Mirabella had married an eminent surgeon who was adamantly anti-smoking, having seen the long-term effects on the lungs. Mirabella soon quit her forty-a-day habit and began trying to raise awareness of the dangers of cigarettes, a tactic that received considerable backlash from the many tobacco companies who were spending millions advertising in *Vogue*. She had started pressuring Liberman to raise editorial wages, pointing out that women now had other options and didn't have to put up with measly pay.[511] As for herself, Mirabella wanted a spot on the board of directors so she could be present alongside Liberman in the conversations that decided *Vogue*'s future. Si Newhouse's depressing opinion was, 'Women don't really mean anything on boards, Grace.'[512] In fact, the boys' club atmosphere of Condé Nast's upper echelons seems to have only ever been cracked by one woman, the same one who pushed Mirabella out. Anna Wintour.

CHAPTER 11

Wintour is Coming

An Icon's Early Years

Anna Wintour and British *Vogue*

There is no name in the industry like that of Anna Wintour. The terror, the fascination, the nervous excitement she produces in even the least fashion-conscious among us is testament to the strength of her cult of personality. But even Anna Wintour wasn't made in a day. How exactly this British fashion editor managed to woo both Alexander Liberman and Si Newhouse we shall never know. Grace Mirabella remembers her materialising at American *Vogue*, a skinny, impenetrable creature.[513] According to fashion legend, Wintour had once been recommended to Mirabella for a job opening. When Mirabella asked which job she wanted, Wintour had nonchalantly replied '*Yours*' from behind her black-out sunglasses.[514]

Born in London in 1949, Wintour was one of five children, though an early tragedy saw her oldest brother die aged ten in a bicycle accident. Her father was the indomitable Charles Wintour, long-serving editor of the *London Evening Standard*. Journalistic proclivity is not the only trait she inherited, Wintour's icy attitude must have come from her father too – he was known on Fleet Street as Chilly Charles.

An ex-employee once said, 'When you meet Charles Wintour, you'll be put off by his rather glacial exterior, but when you get to know him better you realize it's only the tip of the iceberg'.[515] Raised in the leafy enclave of St John's Wood, Anna Wintour was sent to a series of North London girls' schools so posh that students arrived in chauffeur-driven cars. Wilful and complex, she was patently disinterested in anything academic. She made zero effort with her classmates and skipped classes when she could.

Rumour has it Anna Wintour was only fourteen when she tore out a page on short hairstyles from British *Vogue* and went to a Mayfair salon to get her tresses lopped off.[516] She has kept her signature bob ever since. In Jerry Oppenheimer's unauthorised tell-all biography (published in 2005), people remember her being uncharitable and provocative, making fun of the overweight and jeering at teachers who were single or widowed.[517] All the while, she watched her own figure obsessively and had weekly facials in a private clinic in Baker Street. She must have been their youngest client by decades. Although the Wintour family held conservative values they seem to have allowed their clothes-crazy daughter a surprising amount of freedom. By the age of fifteen she would come and go as she pleased, leading a fairly independent life and spending evenings clubbing, dancing and being seen. Those who remember her mostly recall her incredible thinness, her silence, an apparent shyness and her relentless flirtations with older men. At sixteen, Wintour had a final disagreement with her school over uniform, which she thought was hideous. Refusing to conform, she walked out and never returned.

There are no clues to show Wintour had any particular interest in magazines during her late teens or early adulthood, but she did have an innate understanding for what suited her and what to wear to produce a reaction. By the time her parents threw her a twenty-first birthday party at The Savoy she was already the beneficiary of two large inheritances from distant relatives overseas and the sum of these funds was enough to keep her in luxury apartments and expensive cars.[518] More importantly, it allowed her a designer wardrobe which could be refreshed every season without second thought.

At the dawn of the disco seventies, Wintour landed her first role in publishing. The stately *Harper's Bazaar* UK was being merged with the rebellious *Queen* and they were looking for staff. Wintour had no experience but was hired on the merit of her outfits. The pay was peanuts, but of course this was irrelevant. She didn't need the paycheque, what she wanted was to be in with the cool crowd. Although she insisted she had no particular goals, when preparing the December issue of *Harper's & Queen* in 1971, each staff member had to write down their ideal Christmas present. Rumour has it that Wintour's was to be editor of *Vogue*.[519] Her bosses at *Harper's* did not think this was appropriate for print.

As fashion assistant at *Harper's & Queen*, Wintour's success was mixed. She had an original mind when it came to shoots. She was able to organise large unwieldy groups and knew how to manage erratic photographers. She had started wearing sunglasses and seemed to be honing a persona, though it wasn't working yet: people found her imperious and a trifle ridiculous, as she declined to speak or socialise with the team after working hours. There are accounts of some junior staff driven to resign by Wintour's systematic nastiness.[520]

Although Wintour was competent and focused, she only did what she wanted. That complication was heightened by the fact that in those days editorial fashion staff only dealt with the actual photography, not text, and she couldn't communicate her ideas well to the writers. Despite this, she was promoted to assistant fashion editor, which makes one wonder how much accounts of her past can be trusted.

Dissecting recent history is difficult, people have grievances to air.

One fact does seem irrefutable, however: Wintour was ambitious. When the fashion editor of *Harper's & Queen* was being replaced, Wintour was champing at the bit. The manager was looking for someone with writing experience and Wintour had barely any experience in anything – she'd only been working a couple of years – yet she still pushed hard to be among contenders for the opening. When the position went to veteran journalist Min Hogg, Wintour couldn't stand it. Her attempts to persistently undermine Hogg led to recurring disagreements and in 1975 Wintour left and moved to New York.

At age twenty-five in the Big Apple, Wintour slid naturally into the New York equivalent of her London social set. Before it had been weekends away on fancy estates and nights out at Annabel's. Although living on the Upper East Side, she participated in the downtown scene of funky lofts and rooftop cocktails; a life where artists and British expats were much admired. Soon she scored the post of junior fashion editor at *Harper's Bazaar*. Again, Wintour was disciplined, creative and uncompromising. Again, this rubbed her colleagues up the wrong way. Her unwillingness to change fashion shoots to suit editorial briefs was astonishing to her seniors, who were not used to being questioned. She felt she knew better. *Harper's Bazaar* felt they could manage without the hassle. She was fired in nine months.

The sacking was a shock, but it did not change her ways. With the help of some of her boyfriends, Wintour was manoeuvred into *Viva* magazine, published by Bob Guccione and his wife Kathy Keeton. Guccione was the founder and editor of *Penthouse*, a softcore men's magazine and *Viva* was launched as a female counterpart – a companion rag focusing on the erotic for women. Every day Wintour had to walk down the corridors of Guccione's porn empire, flanked with posters of half-naked women, to get to her office. Later she would omit her stint among the 'Penthouse Pets' when questioned about her work experience. Still, it's testament to Wintour's character that she stuck out this less-than-savoury placement, producing fashion pages amid mounting tension with her bosses until the magazine closed. Unemployed again.

Her career continued with jumps and slumps. In 1980 she was hired as a freelancer for a new magazine, *Savvy*, where she was paid a wage even the director thought was embarrassingly low.[521] In return for accepting this indignity, she asked for more space for her layouts, hoping that her work would attract a better job offer from another publication. Nothing happened for a full year, until in 1981 she wrangled another fashion editor title with the help of her contacts, this time at *New York* magazine. Here she finally hit her stride. Her high-fashion, sex-heavy approach struck the right note with the new generation of high-salaried, consumer-loving yuppie couples. *New York* magazine's readership was broader than the other magazines she'd worked for, so Wintour's work now had visibility. It soon attracted advertisers, keen to sell while people were buying.

Wintour's stylised shoots were full of thin, deeply tanned muscular women, set against the backdrop of skyscrapers, wearing masculine shirts with nothing underneath and toting briefcases. Besides this ultra-80s power-woman aesthetic she also had flashes of creativity; in one memorable spread she commissioned contemporary New York artists, including Jean-Michel Basquiat, to draw their interpretation of the latest collections. This particular art-fashion fusion had an effect Wintour could have only hoped for in her wildest dreams: it caught the eye of Alexander Liberman, scion of Condé Nast, who invited her for a meeting.

The big guns at Condé Nast were not ready to offer Anna Wintour anything so concrete as editorship of a publication. Instead, they invented a kind of mid-role; she would be featured on the masthead in 1983 as 'Creative Director', a title that had never been used before. The incumbent editor-in-chief of American *Vogue*, still Grace Mirabella, was furious, especially when Wintour started criticising her in editorial meetings. Mirabella's anger spiked when Wintour did an interview for the trade journal *Adweek*, which produced a sickly-sweet profile extolling her as an innovator in publishing.[522] Any awkward truths were conveniently missing, particularly her lack of tertiary education . . . instead the puff piece lightly mentions a love of English literature.

Now that Anna Wintour is the face of fashion, it is easy to judge her for every misdeed, however small. But while Wintour was used to engendering dislike from her colleagues by being icy and abrasive, what she wasn't used to was dealing with the consequences. In her previous jobs her pushiness got results, but Condé Nast was a corporation and it was filled with big fish. There was a great deal of hostility from every direction, with each senior editor, director, executive and publisher pushing and shoving in a power war that was always trembling with tension. Competition was fierce; everyone was trying to grab a piece for themselves. Mirabella may have resented Wintour's interference, but it wasn't Wintour's ideal set-up either. In the less-than-clear position Liberman had given her, Wintour didn't belong obviously to any department. She could block other people's ideas but they could undercut her too.

Accustomed to working on relatively small fashion departments Wintour tended to take over production, but *Vogue* was a slick business and shoots were their speciality. They had huge teams and Wintour simply did not have experience on that scale. She made matters worse with her own uncooperative attitude. A favourite ploy was to blatantly ignore Mirabella and dance attendance on Liberman. This succeeded in offending Mirabella, who in turn caused problems for Liberman. The intricacies of these infinite feuds are incomprehensible; they go on and on. One wonders if it was a productive working environment.

In the end, Liberman had to ban Wintour from touching the fashion pages as animosities spiralled. It put a lot of strain on Wintour and divorced her from her most beloved subject – clothes themselves. Multiple *Vogue* employees of the time profess to having seen her burst into tears, or to finding her at her desk sobbing on the phone to future husband David Shaffer.[523] Shaffer was a child psychiatrist, making him a good sounding board at the very least; though most pundits credit him with far more, intimating that he behaved more like her personal life coach than a lover. Wintour, under the encouragement of Shaffer, went out of her way to show her colleagues that she meant business. A contradictory report from the same period claimed, far from being caught crying, Wintour was a tyrant who replaced all the walls in the offices with see-through glass because she couldn't bear the thought of underlings whispering about her behind closed doors.[524] This version of events made it into the *New York Times Magazine*, when she was quoted as disliking anything being hidden – apart from, it seems, her own face, hidden behind the fringe of hair and the famous shades.

Walls or no walls, Wintour was dying for the pay-off. There was no doubt in anyone's mind she was waiting for Mirabella to be kicked to the curb and the editorship to be handed over. Even inside Condé Nast people began to take it for granted that, sooner or later, she would become the next EIC of American *Vogue*. Instead – and completely unexpectedly – the British imprint fell into her lap. As Beatrix Miller, then editor of Brogue announced her plans to retire, Liberman saw an opportunity to remove his confrontational protégé without losing her. In the wake of her unpopularity, Wintour had to accept the new plan cooked up for her at Condé Nast, but it was hard. Shaffer, by now her spouse, had to stay in New York for work, but the baby son she had given birth to only a couple of months before had to go with her. Many first-time mothers would have thrown in the towel, but persistence is the key component of Wintour's character. The short period during which she held the post was to be remembered, unfairly in some respects, as a 'Nuclear Wintour' that ravaged the British edition.

Anna Wintour and American *Vogue*

If New York was a rollercoaster, London must have seemed like a traffic jam. To Wintour, British *Vogue* was not hip and Beatrix Miller was almost fuddy-duddy. Taking over in 1985, Wintour was distinctly unimpressed with this avant-garde publication and its indolent ways. Her job was to epitomise style for women, but she didn't seem to believe the English capital had any. New York was all speed and *stop*! Zoom and *skid*! Shrieking yellow cabs; young bucks storming sidewalks; a flinty glint of ambition in everyone's eye. Just joining was an army of career girls, marching in with Starbucks cups. For armour they had shoulder pads, hairspray and hope; but they would need more than that to laser their way into corporate structures. Wintour was itching to dress women for that New York buzz. Instead, she had to start interviewing the members of the London branch to see if there was anyone she thought worth retaining.

It didn't take her long to make changes. The endearing nickname Brogue, which had persisted from the beginning, was abolished. As the American Woolman Chase had in her time, Wintour found European working habits shocking. Her own microscopically scrutinised schedule is public knowledge: Wintour rises between 4–5 a.m. and squeezes in an hour of tennis before getting her hair and make-up done for her daily entrance to *Vogue* at 8 a.m.[525] Back in

New York in the 1980s the whole building was already full when she got in. A London colleague remembered how frustrated Wintour was, remarking: 'I honestly don't know how Anna survived. There was no spirited atmosphere, no determination, everything was deemed "impossible" or "Ooh, I don't think so", and the solution to most problems was "Mmmm, let's have a cup of tea."'

Grace Coddington – who would later hold the lofty position of creative director for American *Vogue* – was one of the few promoted under Wintour in the UK. Just as Coddington was made fashion director, the office faced complete renovation. The walls were painted white, glass partitions were installed, worm-eaten desks were swapped for steel Le Corbusier tables, old carpets were ripped up and pale floorboards were laid down – to fit with the new boss's style.[526] In fact, that was Wintour's overall plan: to modernise and Americanise. Gone were shoots at castles. Bye bye tweed. The eccentric English notes of the magazine were ironed out. No touches of sarcastic humour. No sentimental whimsy. Now there was repetitiveness and regularity.[527] Clean, professional-looking shoots of brawny amazons,[528] meant to represent the working woman of Thatcher's Britain.

Next on the cutting block were the *Vogue* contributors. In her debut issue the masthead was already missing two fashion editors, a living editor, associate editor for features, nutrition editor and the restaurant critic. Soon after came the removal of Milton Shulman, the drama critic, and his wife, Drusilla Beyfus, who was features editor. Film critic Alex Walker was also axed. They were all family friends of the Wintours and long-standing colleagues of Anna's father, Charles Wintour, at the *Evening Standard*. Although discharging journalists who had known her as a child seems pretty harsh, an editor getting rid of a predecessor's roll call and bringing in their own people is not. Wintour was following time-honoured protocol, though understandably, those on the receiving end fumed.

Even those who remained weren't happy or, not wanting to fall out, ended up politely excusing themselves. Grace Coddington was one of these, leaving her post in 1987 to become design director at Calvin Klein. Another of the senior staff members, Liz Tilberis, was also set to defect. She had been one of Beatrix Miller's earliest winners of the Vogue Talent Contest and had delighted everyone so much that she stayed on and on, becoming fashion editor in 1974 and executive fashion editor in 1984. Wintour had unexpectedly promoted her and given her a raise, but the hostility of the editorial department was getting to Tilberis and even she couldn't hack it. She reported that despite the financial perks of Wintour's regime, her demeanour was so unpleasant that Tilberis started getting asthma attacks at staff meetings.[529] Wintour's American way of working – harder, with less fun – grated. Wintour implemented working systems that were unquestionably logical from an operational point of view, but served to alienate everyone. It would have helped if Wintour was charming and apologetic, but she wasn't.

In the end Tilberis, who was adored at *Vogue*, received an offer from Ralph Lauren and decided to take it. Meanwhile, Wintour had become increasingly restless and was vying for a position back in New York. Calls to Liberman and Newhouse were more frequent and more urgent. To make matters worse, neither circulation nor advertising showed any kind of obvious improvement, causing resentment to mount, since her staff felt the punishing new system had no pay-off. Meanwhile, the British press were getting their kicks by crucifying Wintour. They nicknamed this period in British *Vogue*'s life a 'Wintour of Discontent' and a 'Nuclear Wintour'. *Private Eye* received constant leaks from Vogue House and gleefully reported the details of her payment package and the total control she wanted over the content.[530] Jewellery designer Tom Binns designed a badge that read 'VAGUE VOGUE VOMIT' and if rumour is to be believed,

Thom O'Dwyer, style editor of *Fashion Weekly*, wore one. Even her father's paper, the *Evening Standard*, noted her 'habit of crashing through editorships as though they were brick walls, leaving behind a ragged hole and a whiff of Chanel.'

So fast was Wintour becoming troubled at British *Vogue* that Newhouse and Liberman realised they had to move quickly to avoid the loss of this favourite. In 1987, they decided to hand her *House & Garden*, after disposing of editor-in-chief Louis Gropp with a cursory swing of the axe. As an interiors magazine this was a somewhat obscure choice, though at least it was back in the States. Wintour was sick of exile in London and of managing a long-distance marriage, the latter was especially hard since she had just given birth to her second child. Nonetheless, the stint at *House & Garden* was another Wintour special, replicating her previous unpopular methods including mass firings, an overhaul of working practices and the reported destruction of commissioned work worth millions of dollars.

Shortening the name to a trendy *H&G*, Wintour tweaked the format and turned the spreads into lavish fashion scenarios. Instead of home fixtures the pages were suddenly strewn with leggy models. Critics sneeringly nicknamed the result 'House & Garment' and 'Vanity Chair'. Traditional subscribers and advertisers felt misunderstood, so sales tanked. The *New York Times* weighed in again, ridiculing Wintour for wanting to draw parallels between fashion, design and decorating.[531] Today, this seems remarkably forward-thinking, considering the number of clotheswear brands in the lucrative interiors space (Missoni, Versace, Ralph Lauren, etc.), but back then it was not well received. What the article does tell us is that Anna Wintour's desire to be at *Vogue* was popular knowledge; the writer describes her tenure at *H&G* as just another hurdle in the 'crusade' to become editor-in-chief at *Vogue*.

Lasting only eight months, when Wintour was done *H&G* was so crippled it had to close its doors. No matter. By June 1988, she was announced as the new editor-in-chief of American *Vogue*. For Mirabella, who had been clinging on, this was an especially bitter moment. The atmosphere of mistrust and double-crossing at Condé Nast HQ finally came to a head when she came home one day to her ashen-faced husband. He'd just watched a news broadcast announcing Anna Wintour as her replacement. Thinking it had to be a mistake, Mirabella called *Vogue*'s owners, who confirmed she had indeed been made redundant and heard about it on TV.

This kind of shock firing would become Si Newhouse's signature move. Over the next few decades he would earn himself a reputation for brutal and sometimes seemingly random dismissals. Mirabella had lasted seventeen years as editor-in-chief and more than double that overall at *Vogue*, but now her number was up and Condé Nast Publications would never acknowledge her again. For Anna Wintour, ascension had not been easy, but she had finally arrived.

CHAPTER 12

Dying for the Dress

Politics in Fashion and Unfashionable Politics

Photographers in Paris: Art and Erotica

The job of a magazine editor is steeped in prestige and personal glory. Some editors have enjoyed making a celebrity name out of their association with *Vogue*. Others have preferred to act as gurus and guides, providing a platform for creative projects and creative people, directing from behind the curtain but never stepping out centre stage. Francine Crescent, who headed French *Vogue* from 1968 till 1987 was in the second category.

So discreet she almost never gave an interview and so low-key she was never covered by American *Vogue*, Crescent had the strength of character to maintain a balance between her American employers and French advertisers. Her discretion didn't, however, stretch to her dress sense: Crescent liked to clash, offsetting her conservative blonde hair with canary-yellow suits.[532] Later in life she married obese Italian playboy and former gigolo Massimo Gargia. But what she is most remembered for is her role as patroness to fashion photography.

From the early days, a battle had raged between the classic product shot, which showed clothes clearly for prospective buyers, and the atmospheric editorial, which created a mood and seduced the readers into aspirational worlds. Different editors had differing opinions on what would sell more garments. One camp felt product shots were honest, a way of showing the readers what they would really be getting; the other believed women bought not for the clothes themselves, but for the connotations that came with them – beauty, class or a certain lifestyle.

Francine Crescent's strength lay in picking the most talented photographers and allowing them an unprecedented level of freedom. With her support, legends such as Helmut Newton and Guy Bourdin developed their photography into a fully fledged art. It was an era when the power lay with the image-makers: Crescent would rarely give direction, merely telling the photographer how many pages he had to shoot, then letting them develop the concept and hire the team. Such free reign allowed Newton to explore the darker sides of sexuality and produce work with undertones of BDSM, with jackets slung over shoulders, dresses crumpled, torn off or concealed by prone limbs in complicated psychosexual montages. In 1975, for instance, he shot one of his most famous editorials, showing a model with slicked-back hair wearing a mannish Yves Saint Laurent suit.[533] In one provocative frame a female model stands beside her in the street, totally nude and looking vulnerable. Generally executed in glossy monochromes, his oeuvre made a moody splash of drag kings, gender ambiguity, bondage and fetish, earning him the nickname King of Kink.[534] Where Helmut Newton admitted to being influenced by the so-called golden age of porn in the late sixties and seventies, his models reportedly hated the work and emerged from sittings feeling depressed and drained.

The second superstar of this era's French *Vogue*, Guy Bourdin, drew his influences from surrealism. His suggestive way of shooting women's shoes on desolate landscapes, rail tracks or in empty swimming pools created an uncanny tension and suspense, reminiscent of a film drama or a crime scene. In his later work, Bourdin would dispose of the female body altogether and capitalise on suggestions of violence. In one notorious image he places a pair of pink shoes on a pavement beside a chalk outline of a body and bloodstains;[535] in another, a red wedge sandal stands next to a plug socket which seeps blood.[536] These arresting images are clever fashion adverts: one's eye goes straight to the product.

Newton and Bourdin were responding to the landscape around them, turning contemporary motifs into artistic expression. Porn was entering the mainstream in a way it never had before, as filmmakers were waking up to the appeal of using sexually explicit material to boost movie sales. Equally, horror and exploitation were appearing on screens, fascinating mass audiences in pursuit of cheap thrills.

As much as Francine Crescent has been venerated for her daring support of photography, there have been editors who disparaged her. Particularly condescending are the comments of Joan Juliet Buck (who became EIC of French *Vogue* in 1994), who in her memoirs repeatedly labels Crescent and her magazine as banal, limp, empty and stale.[537] She makes a point of declaring it unpopular, claiming that designers and magazine staff hated working there.[538] It's worth pointing out that Joan Juliet Buck was turned down for a job by Crescent.

In any case, it was a cosy environment and much of the staff had grown up together. Every descendant of a prominent aristocrat, every former artist's muse who dabbled in couture, washed up there, from Winston Churchill's granddaughter to various early-year supermodels. This crowd leaned towards the conservative and the overtly French, especially in the wake of France's fear of Americanisation in the 1970s. They set up fashion shoots in grand hotels and filled the office with Labradors, cocker spaniels and dachshunds who snoozed in baskets under their desks. In an increasingly political France, they shied away from taking sides. When a politically aware editor did appear, she took the focus beyond French concerns and made a play for the truly global fashion magazine.

Agitating in Paris: Racism and Spirituality

When there is an opportunity to put right a wrong, Colombe Pringle, author and former editor-in-chief of French *Vogue* believes we have to try. An incident which had taken place a couple of decades before that concerned a fellow writer and editor had stuck resolutely in her mind. 'There had been sort of a scandal in France . . . something rather shocking', she tells me.[539] She was referring to the abrupt departure of Edmonde Charles-Roux from Condé Nast, said to have been precipitated because she was trying to place a black model on the front of the magazine. That was back in 1966. 'American *Vogue* wouldn't have a black woman on the cover either, the English *Vogue* neither. Society was like that at that time. So, I thought for my first issue I would ask a black woman!'[540] She punctuates the sentence with a raucous, throaty laugh. 'I had the office of Edmonde Charles-Roux you see,' she adds wistfully, 'which was a very nice little office.'[541]

It was now 1987, but Pringle's stance would still have been considered radical. There was a scarcity of black models even if you did want to hire one. From a caster's point of view, it made commercial sense to ignore applicants from minority backgrounds since French *Vogue* hadn't used a black cover star so far and perhaps never would. Beauty standards only recognised whiteness and thinness. With all of this in mind, Pringle plotted. To skirt any uncomfortable questions from her superiors and to ensure the greater impact of her message, she saved the idea for Christmas. From the 1970s, French *Vogue* had developed a tradition of inviting a guest editor to collaborate on the creation of a special December issue. Every contributor on the list is a soaring legend: 1971 was Salvador Dalí; 1972 Federico Fellini; 1973 Marlene Dietrich; 1974 Alfred Hitchcock. Need one continue? These covers swapped the usual pretty-girl-selling-fashions formula for the cause célèbre in question, giving the winter numbers a distinctly highbrow feel. No other magazine had access to luminaries of such calibre.

Knowing the holiday edition was their most important – both in terms of advertising and the iconic contributors – Pringle figured an accomplished and powerful black personality could serve as a sort of loophole to the unwritten ban on black cover stars. For her leading lady Pringle selected Barbara Hendricks, an African American operatic soprano and graduate of Juilliard, whom she was already acquainted with, making it easy to reach out. 'She was *extremely* pleased and amazed and honoured,' Pringle recalls.[542] The resulting issue is a victory against racism in fashion; closure for the cause so close to Edmonde Charles-Roux's heart; and a source of enormous personal satisfaction to Pringle. Hendricks is exalted on the cover, a commanding goddess figure draped in a billowing garment of red and royal purple.[543] Her stance is strong, her face is set in a frown. She wears red lipstick, a shimmering headdress. The lettering of 'VOGUE' that stretches out behind her appears in big gold print. Hendricks appears in glorified majesty; her power undiminished by being made to smile inanely and wear the latest trends.

Not that Pringle was ever deluded enough to believe this edition alone would be enough to normalise black faces in the glossy press. To keep the ball rolling she and fashion editor Irène Silvagni (her accomplice and friend who had moved from *Elle* to French *Vogue* with her) hired eighteen-year-old Naomi Campbell for the August cover of 1988.[544] Even then her bosses at Condé Nast only let the issue run when a top designer threatened to pull their advertising if they censored Campbell. Fashion has often been used as a political tool: for solidarity, at rallies, to align with certain groups. Yet the way in which we use clothes is not necessarily connected to the aims of the fashion media. That industry is better known for glossing over the inconvenient truths in life. Fashion is an illusion we like to escape to, but what if it could be the catalyst of social movements, not just the by-product? The debate of whether fashion is – or should be – political, is ongoing. Yet one ought to remember those pioneering editors at *Vogue* who challenged what a luxury magazine is here to do and occasionally paid dearly for daring to do so.

When I quizzed Pringle on how she managed to secure the participation of the notable dignitaries who honoured *Vogue* at Christmas year-on-year, she stops to think. 'I was very stubborn,' she says finally, 'you have to be'.[545] The next special issue after Barbara Hendricks' of 1987 was guest-edited by the Asian auteur Akira Kurosawa, for which she spent several 'crazy' weeks in Japan.[546] Following that she enlisted Mstislav Rostropovich the virtuoso cellist. Martin Scorsese did the 1990 edition, having been easier to convince after he'd seen the efforts of his cinematic confrère Kurosawa. Getting Spanish painter and art theorist Antoni Tàpies, Pringle describes as 'lucky' – she reached him through a connection to Picasso's son and a coincidence involving a ceramics studio.[547] 'I just got in,' she ruminates, 'once you have one end you can keep pulling.'[548] It's a lesson in how to use the six degrees of separation to your advantage. In 1992, Pringle outdid herself by getting His Holiness the 14th Dalai Lama to guest-edit.

'The Dalai Lama was amazing', Pringle comments.[549] Curiously, the door to the Dalai Lama was opened through the intricate web of connections among the fashion industry's elite. Awe-inspiring

former editrix of American *Vogue* Diana Vreeland's grandson
Nicholas Vreeland was a close friend of Pringle, as well as a fully
ordained Tibetan Buddhist monk. Since he had converted and joined
a monastery in the mid-eighties, Pringle, her husband and Nicholas
Vreeland had fallen into the habit of discussing spirituality, with
Pringle's husband even spending time in India following the teach-
ings of his guru. The result was an exposure to yoga and meditation
practices long before they were popularised in the Western world.
With a heads-up from Nicholas Vreeland, Pringle and her publisher,
Prince Jean Poniatowski, went to see the Dalai Lama during a visit
to Strasbourg.

The two French *Vogue* representatives found themselves in a room
surrounded by white-clad monks and Buddhist followers doing
breathy chants of 'Om'. Seated on two tiny golden chairs, they
watched the Dalai Lama do his rounds. Pringle was three months
pregnant, suffering from the heat and lugging around copies of all
the *Vogue* Christmas guest-edited issues she'd worked on. After
showing him these volumes, she looked him in the eyes and asked
His Holiness if he would be their editor for the upcoming winter. His
reply was, 'Come to Dharamshala with one hundred questions'.[550] The
date he set was September. Pringle's immediate thought was, '*Shit*. In
September I'll be seven months pregnant.'[551] In the end, this did not
stop her. She flew back to the office and gleefully announced, '*We got
him!*' Then went on a crash course on all things Tibetan Buddhist by
speaking to monks and questioning people on what they'd ask him
if they could. As an extra precaution, Pringle drafted in the help of
Alexandre Adler, a renowned political journalist in France. 'Come
with me,' she said, 'and bring fifty questions about China!'[552]

Following the long flight they caught a train out of the heaving
metropolis and into the mountains of the Kangra Valley. Accom-
panying the heavily pregnant Pringle was the art editor, the

photographer, her friend Adler and other colleagues, making up a group of six. They were put up in the house of the 14th Dalai Lama's brother, an old colonial property called Kashmir Cottage, which Pringle describes as, 'Exactly like Beatrix Potter. You had little animals going around, and English roses. It was *so* odd.'[553] Each morning they would traipse over to speak with His Holiness and his inner circle of monks. For six days the little *Vogue Paris* outpost asked their questions about freedom, fear, enemies, ego, hate, abortion, women, human rights, politics, politics, politics. After that, they started interviewing. They spoke to his doctor, took notes of monks debating, shot pictures. Pringle found a card in a giftshop featuring a kitschy portrait of the 14th Dalai Lama grinning in front of the snowy Himalayan peaks, a rainbow arching over his head. This unlikely image, evoking a 'crazy peace and love', would run on the front of *Vogue Paris*, that age-old bastion of stately elegance and restrained glamour.[554] Pringle's last question on the last day was, 'Your Holiness, why a hundred questions?' He turned to her with surprise and replied, 'Oh! But it was a joke!'[555]

Pringle makes no bones about the fact that she used *Vogue* as a tool to explore subjects that interested her. When I ask if she kept her readers and their needs in mind during the visit to the Dalai Lama, Pringle snorts with derision. 'I didn't think about that *at all*! You can't think about the audience of *Vogue* when you're talking to a spiritual figure.[556] You can talk beauty – we did – but it's deeper than that, it has to be.'[557] Although Pringle claims they did include some fashion content, the pieces she's referring to are still too thoughtful and meditative to compare to the *Buy! Buy! Buy!* mentality of most consumer magazines. In one article her friend Nicky Vreeland took off his clothes layer by layer to be photographed by Pringle's husband, brought along in case Pringle went into labour.[558] This ran under a playful title roughly translating as 'The Beauty Rules of a Monk'. Flippant though this sounds, the text provides rich insight into Buddhist dressing and grooming habits.

Overall, the fashion stories were more about learning to be at peace with what you have. To any follower of *Vogue Paris* this would have been glaringly out of place amid the prevailing mood of feckless acquisition. A surging stock market in the US churned out yuppies. A slight downturn in Europe did nothing to chill the simmering greed of the moment. People were not yet quitting jobs they hated and retraining as Pilates instructors; they were clamouring to become investment bankers and to seize bonuses. Nobody had learned to pick lifestyle over income yet. To those who sat down and opened the publication that December with the intention of browsing through ritzy designer gowns for New Year's Eve, the lessons from the spiritual leader of Tibet must have verged on incomprehensible. But in dismissing the world of *Vogue*, Pringle was playing with fire. She was not the owner of the magazine, she was a chosen representative. Her penchant for addressing huge topics, embracing the arts and struggling against oppressive systems must have made the C-suite at Condé Nast France swallow nervously.

Final Straw: Mandela in French *Vogue*

Where to go after the Dalai Lama was a real problem. 'At one point I was thinking about Madonna ... Michael Jackson would have been fun,' she remembers.[559] Either of those seems more likely than Nelson Mandela, the first black president of South Africa, the embodiment of anti-apartheid, whose lifelong activism and close on thirty-year imprisonment culminated in a Nobel Peace Prize in 1993. 'I was a bit crazy,' Pringle mused, but crazy or not, she pulled off the superhuman feat of securing a collaboration with Nelson Mandela himself.

She insists she never considered herself political or intended to be controversial, but when she looked closer into Mandela's story, she uncovered a national history so devastated by exploitation that she put down her pen and flew to South Africa.

'No one helped me with that one, I can tell you,' was her summary; while on the reaction of her *Vogue* colleagues she says, 'they were sure it wouldn't happen. They were frightened.'[560] Out in South Africa, Pringle had to hit the ground running. It was an intrepid assignment in a tense and quarrelling country. It was a million miles from the runway collections or the Parisian lunch hour. 'It was like concentration camps, it was something terrifying. I was really in shock,' Pringle recounts.[561] She had gone to visit the townships and witnessed first-hand the appalling living conditions, the harrowing results of racial segregation. When she finally met with Mandela in Johannesburg, she handed him a copy of the Dalai Lama issue and said, 'I want to help you.'[562]

Mandela agreed and Pringle returned to her hotel room to send a fax to French *Vogue* HQ, jubilantly declaring her latest coup. Defiantly, she added a bristling directive: 'And I saw the Townships so you say yes or no NOW.' The top brass in France agreed and for a whole week a tiny *Vogue* offshoot shadowed Mandela, writing and photographing as they went. They walked the bush, visited Mandela's house, attended rallies. In Cape Town they did the editing with Mandela, working in the mornings when he returned from his 5 a.m. run. Pringle was moved by the rallies in particular, observing the experience of being surrounded by 50,000 black people in a group of just 10 white people, '*then* you understand a few things of what it is to be a minority.'[563]

The resulting magazine is not a light read. It featured a piece on Desmond Tutu, the activist Anglican cleric, and the paintings of Willie Bester, a South African artist whose works address heritage, human dignity and government accountability. Photojournalistic stories include a spread entitled 'Violence', in which two women run from a car explosion.[564] Another titled 'Mandela is Free! Joy', shows a South African leaping in the air, waving a trumpet. Sadness and celebration. Pain and victory. A 360-degree report. Pringle goes so far as to print the rules of the apartheid, laying them out in contrasting blocks of black and white text. These laws forbade milk from a white man's cow from being mixed with the milk of a cow belonging to a black man. There were laws banning black men from walking in the shadows of white men on the street. All this cruelty and insanity made it into *Vogue*. For the cover Pringle hired the artist Tommy Motswai, a native to Johannesburg. Motswai, born a deaf mute and an ardent supporter of Mandela, was moved to tears. His resulting illustration is a blue-toned, pop-art representation of the leader smiling warmly and holding his hands together in prayer.[565] 'It wasn't a cover for *Vogue*,' Pringle admits.

When the team returned to Paris, landing in the middle of Fashion Week, Pringle seized the chance to have Peter Lindbergh snap the supermodels du jour – including Naomi Campbell, Claudia Schiffer and Yasmeen Ghauri – all grinning, many holding up two fingers for peace. They wear white T-shirts, each with a black letter on it, together spelling out 'NELSON MANDELA'.[566] This striking image, featured as a three-page fold-out, was inserted at the back of the issue, which totalled a hefty 250-plus pages.

If the response from her *Vogue* colleagues was somewhat chilly, it was nothing compared to the glacial hostility of designer brands. 'A black communist *révolutionnaire*?! On the cover of *Vogue*?! They wanted to pull their ads,' Pringle tells me.[567] How on earth were they supposed to promote lavish spending on Yuletide gifts if the publication was crawling with references to equality and spotlighting stories of white men abusing power? Once again, Pringle proved stubborn.

She held a meeting with De Beers, the fine jewellery tycoons specialising in African-mined diamonds and called them out point blank. 'Listen, I know you've been using the black people to get in your mines to get the diamonds . . . but Mandela *is* going to be elected.'[568] She'd gone for the jugular. 'There was no fight at the time against racism. It was *so* crazy. But I don't regret, I am so proud. If I had to be proud of something it is that.'[569]

Around the time the magazine came out Mandela was nominated for the Nobel Peace Prize. That gave French *Vogue*'s polarising theme a glint of institutional approval. Then, the *Sunday Times* ran a whole feature discussing Pringle's Mandela issue, portraying it as a surprising but commendable step for a fashion mag.[570] Rather than strengthening convictions in Pringle's abilities, the question was raised among the directors of Condé Nast as to whether she'd finally gone too far.

When first summoned to the fold, Pringle had immediately recognised the advantages of living on planet *Vogue*. The name of *Vogue* was like a secret passcode that made the most impenetrable doors swing open. The willingness of heads of state and prima donnas alike to work with the magazine shows just how solid their reputation had become, even outside their remit of fashion. The *Sunday Times* article on the Mandela issue claims he and his political advisors agreed to join forces with Pringle not because they believed in luxury, but because of *Vogue*'s presentation of facts. They could show a different side to politics through beautiful imagery.

There is another possible explanation for the African National Congress's willing involvement. Where most papers have clear left- or right-leaning agendas, a fashion magazine can be more neutral. For her own part, Pringle was aware that the opportunity to expose female audiences to current affairs occurring beyond the Parisian bubble may never come again. Like a campaigner suddenly thrust on stage she grabbed her moment. She capitalised on Condé Nast's resources, knowing she would eventually get caught out, that it would all end. 'Maybe they thought, "she is not made for that magazine",' Pringle states, 'and I agree with them.'[571]

While some commentators imply Pringle's editorial shoots were repetitive, the guest-edited instalments had quickly become collector's items and doubled the circulation figures every time they hit the newsstands, peaking at a reported 100,000 copies.[572] But those buying the December publication didn't necessarily fall into the desired demographic of *Vogue*, especially if they were only buying once a year. Aside from the Christmas issues, Pringle had tried to overhaul the publication during her seven-year stint, battling to change the tone, allocating plenty of coverage to contemporary art, the studios of artists and classical musicians. She supported the work of edgy emerging photographers such as Peter Lindbergh, whose intimate black-and-white style was not yet mainstream. And while *Vogue*'s history has shown editors can be crucified for getting too cultural, Pringle still believes she'd been on the right track. 'Everybody is working with artists now, getting artists to guest-design handbags etc. . . . Fashion is not enough if it's just fashion. You can't just buy all the time, you also have to dream.'[573]

Pringle's fashion editor Irène Silvagni missed out on working on the Dalai Lama and Nelson Mandela issues. The higher-ups at Condé Nast felt her photoshoots didn't show clothes clearly enough and feared backlash from the advertisers. She was fired even though she had been responsible for contracting world-class photographers like Paolo Roversi. Pringle's approach didn't gel with subscribers, who were 'very conventional'.[574] Ultimately, she speculates, 'I think some readers must have said something because I wasn't kept at *Vogue*.'[575] At this Pringle dissolves into fits of laughter. She is not sorry to have been ousted and unlike other editors she came away unscathed.

There was a severance cheque large enough to fund her for a year, allowing her to stay home, write a book and spend time with her infant son. When she returned to journalism it was as an editor-in-chief at *L'Express*, a famous French weekly with a political bent. As far as she was concerned, the Condé Nast company had been 'very elegant' in their handling of her dismissal.[576] Nor did she miss the froufrou of the fashion world.

CHAPTER 13

The Condé Nasties

Rise of the Celebrity Editors

'Nuclear Wintour' vs 'Million Dollar Liz'

The New York social calendar is packed with art openings, theatre shows, film premieres and fundraisers, yet nothing is more coveted than an invitation to the Met Gala. Each May, as an inky-blue dusk drapes the beaux-arts façade of the Metropolitan Museum of Art, a red carpet is rolled out. Oscar-winning A-listers, international tycoons, tech-nerd billionaires and Bambi-eyed supermodels glide up the steps slowly, their practised smiles immortalised by the flashes of hundreds of cameras. Even the attending press have to wear tuxedos. Essentially an opening-night party for the Costume Institute's yearly fashion exhibition, the theme of which is also the dress-code, it gives both celebs and designers a chance to catch the attention of those watching all over the world as they try to outdo each other's outfits. The galleries where the banquet takes place are extravagantly decorated. For the 2006 'AngloMania' theme, the court was transformed into an English garden complete with apple-tree hedges, 35,000 daffodils, 12,000 hyacinths and a carpet of grass layered over the floors.[577] For the 2007 gala, 'Poiret: King of Fashion', two live peacocks in eighteen-foot-tall birdcages flanked the entrance.[578] In 2015, during 'China: Through the Looking Glass', a forest of 6,000 bamboo stems was shipped from Puerto Rico and Hawaii to line the corridors.[579]

The Costume Institute is the only curatorial department of the Met that has to fund itself and with tickets costing approximately $30,000 a head, the gala's contribution is major. According to the *New York Times*, the annual benefit has raised over $145 million since Anna Wintour came on board permanently in the late 1990s.[580] The gala started life in the 1940s as a low-key, black-tie appeal for patronage. But it was Diana Vreeland who, in the 1970s, moved the fête out of fusty hotel dining rooms and brought it into the heart of the museum, transforming the evening into an exclusive event that included the likes of Andy Warhol, Diana Ross and Cher. A surge of Wall Street success stories meant spare cash was making its way into philanthropy and cultural institutions were suddenly all the rage. The Met, profiting from the association with Vreeland, saw donations pouring in. Anna Wintour capitalised on the ground laid by her antecedent and under her direction this local charity night has evolved into a parade of outré design attended by the ultra-elite. Yet even they have to be sanctioned by Wintour first. Chairing the Met Ball is just another of Wintour's ways of monitoring and directing the whole fashion industry. Favoured brands can be promoted, while others might be barred; media coverage is supervised and journalists vetted. Some will be approved, some blacklisted. Quite often, the final decision of which designers will dress which guests is Wintour's. If the gala is valuable to the Met; it is even more valuable to *Vogue*.

Before Wintour had become the de facto host she was simply an editor-in-chief, approached by the museum. They wanted her support for the 1995 gala. After Vreeland's death in 1989, the Costume

Institute was still finding its feet without her and Wintour jumped at the chance. However, the following year, in 1996, they asked Liz Tilberis. Like Wintour, Tilberis was editor-in-chief of a famous American glossy magazine, *Harper's Bazaar*, and she had cut her teeth at *Vogue*. They were both British. They were both ambitious. But while Wintour only made friends with men, Tilberis made friends with everyone. The year Tilberis hosted, she brought in Dior as the sponsor. The man who had just purchased the brand, French magnate Bernard Arnault (who later created the luxury conglomerate LVMH) had recently appointed John Galliano as its artistic director in a high-profile move. This *enfant terrible* of design debuted his risqué collection at Tilberis' Met Gala with a négligée-style dress in deep-blue silk, edged with black lace, worn by the guest of honour: Her Royal Highness, Diana, Princess of Wales. The photos that hit the tabloids nearly all show Princess Di by Liz Tilberis' side, their heads bowed together like conspirators, mischievously grinning at private jokes. This unlikely pair were good friends and there's nothing like bringing a princess to your party to make it memorable. The praise Tilberis received for her gala eclipsed Wintour's the year before and Tilberis' former PR noted that the two were watching each other closely and treating the Met Gala as a personal platform.[581]

Few remember the rivalry between Anna Wintour, editor-in-chief of American *Vogue* and Liz Tilberis, then editor-in-chief of *Harper's Bazaar*. They had worked together at *Vogue* in London; butting heads or begrudgingly collaborating. But when Tilberis moved to New York, she posed the first real threat to Wintour's growing influence. As the two top editors of the two glossiest magazines they were always compared – and the American media did everything it could to fuel a feud, going so far as penning sensationalised reports of imaginary rows. Wintour was considered distant and unlikeable. Tilberis was everyone's golden girl. But although they were completely opposite personalities they were both savvy enough to realise that curating their image would increase their value. A public profile would give them greater bargaining power and possibly even protect them from the disdainful treatment experienced by others in the fashion sector. It was the start of editors as celebrities.

When she left London, Anna Wintour had tipped Tilberis to become her replacement at the British edition and Tilberis snatched at the opportunity to be editor-in-chief. Her aim was to nurse the title to a relative state of calm, stylistically resting somewhere between Beatrix Miller, whose editing she considered a form of magic,[582] and Wintour's aggressive, hyper-American take. But just a few years in, her work began to attract the attention of *Harper's Bazaar* in New York. They were in a terrible position: by the mid-1980s ad pages had stagnated, by 1988 they had fallen a dramatic 11 per cent.[583] Meanwhile *Vogue*'s ads under Mirabella had risen to more pages than any other monthly magazine in the United States.[584] It was a huge discrepancy for two publications which had once been almost neck and neck. Then *Harper's* circulation slipped so low it was being overtaken by new launches, so management had to act fast before the magazine vanished completely out of sight.

Tilberis was first approached in 1991 and in a series of hush-hush, top-secret meetings where she was shuffled in and out of planes like a stowaway to avoid the media catching on, she struck an agreement with Hearst, the parent company of *Harper's Bazaar*. Tilberis wanted a change and she wanted a challenge. As editor-in-chief of *Harper's Bazaar* she would be back in the same city as Wintour, but on a different team. Perhaps knowing this would cause a stir, perhaps playing to the crowds, Tilberis chose to debut in New York at the biggest party Anna Wintour had ever thrown: *Vogue*'s 100th anniversary bash in 1992.

Wintour was presiding over the black-tie affair, held at the New York Public Library, in a sleeveless ivory sheath and for once she did not wear her sunglasses. For Wintour this was a pinnacle moment, the slew of painful editorships at British *Vogue* and *House & Garden* were over and she had assumed her rightful place at American *Vogue*. Now several years into her editorship, it was clear she was on the road to success. The iconic 100th Anniversary Special issue featured ten supermodels on the cover,[585] all of whom Wintour had helped catapult to fame, including Christy Turlington, Naomi Campbell, Cindy Crawford, Claudia Schiffer and Linda Evangelista. Photographed by Patrick Demarchelier, they wore white jeans and white shirts. It is said to be the best-selling issue of *Vogue* to date.

Yet when Wintour's anniversary party hit the headlines she had to share the spotlight with Liz Tilberis, who used the event to herald her own sudden entrance into the VIP room of fashion. The world waited for the claws to come out and reportage quickly turned into a feeding frenzy. Part of this was down to the ancient enmity between *Vogue* and *Harper's Bazaar*. Part of it was rooted in how perfect Tilberis and Wintour were as opponents. Tilberis had gone prematurely white and wore a pixie cut, Wintour dyed her hair chocolate brown and had a bob. Tilberis was plump, Wintour was angular. Tilberis was smiley and approachable, Wintour was sullen and aloof. One article runs: 'One gets compared to royals, the other to nannies. One shops couture collections, the other goes to The Gap. One is a fashion-correct Size 4, the other a free-spirited 14. One is cool, one is chatty. One envied, one liked. One is known as the queen. And one is after her crown.'[586]

A photo of the two editors at the *Vogue* anniversary party shows Tilberis in black with white hair, Wintour in white with black hair. Its caption runs:

Meet the contenders. Far left in a Chanel evening suit is Elizabeth Tilberis. Fresh from England, she'll soon run *Harper's Bazaar*. Adjacent, in Geoffrey Beene beads, is Anna Wintour, empress of *Vogue*. Their weapons: forced smiles. The battleground: glossy pages. And, of course, the spoils: the world fashion crown. Tilberis is the great Hearst hope. Wintour, backed by Condé Nast, has never had a serious challenger. Their rivalry has only just begun.[587]

It's certainly true that as far as recollections go, many colleagues loved Tilberis as much as they hated Wintour. Grace Coddington said she was 'so much fun to work with, one of those jolly English girls who likes a joke'.[588] *Harper's Bazaar* staffer Scott Baldinger saw her as a dream version of a mother protector,[589] while photographer Bruce Weber described her as being so infectiously charming 'she could make you skip for joy'.[590]

Yet, in the late eighties and early nineties, what Wintour stood for was in. Slick career girls with super-thin, super-athletic bodies. The 'dress for success' Mirabella message of the 1970s was replaced by a new eroticism under the banner of health and body-consciousness. Wintour's first cover was groundbreaking.[591] The November 1988 issue featured a mid-shot of model Michaela Bercu, swinging carefree down a street, eyes crinkled with a big natural smile and blonde, windswept curls. Her tummy showed between a pair of $50 acid-washed jeans and a $10,000 jewel-encrusted Christian Lacroix sweater.[592] It was such a huge deviation from the perfect, every-hair-in-place, studio close-ups that the printers called the office to ask if there had been a mistake. It caused a sensation when it hit newsstands; nobody had mixed high- and low-end retail before into a 'look'. It was hip, foxy, about as 'street' as *Vogue* was ever going to get.

Wintour continued to break the mould by putting celebrities

on her covers in place of models – starting with Madonna.[593] This foresaw the development of celebrity culture. 'Fashionable personalities' were just becoming a noted concept, from Nancy Reagan's 'power gang' to Hollywood's 'brat pack'. The newly-famous made themselves accessible through TV shows such as *Lifestyles of the Rich and the Famous* and tabloids like *People*. They opened up their lives, giving brands a new channel for sales. If Kate Moss wore Calvin Klein, then, in the consumer's mind, they could be like her if they had Calvin Klein too. Wintour knew how to harness all of this desire and funnel it into business success.

Liz Tilberis' first cover for *Harper's Bazaar* was the exact reverse of Wintour's aesthetic – a shot of Linda Evangelista, her elbow across one eye, in a black beaded bodysuit. It had ample white space and one solitary headline: 'Enter the Era of Elegance'.[594] It was so different from *Vogue's* approach that the media could keep the rivalry of opposites narrative going strong. Immediately *Harper's Bazaar* boasted an impressive spike. Tilberis' take re-established *Harper's Bazaar* as artistic, a publication full of distinctive image-makers. One obvious way to create an identity for a magazine is to keep the covers consistent, so she made sure the sense of pure elegance stayed. But in order to fill her new property Tilberis needed talent and the best of the best belonged to *Vogue*.

As Tilberis began approaching their photographers and models, swift directives came from Condé Nast Publications. Anyone who worked with *Harper's Bazaar* would never receive another commission from any *Vogue* in any country ever again. On one occasion, Tilberis flew to Paris, eager to pressure photographer Peter Lindbergh into signing a contract. At the airport she bumped into Si Newhouse who'd had the same idea. Tilberis bagged Lindbergh and Patrick Demarchelier, but she did not get Steven Meisel, who was given $2 million to stick with *Vogue*.[595] Tilberis had worked with

Wintour and knew how to use her weaknesses against her: Wintour liked control, photographers liked creative freedom. They were lured over with the promise they could express themselves. These bidding wars, in which each editor consistently upped the ante, came with a price tag that overwhelmed the owners. It is said Tilberis and Wintour overspent their budgets by millions.[596] For much as they were different, they were also similar. They were both ambitious editors-in-chief of legendary magazines.

Every feature at *Vogue* had to be perfectly engineered. Every single month was a statement, which had to result in drama. Thanks to Wintour, these were now productions on an epic scale. 'Everything here is a big story', said the British managing director of Condé Nast, Nicholas Coleridge to the *New Statesman*. The article goes on to vitriolically describe the Condé Nast roster as publications that explore 'the lifestyle of the dementedly rich.'[597] None of the mainstream press had anything that nice to say. A column covering the American *Vogue* 100th anniversary ball derisively describes the guests as 'mention junkies',[598] while 'Condé Nasties' became a popular term for anyone working at Condé Nast. It grated that they were spilling energy and cash on something so non-essential while the country experienced the recession of the early 1990s.

In an interview during New York Fashion Week in 1992, Tilberis professed her amazement at the publicity she'd received.[599] In London no one had known her name; in America she was being stopped in the street. As fashion became more mainstream in the 1980s and celebrities became a fully-fledged cultural phenomenon in the 1990s, magazine editors were pushed into an unexpected limelight. Tilberis was living through the very early days of this. For her herculean efforts, *Harper's Bazaar* won two National Magazine Awards in 1993, but by the end of her first year Tilberis was diagnosed with ovarian cancer. She continued breathing life into the dusty masthead, though her own was finishing. Endless rounds of chemotherapy were completed with layouts and picture edits on her lap. She passed away in April 1999.

Back when her editorship at *Harper's Bazaar* was being announced Tilberis told reporters *Vogue* was tough competition.[600] The idea of competition betrays a desire to beat everyone to the top of the glossy game. A surprisingly moving obituary in *Vogue* itself has Wintour also talking competition, glorifying it as the fire that fuelled them to do better. It is what she laments the most about Tilberis' demise, going so far as to repeatedly mention it, writing, 'Liz was a strong competitor, and even when she was desperately ill put out a magazine that kept us on our toes' and 'I . . . will miss her formidable competition.'[601]

Competition in the Glossy Media

There were other complications in the media landscape. The highly competitive world of American glossies actually had four, not two, high-fashion magazines and they were all struggling to adjust. The soft economy and the competitors who had seemingly sprung up overnight kept the Condé Nast cabal awake at night. In 1985, French-born *Elle* had entered the market with a splash. Its breezy, chatty, fashion-lite approach gained a circulation of over 800,000 in a matter of months, overtaking *Harper's Bazaar* which hadn't yet renovated under Tilberis.[602] By 1992, the number rose to 935,000, second only to *Vogue* (still the front runner with its impressive 1.2 million circulation).[603] Nonetheless, *Elle*'s shot to the top made them uneasy. It had happened too fast. When *Harper's Bazaar* began to gain on them both, alarms went off inside Condé Nast. Then there was the problem of *Mirabella*.

When Wintour's predecessor as editor-in-chief, Grace Mirabella, had been fired, despite being a *Vogue* reject, she was a leading field expert with a scorching list of contacts. Rupert Murdoch approached her to launch a competing magazine, entitled *Mirabella*. Skewing to the slightly older woman with its sophisticated, serious tone, it appeared on newsstands in 1989. Although *Mirabella* took the smallest market share with only 400,000 circulation,[604] it was the most respected publication by both press and readers. Neither Grace Mirabella nor her magazine ever faced the censure, jibes or critical picking apart that everyone else did. The other problem with *Mirabella* was that it had absorbed a huge portion of *Vogue*-trained professionals across editorial, art and writing, since many members of staff had left to follow their old leader in her new venture. In 1992, the battle for advertising budgets had become brutal and it was marked as the year of a 'great sorting-out'.[605] Predictions on who would fall out of the running came hot and fast. Many figured it would be *Mirabella*, as the smallest player, but it was such a favourite that nobody wanted to back its demise. *Harper's Bazaar*, some said, could be dead in a year if Tilberis didn't pull her weight. Losers had to be carved out of this cut-throat competition, winners would be crowned.

As the market leader, technically *Vogue* didn't have much to fear. That didn't stop shock waves from coursing through the management. Alexander Liberman had now become a cultural czar.[606] By nurturing the awkward personality of the billionaire owner of Condé Nast Publications, Si Newhouse, he had gained an immense foothold in the company. In 1962, he convinced his boss and pupil to make a clear departure from the usual Newhouse style of management. Instead of allowing the editors-in-chief of each magazine to have creative control, all editors would now answer to an editorial director. Liberman nominated himself for this role of controlling and homogenising all the Condé Nast properties. By the early 1990s he was eighty years old, self-important, sure of himself, quick, difficult and duplicitous. He still ruled side by side with Si Newhouse, who admitted they had an 'uncomplicated' company structure:[607] it consisted of Newhouse the owner, Liberman the editorial director and Bernard Leser the president of the company. A trinity of old men were putting out thousands of magazines every year aimed at young women.

Newhouse had been an uncertain leader who only developed with Liberman by his side, as consigliere, and relied on market research, statistics and surveys to bring him information about his readers. But as he got comfortable in his director's chair, he developed what writer Thomas Maier dubbed 'The Newhouse Concept'.[608] It advocated the bottom line in every element of magazine-making, meaning *everything* had to boost their profits. So, on the surface Condé Nast kept on publishing beautiful art books brimming with fantasy. But underneath all of that the message to their readers was not style, but: 'BUY'. Today we call this kind of relentless placement 'native advertising'.

It would not be long before adverts became advertorials and product placement became normalised in editorials, blurring the line between PR campaigns and genuine stories. We now expect to see this everywhere, but in the 1980s and 1990s it was received as a tawdry manipulation of consumers, leveraging *Vogue*'s credibility for financial gain. For years the Society of Professional Journalists in America had shunned the 'hybrid' approach,[609] but for Newhouse, Liberman, Wintour and other chieftains of Condé Nast, ethics had become as dated as corsets. So much for competition outside of *Vogue*. The competition from within was far steeper and more insidious.

The Newhouse family, who still own Condé Nast Publications and thus also *Vogue*, are steeped in enigma. Si Newhouse had inherited the sparkling holdings from his father, coming to luxury publishing in middle age. His inclination to secrecy was innate. He hired family members, refused to answer questions about his life, apparently paid high-profile editors their wages from numerous accounts under different subsidiaries within the Newhouse holdings.[610] His need for extreme privacy went as far as arriving at the office before the light of day and walking around in his socks so no one could hear him. More than one person – from his biographers, to former disciple Tina Brown – has called him 'Emperor Augustus'.[611] He was the overlord, benefactor, the final word. Condé Nast was his Ancient Rome.

In the 1990s, the Newhouse family held an estimated $12 billion personal fortune. In this golden era of living under the Newhouse roof, editors could expect six-figure salaries, along with cars, chauffeurs and perks that included beauty treatments as well as daily restaurant dining. When Wintour was at British *Vogue*, the company paid for all her visits to her husband in New York via Concorde. Clothing allowances stood around $25,000 to $50,000 annually. One rumour alleged that when an editor had disliked the layout of their office, Newhouse hired a feng shui master to rearrange it.[612] Subsidised trips abroad included five-star hotels. To help them on to the property ladder, employees were offered no-interest mortgages. To those on the outside, the 'Condé Nasties' were ridiculous, spoiled creatures. Icons of excess. But the money thrown at them was not entirely a waste: if his ring of delegates were expected to hobnob with the social elite, it would cost more than keeping up with the Joneses. In New York you had the Donna Karans and the Donald Trumps, Rockefellers and Rothschilds. Editors needed more than just a party invitation to make the necessary friends in that pool. Many would later lament they never knew how good they had it; the lifestyle was just on loan. As quickly as Si Newhouse could extend his largesse, he could withdraw it and the execution chamber of Condé Nast got as much action as the expense accounts.

Si Newhouse's firing style has made it into lore. Striking unsentimentally and out of the blue, *Time* magazine went so far as to feature a photographic line-up of the severed heads of Newhouse editors in a 1990 profile;[613] *New York* magazine similarly provided a timeline of his discarded employees titled 'The Sacking Solstice'.[614] One with tragic consequences concerned Margaret Case, who'd been society editor since the days of Edna Woolman Chase. After forty-plus years on the job she came into her office one morning to find removal men taking out her belongings. It was an insult from which she never recovered. She was to take her own life by throwing herself out of the window of her Park Avenue home . . . an exit generally considered more dignified than the one she had to effect from Si Newhouse's door.

Fear of the falling blade helped create an uneasy atmosphere among the rain of dollars and Barneys gift cards. It made heads of department forever ask, 'Are we performing well enough? Will management be happy?' Although clearly motivated by revenue, Si Newhouse had favourites who would be forgiven fiscal crimes. Wintour, for instance, does not seem to have suffered any repercussions for sinking *House & Garden*. Many say he cared deeply about status, loved luxury. But Grace Mirabella had succeeded at *Vogue* by making it accessible. What exactly were the rules? To stay ahead, it was crucial to identify and acknowledge some Liberman–Newhouse devices. 'Managed competition' was the cornerstone, according to Tina Brown, another Condé Nast superstar.[615] This meant in-house infighting roiled persistently in the background, lighted and stoked where necessary; it was believed to make staff work harder. Anna Wintour had Liz Tilberis as adversary outside Condé Nast. On the inside was Tina Brown, who'd revived *Vanity Fair* in 1983.

Another of Newhouse's darlings, Brown was eerily similar to Wintour at first glance. Both were from the UK, had privileged backgrounds, were in their thirties, married to older, well-respected men. Tina Brown, a bolshy blonde, had made a sensation of editing *Tatler* in England. Her imprimatur was mixing high and low cultural content, so that a gossipy column about Goldie Hawn could sit next to an investigative political essay on Gorbachev. It was not totally dissimilar from Wintour's mixing of cheap and expensive fashion – both approaches were seen as radical. Just like Wintour, Brown could be 'cold' and 'cutting'.[616] The main difference seems to be that while Wintour was a quiet, simmering presence, Brown was brassy and vainglorious.

The press enjoyed pitting Wintour and Brown against each other as much as Wintour and Tilberis. Headlines from the *New York Times* to the *Chicago Tribune* to the *Washington Post* all tackle the subject of these twin emblems[617] of the Newhouse magazine fortune. Mass media discussed the 'British invasion' of American publishing, using Wintour, Brown and Tilberis as examples. One profile in *Spy* magazine ran with the headline: 'How American Publishing has been taken over by people with charming accents and bad teeth.'[618] In their performance of enmity, Wintour and Brown obliged their bosses, the press and the eager crowds. They sat on separate tables at the same lunch spot every day.

There was a side effect of all this attention on the individual editors. They rose to fame as representatives of the magazine they headed, but as forceful personalities themselves they eventually eclipsed the publication with their own auras. The magazines became a personification of Brown and Wintour respectively. *Vogue* was streamlined into a slinky, sporty, sexy, clever version of itself; *Vanity Fair* was gossip and high culture, ballsy, brainy, brawny. But while Brown seemed like the clear front runner at Condé Nast, riding on the enormous success of *Vanity Fair*, she could not court Newhouse and Liberman with as much dexterity as Wintour could. As the years went by, Brown's smile takes on a manic edge beside her celebrity pantheon of friends as behind the scenes Wintour was making her mark. When Liberman hit his mid-eighties, the speculation on who would be his successor reached deafening new levels.

In January 1994, the company named British-born James Truman, a 35-year-old golden boy, as Alexander Liberman's replacement for the coveted position of editorial director. On this move the papers remained uncharacteristically quiet. Nobody was interested in unpacking the fact that a relatively inexperienced male newcomer had been promoted over two women, each of whom had nearly two decades' more experience than him. Wintour would wait till her next chance, but Brown, who had moved to *The New Yorker* in 1992, fell out of favour and eventually became another Condé Nast casualty.

CHAPTER 14

Addicted to Vogue

A Condé Nast Cautionary Tale

The American at *Vogue Paris*

At French *Vogue* order had to be restored. Once again, an important edition had gone off key: Colombe Pringle had produced rabble-rousing Christmas issues and allowed the fashion pages to wilt, unloved and unkept. In the capital of couture this was unacceptable; the editrix of French *Vogue* had to pacify, persuade, charm and coax the big design houses, playing the game of fashion egos. Pringle was not interested in this pandering circuit, which involved a nonstop frenzy of flowers sent to the office by keen PRs, gifts from major and minor brands pouring in to *gently encourage* the magazine to feature them favourably and friendly deals struck in sugary tones at stylish lunch spots. Condé Nast's job was to find someone more willing to make friendly with a city of fashionistas.

It was good common sense to pick someone who was already on their books and Joan Juliet Buck belonged to *Vogue*'s realm of unimaginable privilege. She had been born rich enough to be hired on a typically low salary at British *Vogue* and had worked for the company long enough to be on familiar terms with the executives.

Offering her the editorship of French *Vogue* would be safer than gambling on another newcomer who might have loyalties elsewhere.

The daughter of a Hollywood movie producer and his supermodel wife, Buck was an American girl who'd been raised in a pink palace on the outskirts of Paris. Greats such as Lauren Bacall and Peter O'Toole were dinner guests during her childhood and her first best friend was Anjelica Huston. At the tender age of seventeen she met Tom Wolfe, who made her the subject of an essay titled 'The Life & Hard Times of a Teenage London Society Girl'. She would move to NYC to be closer to him and dropped out of college to become a reviewer for *Glamour* when she was still only twenty. From there her career snowballed.

Buck worked often, prolifically and internationally, cleaning up with the giants of journalism. She became features editor of British *Vogue* at twenty-three, then the London correspondent of Andy Warhol's *Interview* magazine, a correspondent for *Women's Wear Daily* in London and Rome, associate editor of the *London Observer*, contributing editor to American *Vogue*, *The New Yorker* and *Vanity Fair*. Those heady years of flurry and stardust were all air travel, delirious parties, experimental love affairs. She had a romance with Donald Sutherland. Leonard Cohen asked her to run away with him. Friends throughout her life included Jackie Kennedy, Yves Saint Laurent, Hélène Rochas, Karl Lagerfeld. Suffice to say the pages of her memoirs are generously spiced with stories concerning the socially prominent, fashionable, political and entertainment elite of several continents; so full of name-dropping that entire paragraphs are at risk of turning into lists. Despite being born into a rarefied circle, her success is down to talent as much as it is to luck. Buck was – and still is – an accomplished writer, versatile and playful. *Vogue Paris* gave her the opportunity to explore both her kooky style and her creativity more broadly.

It was 1994 when Joan Juliet Buck signed her contracts and committed to a new routine as editor-in-chief of French *Vogue*. She would have to please the business-minded Newhouse family. She would also have to manage an unruly and unreceptive team, learning to fire and hire. Buck had held a grudge against Francine Crescent, an earlier French EIC who had refused to hire her, and had commented frequently on her bland, non-committal manner. Now, Buck would have to cultivate her poker-faced smile as a necessary evil, her only shield against an avalanche of PRs, new brands, old brands, modelling agencies, emerging photographers, established photographers, writers, stylists and anybody else who recognised her as a *Vogue* editor-in-chief and hounded her for it.

Buck had been courted for the position before. The French *Vogue* publisher, Prince Jean Poniatowski, had lunched her at Maxim's at a time when it wasn't fashionable. She had been living in a carefully constructed bohemia, taking freelance commissions and working on novels. In the evenings she went for cosy dinners with sophisticated intellectuals. She could borrow couture whenever she felt like it thanks to her connections and was satisfied penning regular pieces for American *Vogue* and *Vanity Fair* reporting on French culture. She turned down the prince's offer.

Some years later, having returned to New York, a series of taxing events in her personal life and a steady disillusionment with the rampant glitz of her world began to grate. 'I lived from one adrenaline-filled magazine deadline all-nighter to the next',[619] Buck wrote, 'I prayed that something would happen to liberate me from the infernal cycle of writing profiles to pay for new dresses to wear to old parties.'[620] When Liz Tilberis left British *Vogue*, Buck called Si Newhouse to ask for the job. It was already taken. Newhouse expressed surprise that she was interested in editing, to which Buck replied she was desperate to leave New York.[621] The message must have hit home since not long after, Anna Wintour got in touch warning Buck to expect a phone call from Jonathan Newhouse, head of Condé Nast International.[622] A meeting was set up and Buck asked to be sent a year's worth of back copies of *Vogue Paris*. She stayed up in her hotel room all night, skimming, critiquing and covering the pages in notes.[623] When she met Jonathan Newhouse she insisted one of the magazine's greatest weaknesses was the soft-porn Helmut Newton-style sex-infused shoots. Women, in her opinion, ought to be treated with more respect.[624] Six months of silence followed before the call from Newhouse came, offering her the position of editor-in-chief.

Just like others suddenly propelled into the spotlight of a *Vogue* editorship, Buck was shell-shocked by the reality of the job. Obstacles sprung up everywhere. To start with, she had to clear out the old staff and create a new team, a problem for which Jonathan Newhouse recommended a curious solution: poach from other Condé Nast interests.[625] Thus, the art director Donald Schneider came from German *Vogue*, while fashion editors included the darlings of Paris – Carine Roitfeld and Delphine Treanton, who'd been at *Glamour*. These shifting alliances caused their own problematic knock-on effects. The French staff mistrusted her and made sly digs about her being American, insinuating she had no right to teach French women anything. They suspected her of being Anna Wintour's spy. They spoke to her in English instead of French, although she was fluent.

She was assigned a cramped, second-rate room and no one found her a chair for days, forcing her to float uncomfortably over the desk. These slights added to the already mammoth task of reordering a publication and unsurprisingly Buck made blunders. An art director she'd been planning to fire for days kept disappearing and in the end she found herself sacking him unceremoniously on a crowded flight of stairs – a terrible faux pas, gossips said, showing all too clearly the ill-breeding of Americans.[626] Another incident would be comical if it wasn't viciously used against her. Buck had been burning cedar incense sticks in her office, attempting to cleanse the space of bad energy, when a HR executive appeared, sniffing about and dropping hints that someone had been smoking a joint in the building.[627] Embarrassed, Buck didn't confess to lighting the cedar; she felt reasons were being compiled to get rid of her before she'd properly started.

Meanwhile, talent was as self-absorbed as ever and egos had to be massaged. Buck recounts tiresome incidents with Mario Testino, who, needing constant reassurance, had a frustrating tendency to sit in her bureau no matter how busy she was, insisting he was the epitome of *Vogue*.[628] Because the budgets at French *Vogue* were low, even superstar photographers couldn't expect big fees, so instead people had to be bribed, sweet-talked and treated like gods, since in a way they were doing Buck a favour every time. Then there was the constant fielding of gifts and bribes from the *maisons* of Paris who air-kissed and hand-held and made compliments to her face, but spread rumours behind her back. The bubbling brook of bad feeling that streamed unchecked through the corridors poisoned relationships and fed the toxic atmosphere. In the midst of all this, Buck still had to put out a magazine every month. Her private life melted into nothingness. Like so many other editors, she recollects only the relentless work cycle, the eighteen-hour days. All she remembers for years was passing out half-dead at the end of the day, only to wake a few hours later to start again.[629]

Scandals that Rocked the Fashion World

Part of the reason Buck's editorship had such a rocky start was her nationality. Of the twenty-seven or so countries which have a *Vogue* edition *Vogue Paris* is the only one to be known by city rather than country. Paris considers itself not just the capital of France, but also the capital of fashion and they have always been protective about their status as the home of haute couture.

The country is also recognised for their rich cuisine and fine wines, beautiful language and classic literature. There are other cultural particularities, among them another Parisian institution: *la conversation*. In the eighteenth century eloquent discussion flourished in cafés, salons and private houses. Quick wit, elegant turns of phrase and a vast general knowledge showed education in a speaker and could demonstrate intelligence. This is not as irrelevant now as it may seem. To this day, philosophy is a compulsory subject in the French curriculum, teaching students from a young age how to cultivate thought. France's attitude is – and always has been – that the ability to engage critically is a mark of civilisation. The result is Paris's self-conscious image of itself as the centre of high culture, with the Parisians as innately refined taste-makers. Much like *Vogue* itself, Paris stands for the best of the best, in theory. In practice, the restrictions of this echo chamber had long stifled any originality, leaving the Parisians insulated by their snobbery.

Paradoxically, it was Buck who restored the magazine's identity to a far more authentic semblance of Frenchness. The essence of spirited natural beauty and easy cool which had defined Parisian chic was in danger of being lost. The country was going through a phase of political polarity, with fidelities to either right-wing or left-wing parties dividing people. Buck felt that *Vogue Paris*, before her arrival, had hoped to skate over these rivalries by concentrating on lingerie as more politically neutral. Blazers and pencil skirts were shamelessly conservative; designer jeans and battered Burberry coats were the marks of a champagne socialist.[630] Clothes of any kind seemed to come with connotations, so the fashion pages just stripped their models. Looking at back issues before she became EIC, Buck felt it was a glossier, thicker, denser *Vogue* than any other *Vogue*, shiny and slick and practically empty.[631] Buck made it her mission to turn her *Vogue Paris* into an embodiment of France and a reflection of France's greatest achievements.[632]

Buck's first full issue, September 1994, was an ode to the French woman, 'La Femme Française'.[633] The cover was a statement of simplicity. Wearing a loosely tailored black trouser suit, the statuesque model had a shock of black hair and is beaming at the reader. Gone was the sultry pouting, the S&M. Actress Kristin Scott Thomas appears for a feature, humorous horoscopes are included and wardrobe staples are shown by matching them with the 'type' of French woman they were associated with. Turbans were for Simone de Beauvoir, trainers were Jane Birkin, pearl necklaces were Chanel, push-up bras Brigitte Bardot and so on. Posters of the September cover were strung on the sides of kiosks across the whole city and according to Buck it outsold the magazine's usual figures, though every so often someone would make a sly remark or laugh inexplicably when they saw the theme.[634] It was only much later that Buck was told 'La Femme Française' came across like a rallying call to the far right and the cover even looked like an advert for the National Front.[635] So much for her attempt at political neutrality.

With December fast approaching, Buck had to start thinking about the all-important guest editor. But finding someone to follow

Nelson Mandela would be nigh on impossible. In the end, Buck decided to abolish the guest-edited Christmas issues. Instead, they'd be made in-house, with multiple contributors, planned side by side with photographers where possible.

The ambitious theme Buck chose for December 1994 was 'Cinéma'.[636] Inside, they traced the history of film from the Lumière brothers and turned blockbuster masterpieces into fashion stories. She had managed to whip her team into a frenzy of excitement. Thierry Mugler agreed to send a metal robot costume he'd used in a show once, but this was impounded by US Customs. Photographer Enrique Badulescu and an editor managed to shoot illegally in Grand Central Terminal. Afterwards, they discovered the film had been accidentally left out in the sun and ruined. The team redid Bond girls in white fur and spoofed movies from sci-fi thriller *Blade Runner,* to the opulent drama by Jean Renoir, *The Rules of the Game*, shot by Mario Testino with Isabella Rossellini. Buck claims that when she showed the result to Si Newhouse back in New York he was amazed.[637] Her words only.

The editions made by Joan Juliet Buck zing with a sense of fun. Like the best editors, she had an instinctive way of thinking outside the box, repackaging old ideas to make them sparkle again. But it does seem she was constantly hampered by bad luck and bewildering complications. The Christmas issue of 1995 celebrated seventy-five years of *Vogue Paris* and published nostalgic material from the archive,[638] but as they outwardly celebrated their past, Buck and the American-born publisher Gardner Bellanger were cloistered in secret meetings with lawyers about their future.[639] There was a severe economic crisis in France and magazines were vanishing into thin air. *Vogue* was trying to get its hands on some of the newly unemployed with long-standing reputations. They also debated which of their own they might be able to foist out without directly firing.

Rumours circulated that *Vogue Paris* would be one of the many casualties of the crisis. It wasn't, but four other Condé Nast France publications folded, including French *Glamour*. Buck, Bellanger and other senior employees busied themselves looking happy and confident so that advertisers wouldn't get jumpy and pull ads out of their pages.[640] When each storm was weathered, cold winds would blow in from some new direction and black clouds would gather above them once more. A relentless turnover of staff made it hard to get systems in place. Then there was the problem of American *Vogue* always taking priority. If they suddenly decided they wanted a dress or a celebrity interview or a photographer that *Vogue Paris* was already using, the French team had to give up their plans and start from scratch.[641]

In December 1996, Buck tackled the topic of music, trying to give *Vogue Paris* some of the edginess of the nineties rave culture but it fell flat.[642] In September 1997 she commissioned an interview with Madame Claude, a notorious procuress now in her seventies, who'd invented the term 'call girl' because she used to send out to clients directly instead of maintaining a bordello.[643] Servicing only the upper echelons, her girls were coached in speech and deportment, taught never to wear perfume in case it lingered on men's clothes and carried a wig in case they hadn't had time to visit a hairdresser before an assignation. That raunchy little number resulted in many whispered propositions from male acquaintances, who suddenly wondered whether Buck might be interested in orgies or sex clubs.

On the cusp of the millennium, Buck was brainstorming ideas for the December 1999–January 2000 issue. The theme she settled upon was quantum physics.[644] The result is a fascinating experiment. It includes a Paco Rabanne dress of plastic scales used to emulate the first vertebrae; a Ralph Lauren crocodile jacket shot to symbolise the first reptile; and a Primavera goddess dress signalled the arrival of *Homo sapiens*. They photographed landscape designer Charles Jencks's quantum garden, played on tropes of cloning and optical illusions. Except again, it was a case of one step forward, two steps back. In an interview with the *Wall Street Journal* about the science copy – officially named 'Archives of the Future' – she was asked if she hung out with Parisian designers. Buck accidentally made a dismissive remark which went down badly and got Paris muttering behind their hands again.[645]

By now paid circulation had nearly doubled since the beginning of her editorship, going from 60,000 to 120,000 in 1994.[646] Ad sales from 1998 to 1999 jumped 16 per cent.[647] Still Buck's job was not getting any easier. Mario Testino walked away and there were more staff resignations. The fashion pages went stale, then curdled, because star stylist Carine Roitfeld had also moved to pastures new. Buck had a knack for cerebral and playful issues, choosing broad themes from theatre to science. The danger was that this could look gimmicky after a while and frustrated advertisers, who just wanted to see their clothes modelled normally. Buck's problems were compounded when she began to clash with her publisher, Gardner Bellanger.

When Buck had taken the role as editor-in-chief, she had brought another American native living in Paris, Gardner Bellanger, on board. Bellanger had held the post of associate publisher in Europe for American *Vogue*, she was competent, hands-on and knew her way around Condé Nast. During the early days they had muddled through together, struggling against the tide and clinging on through the many bumps in the road. Of this period, Buck wrote, 'Some days it felt as if Gardner and I were standing back to back, fighting off enemies with broadswords'.[648] But as the years went by, their closeness began to slip. They turned the swords on each other.

By 1999, Bellanger had been promoted to president of Condé Nast France and appeared to have gone power mad. Buck had begun dating a hard-nosed banker and best friend of Jonathan Newhouse. The new relationship gave her a false sense of security that company loyalties would now lie with her. Unfortunately, this self-assurance meant the collisions with Bellanger intensified. Doors would be slammed, high-pitched swearing would ring out from behind them, there was even blackmail and threats. It was unsustainable.

When Buck met Jonathan Newhouse before the next Milan collections she was single again. She must have known, as we all do in such situations, that her ex would tell his friends the details of their washed-up romance – not easy when one of his closest confidants is your employer. Buck and Newhouse's meeting was brief: Newhouse urged Buck to take a sabbatical. Two months. Buck refused. Newhouse insisted. He wanted her to spend some time in Arizona, supposedly for therapy, before her title of editor-in-chief was officially handed over to someone else. Surprised and confused, Buck asked why, to which Newhouse replied that he didn't want her to end up like one of his London editors, who'd died in 1995 from a cocaine overdose following an orgy. Buck was stunned. She was not on drugs – didn't even drink – and reminded Newhouse of this. The imposed sojourn in rehab was supposed to act as a transition to ease Buck out of her job and possibly used to decide what to do with *Vogue Paris* while she was far away and out of touch. Newhouse told her that if she refused to go, this would be construed as a resignation and she would forfeit her severance pay. Buck needed those funds, especially since she was responsible for her elderly manic-depressive father.

At Cottonwood, a treatment centre outside Tucson, Buck had her Guerlain deodorant confiscated for its alcohol content, gave a urine sample, then a blood sample.[649] The next day she was told she had to

leave because her tests had all come back clean, but she insisted she
was under orders to stick it out. Even hiding out among addicts and
attempted suicides who cried publicly day and night, Buck caught
snatches of nasty gossip from her old world.[650] There were rumours
circulating Paris that she'd punched Bellanger at the Milan shows
– this had started as a joke because Bellanger had so much lip filler
put in, but gossips who hadn't seen her took the story literally. Other
rumours said she'd been caught with syringes on her desk – but these
were vials of seawater she was given by a spa in Italy, intended to
balance her electrolytes after meals. There was even a rumour about
her and Bellanger having been lesbian lovers, which Buck decided
was a crack at her cropped haircut.[651] Meanwhile, Newhouse still
wouldn't explain why she had to do a course in rehab and her own
lawyer doubted every word she said.[652]

While hanging around support groups she had no reason to be at,
Buck had the epiphany that she was addicted to *Vogue* the way her
fellow inmates were addicted to cocaine.[653] Suddenly, the glamorous
life with all its beautiful add-ons was nothing more than a drug to
her mind.[654] While there might be room for philosophical discussion
around fashion as a 'drug', the idea of a cosmopolitan career woman
babbling this to a roomful of people with addiction problems to hard
substances seems disingenuous. Though Buck had been through a
genuine ordeal. Condé Nast and its representatives had been cruel,
manipulative, condescending. A letter Jonathan Newhouse wrote to
her in rehab is laced with patronising judgement: 'I write to you as
your employer, as well as a friend who cares deeply about you . . . I
expect you to have a healthy lifestyle and not behave in ways which
could jeopardize your physical or mental health. (I understand you
smoke and accept this.)'[655]

And yet, time passed. A new editor took over in Paris. Bellanger
was found to be manipulating behind the scenes and was fired in

2002. The gossip mill moved on. And eventually – most unbelievably of all – Buck began writing for American *Vogue* again. A reconciliation? Financial necessity? Lack of pride? Or maybe there really is something to the drug theory. Buck's 'luxury-is-a-drug' revelation does hold some merit and her story reads like a cautionary tale to those obsessed with wealth and glamour. Her cushioned life at the heart of *Vogue*, full of five-star hotel suites and haute couture, still had to be paid for. The work was difficult, debilitating and draining, but ending up in a rehab facility because you'd burned some cedar incense and fell out with a co-worker is insane. Perhaps her story should be taken as a modern fable and summarised with that old adage 'all that glitters is not gold'. Still, Buck had not learned her lesson.

Moving back to America, she vowed to use her substantial severance money to set herself up away from the action, but after a quiet period in New Mexico she returned to New York. She began slowly accepting commissions from Anna Wintour, first a little guiltily and then, when the recession hit, with gratitude. In December 2010, she was given a somewhat unusual assignment: to interview the First Lady of Syria, Asma al-Assad. Unsure of the relevance of Middle Eastern dictatorship to fashion, Buck questioned the commissioning editor, who reportedly sold it as an exciting chance to talk culture and museums with an elegant, English-born First Lady.[656] Curious to see the ruins of Palmyra, and figuring it would be a once-in-a-lifetime opportunity, Buck accepted the job.

The result of this trip was a treacly puff piece titled 'A Rose in the Desert', which describes in tones of awed reverence the beauty, charm, youth, magnetism and energy of this dictator's spouse.[657] Syria is described as the safest country in the Middle East and Asma al-Assad as a hard-working former investment banker whose new mission was to save the children of Syria.[658] In February 2011, the

piece went online at Vogue.com; in March it was printed in American
Vogue, in the so-called 'Power' issue. That month, uprisings began
in Syria as part of the Arab Spring, forcing to the surface the truth
of an oppressive regime, known primarily for extreme corruption,
mass killings and the torture of children . . . a regime run by a family
Vogue had just called 'wildly democratic'.[659]

The public responded with shock and incomprehension at *Vogue*'s
bizarre interview of a high-profile murderer's wife and Condé Nast
was swept off in a storm of criticism the likes of which it had never
seen. By May the piece vanished off the website and soon after an
experienced official apology was issued. It is pretty tricky to find
copies of the article as *Vogue* determinedly works to remove traces
of the gaffe, though various blogs continue reposting the evidence.
But the harshest repercussions were felt by Buck, not Condé Nast.
Asked not to comment on the scandal as it unravelled, Buck was
left in the dark as decisions were made in meetings she wasn't
privy to.[660] She endured a torrent of hatred online and at the end
of the year, her contract with the company was terminated.[661] Her
association with *Vogue*, spanning some forty years, had come to
a sticky end.

In a long article for *Newsweek* originally titled 'Mrs Assad
Duped Me', Buck tries to tell her side.[662] She admits to being gul-
lible and naïve, to wanting to visit Syria and to misunderstanding
how much research she should have done in preparation.[663] Unfortunately, this still leaves unanswered questions. Buck claims to
have been followed during the trip, but never says why she didn't
question this; she also never seems to have wondered why her
British-born interviewee would marry into a family responsible
for the deaths of thousands. The *Newsweek* article betrays a writer
used to giving her subjects the glossy treatment unthinkingly.
Buck comes across as out of touch and clearly considers herself

a victim of callous management at Condé Nast. She admits she should have never accepted the assignment and obviously feels betrayed by her bosses who, instead of taking the blame, cut her loose. Buck paid an enormous price for the dazzling decades at *Vogue* – for nothing in life is free.

CHAPTER 15

The Digital Curveball

Fretting, Restructuring, Franchising

The Glossy Media and the Internet

A great deal has happened since 2000 when we were all contemplating the dawn of a new millennium. There were a few who guessed what was coming. We all know about Bill Gates and Microsoft; Jeff Bezos and Amazon; Steve Jobs and Apple; but for your average Joe, a world online was uncharted territory. The internet was born in the 1990s, so the web was still in its earliest infancy at the start of the 2000s. How quickly it has developed since has shown us what a unique moment in history we have witnessed. The internet has had infinite and far-reaching effects on the way we live, more than we could have imagined possible, and one of its pillars is interconnectivity.

Facebook appeared in 2004, Twitter in 2006, Instagram in 2010. How we communicate has been complicated by smart technologies with the launches of the iPhone in 2007 and the iPad in 2010. Now we all carry computers in our back pockets. In fashion production, progress in manufacturing has meant clothes can be made faster and at shorter notice. With the web they can also be sold and shipped at lightning speed. This can be best seen with the rise of e-tailers. Net-a-Porter was created by Natalie Massenet in 2000 as an online store selling high-end apparel. ASOS, which produces cheaply for the mass market, emerged the same year. Nobody had much faith in the model – why would we want to buy clothes without being able to see them or try them on? – yet by February 2014, Net-a-Porter had a turnover of £500 million with 6 million monthly users.[664] ASOS had a turnover just shy of £770 million in 2013, with 9.1 million active customers by the end of 2014.[665] The way in which consumers buy clothes, browse sales and discover new brands has changed for ever. And if brands can build their own followings online and market them through social media, where would glossy magazines fit in? Today, printing cycles are out of date as soon as the ink dries on the page, so advertisers are increasingly diverting budgets away from traditional press and channelling them towards influencers instead.

As a result, the secretive fashion industry has been forced to open up, allowing consumers access behind the scenes for the first time in history. Fashion photographer Nick Knight played a significant role in this by founding SHOWstudio in 2000. Knight recognised the potential of the digital medium and wanted to challenge fashion communication by widening the circle of accessibility. SHOWstudio provided us with some of the earliest insights into day-to-day operations such as running a studio, making a collection and the nitty-gritty of photoshoots; anything to help precipitate an intense period demystifying fashion.

Some favourites among his SHOWstudio experiments include 'Moving Fashion',[666] a series that re-examines clothes through film shorts instead of frozen still imagery, and 'The Sound of Clothes',[667] which looks at the noises garments make. These are strangely simple, strangely hypnotic sound and video clips. SHOWstudio.com was groundbreaking in its approach to the creative possibilities in tech, though it eventually accepted advertising – a step that usually signals commercial priorities over artistic ones. The platform continues to provide experimental fashion shoots and panel discussions, telling us Knight intends to continue his crusade to democratise the industry. His invention of the 'fashion film' has since been adopted as a staple by magazines and brands alike. The result is that anyone anywhere can now feel part of the fashion world in a way it was impossible to before.

If social media and alternative methods of fashion storytelling presented competition, it was only the beginning. Another tidal wave that rose out of nowhere to eclipse the glossy media was blogging. The first slew of important fashion blogs appeared in the mid-2000s and received a definite cold shoulder from the mainstream. In 2004 Bryan Yambao, a web developer from the Philippines, started Bryanboy; in 2005 Kevin Ma debuted Hypebeast; in 2006 Susie Lau entered the sphere with Style Bubble. For a while nobody noticed these excitable, relatable, outsider voices who snapped themselves posing in streets and gushed over collections they could only see in pictures and only dream of wearing. As late as 2008, the *New York Times* claimed *Vogue* still had a monopoly on luxury advertising budgets. But soon enough, someone came up with an idea: bloggers loved fashion, had thousands or even millions of staunch fans and wanted desperately to be part of the industry. Brands could bypass magazines and access their desired audience through these new individuals . . . a strategy that would rock the glossies' place as the ultimate arbitrators of style.

A turning point came in the form of a pixie-faced Chicagoan. Some will remember the stir caused when 13-year-old blogger Tavi Gevinson was flown to Paris to see the Dior couture show, then irritated seasoned editors and the fashion savants by donning an enormous bow on top of her diminutive figure and blocking their view of the runway. Gevinson had started sharing her thoughts online at age eleven and is widely considered to have flown the flag for the blogger generation. Plenty of journalists were upset at this high-stakes exercise in PR, feeling that their career-long experience was being dismissed for the sake of a few lines put on the free web by a child. Nonetheless, Gevinson continued to appear on front rows, flanked either side by fashion royalty and was even invited to judge an award in 2010 by the Council of Fashion Designers of America (CFDA).

Dubbed the 'know-nothings'[668] this generation were willingly shoehorned into the scene by hungry publicists determined to promote their brands at any cost. And along with the prepubescent prodigies, a new vocabulary emerged. The stuff that counted now was: visibility, customer conversion, engagement, follower counts, pay-per-clicks, affiliate advertising. Today, bloggers are recruited by industry officials and placed next to the likes of Anna Wintour at international fashion weeks. Once kids in bedrooms leafing through magazines with unbridled enthusiasm and sharing their thoughts in forums, bloggers have become mini business people, cashing huge payments from sponsored posts in partnership with both high-street and luxury retailers. By the middle of the 2010s, the stewing animosity of professional media spokespeople towards the bloggers broke free from the confines of offices and spilled into public view. In a vitriolic campaign, a number of senior *Vogue* staffers lashed out at the blogger phenomenon during Milan Fashion Week in 2016. The tension had been building for a long time and the Condé Nast coven really went for it.

Creative digital director Sally Singer, wrote: 'Note to bloggers who change head-to-toe paid-to-wear outfits every hour: Please stop. Find another business. You are heralding the death of style.'[669] Sarah Mower, chief critic of Vogue.com added it was 'pathetic for these girls, when you watch how many times the desperate troll up and down outside shows, in traffic, risking accidents even, in hopes of being snapped.'[670] It continues. Nicole Phelps, director of Vogue Runway, said it wasn't just 'sad for the women who preen for the cameras in borrowed clothes, it's distressing, as well, to watch so many brands participate.'[671] The queen of claws has to be Alessandra Codinha, fashion news editor of Vogue.com who dubbed paid appearances 'embarrassing', adding: 'Rather than a celebration of any actual style, it seems to be about turning up, looking ridiculous, posing, twitching in your seat as you check your social media feeds, fleeing, changing, repeating'.[672] She went so far as to say looking for style amid fashion bloggers was 'like going to a strip club looking for romance. Sure, it's all kind of in the same ballpark, but it's not even close to the real thing.'[673]

Strong words all round, though who can blame them? It's galling to imagine working for years, honing your craft, then being unceremoniously replaced by those you might see as hobbyists hoping to make a quick buck, especially tiresome since bloggers are no longer 'outsiders', they've been sucked into the system. Originally, they appealed to audiences as 'real people'. But their place as the 'voice of truth' is compromised. Bloggers have developed as multi-pronged selling channels, as influencers and vloggers, all of them forever hawking, hardly distinguishable morally from magazines that publish articles sponsored by commercial brands. For Vogue, what these web-based platforms really mean is a dilution of focus.

Around the mark of the first decade of the twenty-first century the cry had gone up that print was dead. Glossy magazines had no place in this brave new world. Panicking about shortened attention spans, many publications adopted a drive-thru approach to editorial in a bid to compete with digital. Condé Nast, with its bulging portfolio of high-end properties had seen enough to worry

them and in 2009 they hired McKinsey & Company to investi-
gate their holdings one by one and sniff out the culprits guilty of
haemorrhaging the Newhouse fortune. Sarcastic articles ran with
gloating titles such as 'Condé Nast, McKinsey and the Death of
Endless Dreams'[674] and 'Condé Nast Hires McKinsey, Staffers Suffer
Shock'.[675] Clearly onlookers – particularly other media – wanted
to see the corporation suffer. Sadly, McKinsey fed into this beautifully when it produced a report that was widely received at the
time as one of the most uneducated memos imaginable, derided
as demonstrating that the management consultants knew nothing
about media. *The Atlantic* managed to get its hands on a draft of
this early memo and reproduced it gleefully to the groans of journalists and readers everywhere:

> In the interest of vertical interconnectivity and maximum
> impactfulness, we just wanted to share some of our initial
> observations/questions with you. We hope these don't seem too
> obvious:
>
> 1. The role of writers in the magazine production process
> seems worthy of examination. What do they do? Why are there
> so many?'
> . . .
> 4. Has the company considered using the World Wide Web as
> a platform for its magazines?[676]

And yet, as hilarious as the suggestion that writers are un-
necessary to a magazine seems, it is becoming increasingly true. The
written word is giving way to the photograph which is slowly giving
way to the video clip, GIF and viral meme. The once-reviled bloggers
have been hired as permanent staff or to produce regular columns.
If McKinsey couldn't see why magazines needed writers, they also

struggled to see why publishing companies needed magazines. That year they proposed the Newhouses axe four titles to lessen their expenses. Since, there have been many other print casualties, from *House & Garden*, to *Portfolio*, to *Glamour* and *Teen Vogue*. The Condé Nast policy of constant expansion was suddenly in reverse gear.

Between 1975–2010 twelve more editions of Vogue had been launched: *Vogue Brazil* in 1975, *Vogue Germany* in 1979, *Vogue Spain* in 1988, *Vogue Korea* and *Vogue Taiwan* in 1996, *Vogue Russia* in 1998, *Vogue Japan* and *Vogue Mexico* in 1999, *Vogue Portugal* in 2002, *Vogue China* in 2005, *Vogue India* in 2007, *Vogue Turkey* in 2010. Soon enough, the appearance of a *Vogue* in an emerging economy became a kind of barometer for the country's financial state: the wealthier a nation became, the more likely *Vogue* was to enter the market. As soon as a growing middle class was successfully identified in Russia after the collapse of the Soviet Union or in Turkey following economic progression, low and behold, *Vogue* swept in to tempt the newly created wealth. Although the rate of new launches has since slowed, new editions have continued to spring up, including: *Vogue Netherlands* in 2012, *Vogue Thailand* and *Vogue Ukraine* in 2013, *Vogue Arabia* in 2016, *Vogue Poland* and *Vogue Czech Republic and Slovakia* in 2018, *Vogue Hong Kong* in 2019 and *Vogue Singapore* restarted in 2020.

Condé Nast has not replicated this scale of growth with any of its other titles. *Vogue* is their prize thoroughbred and the paper on which the Condé Nast reputation is built. It was a time to shed its smaller stablemates and knuckle down on getting the best perform-ance possible out of it.

Vogue Raises its Profile, and Gets into Politics

When *The Devil Wears Prada* hit the cinemas in 2006, Meryl Streep's performance as terrifying fashion editor Miranda Priestly sent a thrill through audiences. With her ash-blonde up-do, faux-stern stare over black-rimmed spectacles and cutting one-liners, Streep enshrined the fashion editor character. The film turned the inner workings of a fashion magazine into a juicy romcom. The plot followed a young ingénue played by Anne Hathaway who has to manoeuvre through the endless trials put upon her by a glacial boss, discovering herself along the way. Stripped bare, it's a simple narrative about finding your calling and navigating adulthood; dress it up in Prada and it's a big-time blockbuster. Ranked by IMDB as the second-highest-grossing Meryl Streep movie, it captured popular imagination.[677] And since it was based off a chick-lit *roman-à-clef* by Lauren Weisberger – a former assistant at *Vogue* – it for ever cemented Anna Wintour's celebrity. *Everybody* said she was the devil.

Wintour identified the change in public mood, maybe even identified the PR opportunity. After *The Devil Wears Prada* came *The September Issue*, a documentary following Wintour and other staffers as they put together the 2007 September issue of American *Vogue*. Premiering in 2009 and often focusing on the working relationship between a restrained Wintour and a sparky Grace Coddington, the film opens more fashion doors. Creative director Coddington shines, whether storming through the corridors cussing passionately about photoshoots Wintour won't include, or sitting grimly, lips pressed in disapproving silence. Again, the age-worn motif: clashing personalities. It was with a delighted sense of voyeurism that audiences poured back into theatres to watch more fashion magazine antics. Wintour, who had never been big on interviews, was becoming more accessible. In her autobiography, Coddington insists the friction between the two was grossly overemphasised and edited for dramatic effect.[678] How Wintour and Coddington felt about their day-to-day lives being projected for the enjoyment of the masses is a whole different story. In any case, between *The Devil Wears Prada* and *The September Issue*, fashionistas were now subject to a new level of celebrity in the mainstream, with *Vogue* employees in general and Anna Wintour in particular at the forefront of people's minds.

So often photographed, so rarely revealed, Anna Wintour has been said to part crowds like the Red Sea.[679] The page-boy haircut, the sparse frame, the shut-out sunglasses; a clicking of stilettos, a sip from a Starbucks cup. Wintour's reputation was built up in layers by her unmistakeable features, wagging tongues from Manhattan to Mayfair, vendettas of colleagues both current and former, and an avalanche of bad press. From arctic[680] to icy,[681] from devilish to satanic,[682] there's nothing Wintour hasn't been branded. She cannot be as one dimensional as Meryl Streep's portrayal. Wintour has taken much vitriol over the course of her career. In 1995, while having dinner in a restaurant, an anti-fur protestor screamed 'Fur hag!' and flung a dead raccoon into her plate of food. In 2005, she had a tofu pie thrown forcefully at her face as she walked into a show (her dry response: 'I think it was organic').[683] In a ten-year period there were countless incidents with fake blood, parcels of maggot-infested animal guts sent to her desk,[684] harassment, near-attacks. Ten years is a long time to put up with inhuman behaviour.

Wintour has never cracked, never snapped, never taken prescription meds and had it leaked to TMZ, never been papped running out of rehab, never been seen with tears in her eyes, never crumbled. Having said that, Wintour has been eroded. Chiselled down to a cartoon version of herself. She's the comic villain we all love to hate with a trademark look so recognisable you could stick a wig and sunglasses on anyone and send them to sit in her place in the front row. We love to hate her so much that the hate has dropped clean away and the love has become blind adulation. She's a celebrity all right, as high up as Beyoncé and Kim Kardashian. Elvis and Marilyn. Michael Jackson and Queen Elizabeth. Show me the person who won't recognise Anna Wintour.

In her fourth decade as editor-in-chief of American *Vogue*, Wintour is the second-longest-serving editor in the history of the magazine (Edna Woolman Chase still sits at the top of the category). Back in the late eighties, Si Newhouse and Alexander Liberman liked her because she seemed to embody *Vogue*. They wouldn't live to see to what extent she would become the walking, talking manifestation of their glossy journal. Part of the zeitgeist now is to constantly add to the layers of myth-making around her. Her popularity is part of how *Vogue* stays relevant. This is particularly valuable as our culture shifts in focus from trusting big brands, to trusting individuals like celebrities and TV personalities. For all the whittling of her image, it seems improbable that Wintour is even half as farcical a creature as she is made out to be. Her edition has published everything from political pieces by Donna Tartt[685] to long-form essays about the 'heroin chic' trend, complete with an admirably responsible tone and gentle admonishment of the deadly waif 'look'.[686] Much has been said about her homogenisation of the magazine into an identifiable template, one she is said to have pressed on other *Vogues* and, since her appointment as artistic director in 2013, other magazines under Condé Nast. But then brand recognition is a much-used, much-lauded business tactic. She is continuing the legacy of Alexander Liberman and Si Newhouse, both of whom had been zealous in pursuing consistency of agenda and tone. It was a killer strategy in the boom years of the 1980s. It's a little less *au courant* now, as people are slowly veering towards niche publications and the more personal, less corporate touch.

Business savvy has always been one of Anna Wintour's strongest traits: from popularising the use of celebrities on front covers, to keeping the Condé Nast colossus afloat in times of crisis. But the conglomerate still had to weather the Great Recession – that era of economic decline during the late 2000s and early 2010s. Subscriptions were uncertain, newsstand sales even more so, and digital was taking over but execs everywhere were still scratching their heads wondering how to monetise it.

Condé Nast International developed a restaurant and hospitality arm and – through a number of high-profile partnerships – licensed the names of its major properties. A Vogue Café was unveiled in Moscow in 2003, giving the socially keen a place to peck at European-style salad and flash Rolexes. In 2013 a Vogue Café opened inside a mall in Dubai, within what is billed as the world's largest shoe store. There are Vogue Cafés in Ukraine, Saudi Arabia and Portugal. There's a Vogue Restaurant in Turkey and a Vogue Lounge in Malaysia. This does feel like a dilution of the *Vogue* label, and all are located in emerging markets with new money. Condé Nast might fear the concept of Vogue cafés would be perceived as tacky in America and much of Europe, although it dipped its toe into London with a pop-up for the 100th birthday of British *Vogue*. Their global revenue has swelled to include an advertising branch, creative agencies in New York and London, conferences, events and a licensing department to leverage their own assets. The emphasis is firmly on business and on harnessing the legacy of *Vogue* to maintain the stronghold of their cultural influence. It's nothing short of genius that Condé Nast can get paid to create a marketing campaign for a brand, then charge the brand an advertising fee to publish the campaign in its magazines.

Developing multiple income streams is not Anna Wintour's job, but there are tangible clues that reveal her involvement. In 2011, *Women's Wear Daily* (*WWD*) reported that thanks to a Lady Gaga front cover (then at the height of her *Born This Way* fame), *Vogue*'s sales in the USA shot up by 100,000 copies.[687] In fact, *Vogue*'s numbers rose almost 13 per cent at a time when the industry overall was down a whole 9.2 per cent.[688] They were just about the only fashion magazine with any earnings. And while Lady Gaga didn't seem *Vogue* enough to many critics, they might have missed the point. She was commercial.

Times of trouble are good for consolidating power – the weak drop out of the race. Just as *Vogue* had the means to put high-selling celebrities like Jennifer Aniston on their cover, they also had the reach to expand beyond both competitors' budgets and their own pages. As print floundered Wintour launched 'Fashion's Night Out'. Citing New York City as a partner after a successful meeting with the mayor, the *Vogue*-sponsored shopping event included free drinks, celebrity appearances, parties and slashed prices on designer garb. It was intended as a pick-me-up to the recession. Sales were sluggish, the people weren't spending. Wintour weighed in to inject some pizazz into the proceedings again. Supporting the fashion industry at large is something *Vogue* has always done; it serves to encourage the world they write about and it's a good way of building sturdy connections with designers and other talent.

Wintour does still more to assert *Vogue*'s power. Designers such as John Galliano, Michael Kors and Marc Jacobs might not have made their fortunes without the editorial boosts she gave them. Reports say Wintour has gone so far as to educate senators on international fabric trade and the effect of tariffs.[689] She put Hillary Clinton on the cover – the first First Lady to front *Vogue*. In fact, Wintour is a major player in politics. For Obama's re-election campaign she raised over

$500,000 (landing her on the list of top-tier patrons), filmed a promotional video and hosted fundraisers in her own house. Michelle Obama got three *Vogue* covers and it's said that Wintour styled her for public appearances. Her relationship with the White House went as far as discussing partnering up for a fashion workshop[690] and there were rumours of her being awarded an ambassadorship.

Under Wintour, *Vogue* has not been shy in declaring its political bias towards the Democratic Party. In 2016 they endorsed Hillary Clinton as their favoured candidate over Donald Trump; the first time *Vogue* has openly picked a side in an election.[691] Wintour may be many things, but most of all she shows exactly how much soft power there is in the fashion industry, which was estimated to be worth $2.4 trillion in 2017.[692] Fashion has enough influence for the woman who runs *Vogue* to impact presidential campaigns in America, a global economic and military superpower. Let that sink in.

CHAPTER 16

From 'Porno Chic' to 'Parisienne Chic'
Selling Stereotypes

2000s: Defying Beauty Standards

The 1990s and early 2000s were still preoccupied with promoting the thin ideal; an undernourished body with a gaunt and angular face.[693] But even with rib cages jutting, young girls on front covers smiled, happy or sensual, in turn. The toxic subtext so often present in female magazines is that women are here solely to please men. Columns on how to incite desire were resoundingly popular, resulting in an entire generation of girls coached by the glossy media. Women should be tempting, but not too readily available; free-spirited without being wild; confident without being pushy. No matter what changes occur in the law, societal pressure can feel like the real struggle.

Appointed editor-in-chief of French *Vogue* in the millennium, Carine Roitfeld put together a Molotov cocktail of a magazine, a zany, overtly sexual, sometimes offensive, onslaught upon the senses. New ways to be a woman were finally being chiselled out of the sex wars that fought for sexual liberation.[694] Roitfeld's high-fashion, all-sex take on *Vogue* was enormously successful and extremely polarising. It was certainly experimental; it seemed to show every possible version of womanhood. The 'girl' of old mainstream media had all but disappeared, while many new versions of femininity glistened on the pages, beckoning us into the future.

Emmanuelle Alt, the successor who stepped into Roitfeld's shoes in 2011 and is still editor-in-chief today, found a vastly different terrain before her. From needing to show themselves as sexual beings and reclaiming their sexuality in the early 2000s, women had now shifted to self-sufficiency in the 2010s. From wanting to acquire material belongings, they increasingly consume digital ephemera and value knowledge. Diversity, empowerment, body positivity and inclusion are the bywords of this era.

Therefore, the product that Alt offers has to bring a sense of self, an identity and an attitude. As technology manipulates our perceptions and taps into our insecurities, we need to be more grounded than ever. Alt's back-to-basics approach, with an emphasis on motherhood, confidence, simple dressing, the natural ageing process, access and education, turns *Vogue Paris* into as close a reflection of real life as possible. We need to be uplifted and encouraged, while the truths of human biology, like giving birth or growing old, need to be accepted and normalised once and for all.

Yet even wholesome imagery and identities will crystallise into new stereotypes. As a mirror of society and its ambitions, fashion publications are fulfilling a need. Some critics are beginning to suggest that glossy media employees are no longer journalists, but salespeople. And much as they are ambassadors for the *Vogue* brand, they also have to make a brand of themselves. Roitfeld and Alt had long careers as stylists before becoming editors, and although Roitfeld is XXX while Alt is PG, they are both well versed in visual coding and know how to portray social values. How *Vogue* responds to the world around it has always been its key to success.

*

When Joan Juliet Buck was preparing to take over as editor-in-chief of *Vogue Paris*, she was advised to snap up Carine Roitfeld, the slinky-limbed, thickly browed, freckle-faced stylist who'd spent fifteen years at French *Elle*. At the meeting, Buck felt instinctively that Roitfeld would one day replace her as the EIC . . . and she was right.[695] Formally enshrined at the head of French *Vogue* in 2001, Roitfeld has become another of the industry's mythic creatures. To *The Observer* she's a 'Parisian vamp . . . best known for black ensembles, high-slitted pencil skirts and towering stilettos'.[696] Elsewhere she is 'Sultry. Decadent. Dusky'.[697] She's important enough to appear on *The Business of Fashion*'s BoF 500 index of global figures shaping the sector, where they describe her style as 'invariably involving towering heels' with 'the hair and makeup of a night owl.'[698] To the *Financial Times* she's the 'editrix with a hint of dominatrix',[699] though in all these sketches what's missing is any trace of her healthy sense of humour. In interviews she waves away bombastic praise, preferring instead to boast about being compared in looks to haggard punk legend Iggy Pop.[700]

If her fame rests on the image of a rock 'n' roll femme fatale, it is because she portrays this aesthetic as faithfully in her editorial work as in her sartorial choices. When a company memo was sent round to welcome Carine Roitfeld on board it named her creative director of the French Condé Nast group. Under her management, *Vogue Paris* alleged its focus was to make the magazine truly French again – though this meant something quite different to Buck's elegantly cerebral editions. Buck's core principles for *Vogue Paris* included tireless promotion of French culture and a desire to stimulate women intellectually. Buck was against showing pages and pages of lacy unmentionables and feared this was the kind of 'Frenchness' Roitfeld stood for: the sexy cliché.[701] She felt without her influence, French *Vogue* would slide back into its old formula of nipples and cigarettes.[702] This turned out to be true, though in the most un-expected way possible. During Roitfeld's ten-year stint she laced her magazine with scandalous images, not few of which sparked international outrage.

The trope of cigarettes immediately reappeared, as Buck had dreaded. The summer of 2003 produced a bestselling cover, a close-up of actress Sophie Marceau squinting with a thin roll-up dangling from her full lips.[703] An editorial in April 2009 called 'No Smoking' centred on model Lily Donaldson pulling faces and playing with a baby doll.[704] While the model is portrayed as a mum-to-be, complete with false pregnant belly, she is also dressed in garments which both sexualise and infantilise. One image shows her baby bump barely covered by a pink-and-white frilly gingham apron which stops just short of her knicker line. Most of the photos are full length, drawing attention to her long, naked legs. Commentators levied their criticism of this not-so-tender portrait of motherhood, mainly at the title shot, which shows the expectant parent smoking a cigarette.

Bare breasts return as a general theme, sometimes in mind-bogglingly weird scenarios, like the fashion photo of a woman crawling across a table and sticking a big pair of scissors in a gold-fish bowl.[705] In 2007, Roitfeld published model Karen Elson looking languid, her alabaster-white limbs bound by coils of shiny black rope and complex knots.[706] The pallor of her skin is stark against the shadowy background, the blaze of her red curls adding the only lick of colour. Despite the languor, the positioning of her body references BDSM practices: wrists tied together behind her back, arms tied together over her head, hands tied together in front of her crotch. Photographed by David Sims and originally placed in the *Vogue Paris* calendar of December/January, this went down particularly badly, not just with feminists, but with subscribers too. The office phones rang off the hook with complaints. In response, Roitfeld shrugged. She called it 'glamour bondage'.[707]

Another shoot, dedicated to icons of French sensuality and one-time lovers Serge Gainsbourg and Jane Birkin, features both sex *and* cigarettes. Appearing in May 2010 and shot by Mario Testino, 'La Decadanse' shows model Daria Werbowy and artist Francesco Vezzoli fondling each other over ten sizzling pages.[708] Set in some nondescript office with tubular 1970s furniture, he wears a slate-grey suit, she a metallic-grey dress which quickly comes off to reveal dove-grey lingerie and the sheerest of sheer grey stockings. In the absence of colours, the effect of textures – silk, Perspex, leather, nylon – is dramatically heightened. All the hair-pulling, back-arching and tearing of clothes (hers, not his) succeeds in looking both authentic and extremely staged.

October 2010 included the story 'Festine' (roughly translating to 'feast') shot by Terry Richardson.[709] Clearly a play on the idea of appetite, the series is a dichotomy. A glamorous beauty draped in statement jewellery goes full cavewoman over platters of food. She bites rabidly into a handful of raw steak. She rubs her hands in tomato spaghetti. She swallows a whole squid. The model hired for this was Crystal Renn, a former anorexic turned plus-size model. Even the name of her autobiography is *Hungry*. It seems more than a little uncomfortable, but presumably Crystal Renn would not have taken the assignment if she was offended.

Up there with the more controversial is the 'Spécial Top Models' issue of 2009.[710] Pitched as an homage to the best in the modelling business, not one of the stars included is black. This feels like a surprising misstep. Worse, it includes a fourteen-page spread of Dutch model Lara Stone completely blacked up . . . apparently no-body thought to ask any questions as they painted her white body in brown. The French edition historically has a tense relationship with its representation of ethnic minorities; this episode can't have helped.

French *Vogue* claimed it knew nothing of blackface controversies. If they thought it might pass under the radar because of their relatively small circulation, then they must have forgotten we live in the internet age. An explosion of protests carried the torch against the racial insensitivity in *Vogue Paris*, reaching across continents via blogs and social media, even formal news channels and papers. In a piece on CNN, a guest expert identified blackface as predominantly tied to American history, but rightly points out this does not provide any kind of justification.[711] To suggest Europeans might be that ignorant on the topic of colonial inhumanity is ridiculous. Furthermore, if the French editorial team really were so naïve, then the American photographer Steven Klein, who shot the pages, should have been able to clue them in on exactly how offensive this was. All of these shoots had been styled by Roitfeld personally.

A supermodel in blackface is not necessarily Roitfeld's most scandalous composition. In December 2010–January 2011, *Vogue Paris* ran a glittering forty-page editorial displaying a treasure trove of branded presents, a sort of early Christmas shopping guide for readers and their loved ones.[712] It had emeralds from Harry Winston among other haute jewellers like Cartier and Boucheron; leopard-print mules with crystal spike heels by Christian Louboutin; ballgowns by designers from Lanvin to Valentino, with a sheath dress in gold lamé by Balmain a particular standout. It's the usual stuff for a glossy mag marketing luxury goods and was photographed on a group of female models in classic poses, pouting and sultry, complete with fancy up-dos, full make-up and red manicured nails. What's unusual is that these models are all children, some reportedly as young as six.

Even more uncomfortable than the sight of little girls whose babyface complexions are smothered in smoky eyeshadow, lip gloss and blusher, is the subtext of the piece. Titled 'Cadeaux', the viewer is left with the uneasy impression that these children are themselves a present to the adult audience. Their positioning doesn't help. They are pictured lying supine on sofas, reclining on tiger skins and sprawling under a decorated tree among wrapped boxes, looking up at the camera, baleful, unsmiling.

The outpouring of condemnation online was immediate, criticism explicit. For a sample of the tone: blogger Xeni Jardin, under the heading 'Pedocouture', wrote that it 'features an extensive spread of child models presented more or less like whores'.[713] A post from a user on Frockwriter runs: 'this is NOT little girls playing dress up! It's marketing luxury clothes with baby girls dressed like prostitutes, posed in porn come-hither situations'.[714] Another Frockwriter comment: 'If any of these looks, coupled with that clothing/makeup, were from a grown woman in a nightclub, the message would be pretty clear. You cannot just separate that kind of body language from the usual meaning just because the body performing it is a child.'[715]

A more analytical reading of 'Cadeaux' can provide more context. A blogger from the UK observes that in a consumer society where women have to look like prepubescent teens to sell adult clothes, it is perhaps our own 'fault' that children are now being roped in.[716] A former model writing for feminist blog Jezebel felt it was 'a parody and a critique of the fashion industry's unhealthy interest in young girls, not an endorsement or a glamourization of it'.[717] Possibly Roitfeld really did hope to highlight the hypocrisy of a world that happily takes advantage of teenage girls, yet feels a deep moral indignation if the subjects are just a few years younger.

A theory advanced by cultural academics Reimer, Tosenberger and Wodtke, suggests that the entire holiday issue aimed to challenge and satirise the narrow ideals of beauty in fashion.[718] They arrived at this conclusion by examining the three main features as parts of a cohesive whole. First comes 'Cadeaux', raising complicated questions about the exploitation of youth. In the middle of the magazine is 'Forever Love', a shoot of an elderly couple – complete with grey hair and prominent wrinkles – groping each other in throes of ecstasy, French-kissing passionately while plastered in a ransom of fine jewels.[719] This confronts the invisibility of older men and women in mainstream fashion publications, whose aim is often to glorify the young.

The last provocative editorial parodies elective plastic surgery. 'La Panthère Ose' plays out a powerfully disturbing narrative of a middle-aged woman, clad in animal print to hint at her status as a cougar, recovering from a mix of cosmetic procedures while being waited on, even sponge-bathed, by a parade of boy toys.[720] Face and body stitched and bandaged, she is nonetheless carefully arranged in each frame to show off an abundance of designer items. Collapsed in a wheelchair she wears jungle-green Gianvito Rossi sandals and a zebra-print coat by Azzedine Alaïa. Reclining painfully in bed, her torso in a cast, face covered and lips crusted with blood, a suitor dabs her with Chanel No 5, while an Hermès purse lies close by. Enormous, costly gems flash on the body parts that are not bandaged. Rings are crammed on fingers. Thick bangles heaped on weakened wrists. It may be an anonymous construct, but it's also a recognisable stereotype in modern society: countless women are willing to risk the surgeon's knife, desperate to fit impossible beauty standards.

The photo story draws attention to the complicated relationship between wealth and sex appeal, style and suffering. It might prompt one to ask how we learned to prize the beauty of Chanel, Gucci, Bulgari, while rejecting and devaluing our own natural beauty? Our flesh-and-blood bodies can never be replaced by stones and metal ore, butter-soft cashmere or leather goods. At its deepest level 'La

Panthère Ose' could be interpreted as a cautionary tale for fashion victims.

Roughly halfway through her memorable reign, Roitfeld gave an interview in which the reporter says, rather flatteringly, 'You're actually redefining Paris, aren't you?'[721]

The capital was indeed regaining cultural gravitas in the nineties and early noughties. Restoration projects saw boulevards revamped and a refurbishment of the Grand Palais tackled. Along with this injection of energy there was a revival of some of Paris's most storied fashion houses. Givenchy, Balenciaga, Lanvin and Dior all appointed young creative directors on a mission to spin old-world heritage into happening design. A high-profile partnership with Tom Ford meant Roitfeld helped define the hypersexualised new Gucci and concoct the Los Angeles 'power slut look' of the 1990s. It was during these days that Roitfeld's style was first dubbed 'porno chic'. Such experiences earned her the seal of approval from fashion leaders and budding prodigies on the verge of superstardom, giving Roitfeld a certain cachet which she in turn would transmit to *Vogue Paris*.

The term 'porno chic' emerged as society became progressively more sexualised, beginning in the 1960s when legislation and media regulations around nudity began to relax. It refers to a 'pornification' of mainstream culture. With the boundaries between fashionable nudity and graphic porn increasingly broken down, deciding where to draw the line is not always obvious. Roitfeld prefers to think of her work as 'erotic chic', even though she acknowledges that 'porno chic' slides more glibly off the tongue.[722] The difference is subtle: she explains porn as leaving nothing to the imagination, while erotica retains some mystery and allure. These definitions make sense, though it's hard to see Roitfeld as using the softer brush of erotica when she is publishing a full-frontal shot of model Crystal Renn's pubic hair.[723]

Picking out extreme examples of Roitfeld's work is not hard, but there is merit in this too, which shouldn't be overlooked. When her interviewer discusses 'redefining Paris' what they really mean is Roitfeld's inclusivity. The ideals of Parisian beauty have traditionally been very fixed, but in her version of *Vogue Paris* Roitfeld explores and embraces. She is unafraid of printing pictures of the old, young, plus-sized or gender ambiguous. She certainly does not falter at exploring taboos, whether they're gender related, connected to sexual orientation or purely erotic. Some of her editorials, distributed at a time when they were deemed scandalous, would be received with applause now. A cover shot from 2007 shows party promoter Andre J rocking a turquoise mini and heeled ankle boots.[724] Placing a black bearded male model, grinning and frolicking in a feminine pose was unthinkably daring. Although not that long ago, this was still before TV shows such as *RuPaul's Drag Race* had normalised drag queens and back when Andre J was still being called a tranny and a cross-dresser.

It is easy to say that Roitfeld trades on shock value and she has previously admitted she likes the role of provocateur.[725] *Vogue Paris* used to be considered a 'snob' magazine; Roitfeld made it sexy. She gets away with a lot of her edgier themes because of the genuine beauty and aesthetic appeal of her imagery. There's also her cult of personality. All the little buzzwords we use to try to sum up a particular sort of charisma apply to Roitfeld: 'it girl', 'wow factor', 'star power'. And it is no coincidence that she was profiled several times in American *Vogue*. One might even argue she was the fetishised item in the columns of 1999 and 2001, where she is hailed as the 'stylist's stylist',[726] a 'luminous beauty',[727] 'one of the most head-turning sights'[728] and a 'decisive influence over the clothes millions of women have rushed to wear in the past decade'.[729]

Her rapport with photographers and popularity among celebrities goes further. Under her jurisdiction guest editors returned to *Vogue Paris*, among them A-listers and supermodels drafted in from her own seemingly endless list of very glitzy friends. These included Penélope Cruz, Kate Moss, Sofia Coppola, Charlotte Gainsbourg and, of course, her bestie Tom Ford. The guested features have a photo-album feel, with layouts reminiscent of schoolgirl scrapbooks, turning the mundane details of life into voyeuristic fodder. Roitfeld is able to transfer the essence of her human subject into the physical product. The Sofia Coppola cover shoot, for instance, is all elegance, as dreamlike and lonely as her films.

The Roitfeld system was lucrative. Suddenly the glossy pages were bulging with advertising and circulation figures soared, reportedly skyrocketing by 40 per cent between 2001 and 2005, a fact that Jonathan Newhouse rightly took pleasure in boasting about.[730] Still, Roitfeld alleges it took at least two years for the commercial turn-around to take place; and three years to feel comfortable with the rate of incoming adverts. Selling space is hard, even if you're *Vogue*. What works in a smaller market like France would not work in America. It is to Condé Nast's credit that they acknowledged this despite being a conglomerate and allowed a certain margin of creative freedom for image-makers like Carine Roitfeld.

Although venerated in the USA, it would be hopeless to try and transplant someone as staunchly Parisian as Roitfeld. Her *Vogue Paris* talks to an omnivorous audience that have not had their self-esteem eviscerated by consumerism and are not insecure enough to buy anything a magazine tells them to. There is not much pandering to trends. Instead there is a commitment to make everything high fashion. It is clearly a magazine edited by a former stylist.

Exactly under what circumstances Carine Roitfeld left *Vogue Paris* is, of course, classified. The official statement claims she resigned, though this is often the line taken by big companies negotiating severance payments.[731] Multiple commentators have been convinced she was fired (or pressured into resignation) after publishing the 'Cadeaux' shoot, with rumours circulating that major advertisers were threatening to pull their ads in disgust.[732] Meanwhile, Roitfeld claims she'd been thinking about leaving for a while, having completed a full decade as editor-in-chief.[733] Others have said Condé Nast was fed up with her consulting for big fashion houses on the side, a charge she firmly denies.[734] If true, this would have been equal to taking bribes, since she could encourage brands to make clothes she would feature. What is malicious gossip and what is Roitfeld's abuse of power (if any) is tough to separate, though being blacklisted from Balenciaga was certainly one of the more blatant embarrassments for Condé Nast during her tenure. In any case, that *Vogue Paris* is extremely cliquey and largely promotes its own favourites without bothering to break new talent is a criticism they are often faced with.[735] A tiny group of already-famous photographers are frequently the only ones getting commissions; new names are harder to find on a *Vogue* masthead than needles in a haystack.

In one interview following her departure she claimed she had increasingly less freedom. There was also the mounting pressure of political correctness.[736] Whatever the reason, it seems Carine Roitfeld and *Vogue* outgrew each other. Since then she has done it all, from releasing books, to being the subject of a documentary. Roitfeld retained her A-list pals and even went on to launch her own magazine to great fanfare. Like anyone who makes a name for themselves in fashion she knows how to promote herself and, despite feigned ignorance about branding,[737] continues to trade on her own star power, going so far as to pretend she was the first person to break taboos in *Vogue*.[738]

2010s: Setting Wholesome Standards

The French headquarters of *Vogue* are located at 56A Rue du Fau-
bourg Saint-Honoré, a street in the 8th arrondissement of Paris
with the highest density of fashion houses and boutiques in the
city. Saunter along a few steps and you'll come face to face with the
Hermès flagship. Right behind is the glowing neoclassical splendour
of Hôtel de Crillon. *Vogue* is truly in its natural habitat.

Midway through 2011 there was movement up on the sixth floor.
A fabled, dynamic editrix had vacated and a relatively discreet
fashion director was taking her place. Just like Carine Roitfeld,
Emmanuelle Alt used to work for *Elle*. And just like Carine
Roitfeld, Emmanuelle Alt joined *Vogue Paris* in 2000. For over a
decade she had poured Roitfeld's visions on to the pages, working
her way up through fashion departments as assistant, stylist, editor,
director. She produced countless sittings and an infinity of call
sheets to briefs; had been on hand to help with the hedonistic
photoshoots published in the glory days of 'porno chic'. She knew
the drill and now she was in the driver's seat.

When Carine Roitfeld had the office, it remained clinically white
with empty white shelves. An enormous close-up of her own face
and a diamanté skull were among the only ornaments.[739] Coinci-
dentally, Alt had also brought a decorative skull and kept the space
super-simple, sparsely populated with art books, scented candles and
a framed photograph of herself at nineteen with best friend Carla
Bruni Sarkozy. Alt has influential connections and she wants visitors
to know it. Yet she was considered the safe choice for editor-in-chief;
a long-time staffer who would provide continuity after Roitfeld's
departure. The two are no longer on speaking terms.

Alt's background was in styling, again, like Roitfeld. Here the similarities end, for their aesthetic is polar opposite (despite the semi-identical take on offices). Alt champions the 'au naturel' approach; the understated tomboy simplicity of jeans, blazers, plain T-shirts; the practicality of sensible shoes. In interviews, she takes the stance that confidence and comfort make a woman attractive, tottering in sky-high heels or wriggling in restraining ensembles is not cool.

It's just as well, because in the ten years or so between the inauguration of these two editors the fashion scene has been disrupted. Forecasters are constantly threatening a dip in sales. Magazines were left open-mouthed with astonishment as an internet generation began to eat away their audience. The industry at large faced even more change. By 2012 fashion was a global industry worth over \$1 trillion.[740] In terms of trade intensity, this made it the second biggest economic activity worldwide. Online retail was on the rise, creating a decentralised global high street; a trend that was mirrored in global newsstands as publishers rushed to create digital channels to combat falling print circulation. Global brands like *Vogue* had to reconfigure their operations and consolidate their dominance – acting quickly against the growing authority of bloggers. In a 2019 interview with *Vogue Business*, Alt tellingly comments, 'I used to work for a magazine, and today I work for a brand.'[741]

As much as defining *Vogue Paris* could be a problem, so is living up to expectations. Just try finding an article, blog post, comment or even a caption online or in print that doesn't salivate over Alt as a walking, talking representation of her country. 'Could you get more French?' cries *The Telegraph*; 'quintessentially Parisian' says StyleCaster; she 'embodies Parisienne chic', comments *The Business of Fashion*.

Negotiating the perception of Frenchness is important as it drives her substantial online audience to Vogue.fr and keeps the follower count on their Twitter profile growing (in 2020 the number stood at some 2.4 million, an extremely high number for a magazine whose print circulation doesn't reach 200,000).[742] Tellingly, the Twitter page is written in the English language; they are catering less for locals and more for international readers hungry to be part of the *Vogue Paris* dream. The internet may have released entire industries from their geographical anchors, but if anything, it has only further cemented a worldwide obsession with the French capital and its historic connection to haute couture. Although Alt professes her pride at meeting people from New York to Madrid who are keenly in tune with *Vogue Paris*, there must be times when upholding the stereotype becomes a bore.[743] When asked in an interview, 'How mindful do you need to be of the Frenchness of French *Vogue*?' Alt's response is honest:

> It's funny, I'm not sure French women see themselves in the same way as the rest of the world does: those books about why French women never get fat, as if we have miraculous metabolisms. It's fantasy! What's particular to this *Vogue* is that . . . we are the name of a city, *Vogue Paris*. Everyone has a clear conception of *La Parisienne*.[744]

The pursuit of increasingly international patrons has had a somewhat neutralising effect on *Vogue* by Alt. Political correctness has become too great a force to go against, so any Roitfeld treatment of the female body as a sexual object is out of the question. These changes could also be a result of changing company policy: the French edition can no longer show drinking and smoking, although they have retained their topless permission. Alt was hailed by the creative director at *Vogue Paris* for being more commercial[745] and exalted in the media for a more consensual portrayal of the sexual body. Yet some commentators have attacked Alt for leaning too much into the mainstream. An in-depth essay posted on a culture blog labels her first issue 'a bitter disappointment',[746] proceeding to passionately discuss Alt's editorial choices and their meaning within a broader social framework:

> In this global battle for women's bodies, Carine Roitfeld is my rock of Gibraltar, the editorial heroine of the fight that lies ahead for women everywhere and especially in America, where the conservative tide is turning against women.
>
> *Vogue Paris* is now an international publication, one that could advance French influence and attitudes about women's emancipation worldwide, especially if Conde Nast would consider the unthinkable and publish it in multiple languages online.
>
> I don't need Emmanuelle Alt to show me women's everyday reality; I need her to show women a way out of it.[747]

Although insightful, this is a contestable opinion. France is in no way a leader of female rights. Further, Alt attaches value to realistic representations and has done much to naturalise the image of women, as well as to celebrate femininity in all its guises.

The November 2012 issue shows three renowned bombshells, photographed wearing matching faded blue jeans and crisp white shirts: Daria Werbowy in her twenties, Stephanie Seymour in her forties, Lauren Hutton in her sixties – each looks effortlessly attractive. The heading reads: 'From 20 to 60, in the prime of life'. The message is blatant: age is irrelevant.

Family is included – and praised – with extra focus on mother and child, another motif frequently deemed too messy by fashion. An emphasis on including France's best-loved faces betrays an admirable national pride. Tributes are paid to the likes of: retired icon, aristocrat, and Karl Lagerfeld's muse Inès de la Fressange (who guest-edited the special edition of 2014);[748] Vanessa Paradis, the former child star and Chanel spokeswoman;[749] and Marion Cotillard, Academy Award-winning actress.

Adhering to the tradition of pushing social boundaries at *Vogue Paris*, Alt broke the mould by putting the first transgender model, leggy Brazilian brunette Valentina Sampaio, on the cover.[750] Alt extols Sampaio as an 'icon' and a 'beauty', writing in her editor's letter that she hopes a more accepting era is on the horizon.[751] Shot by Mert and Marcus and released in March 2017, Alt proves again that she sees the French publication as a global magazine. This issue hit newsstands the same week President Trump reversed a policy protecting transgender students. Her latest foray into identity politics was the unisex issue of February 2019, which celebrated androgynous style throughout.

As an image-maker and stylist, Alt misses being more involved. When she took the editor's position, she promised herself she would still contribute a fashion story every issue, though sometimes this isn't possible.[752] Nowadays, she claims there are a minimum of twenty people working on a shoot – comparable to a small film production.[753] This is a stark difference to the early 2000s, when creative duo Mathias Augustyniak and Michael Amzalag (M/M) art-directed. It was informal, experimental. As a novice, Alt had once made the faux pas of reminding M/M of the *Vogue* archive, but they snubbed the idea of using the resource for inspiration. Yet the archive is priceless and denying the influence of legends from Helmut Newton to Norman Parkinson is a sin. These cameramen developed styles, artistic touches and visual cues that are still at the core of fashion photography. In today's fashion landscape, these on-set skills are forgotten and the conversation tends to fixate around graphics, retouching and post-production. Though this again is a question of trends: heritage is fashionable now. Of course, Alt – now the boss, no longer the rookie – can impress the magnitude of their collection on other employees and encourage them to develop their artistic sense, not just their understanding of Photoshop and other software. 'I want the people around me to understand how lucky they are . . . This is a gift. There is no other magazine that can present that. *Vogue* has the sense of something exceptional . . . You arrive every day, and it's historic.'[754]

As a study, Alt is interesting in her perfect rendition of a *Vogue* employee. She plays by corporate rules. And yet she's subversive in her own way. French *Vogue*'s circulation may still be a drop compared to the tidal waves incoming at American *Vogue*, but it has cult status. Sitting at the top of fashion's hierarchy in France, it is her job to personify *la parisienne*. And what exactly are *la parisienne's* qualities in the twenty-first century? Not vanity, for Alt does not enjoy the attention of being on the front row. Not eternal youth, since Alt refuses to package it as a commodity to sell to older women, choosing instead to present maturity as aspirational. Not *politesse*, since Alt is willing to call out injustice and champion equality. She's not covetous or celeb-worshipping; empty idolatry is replaced by inclusivity here. In a media-mad world, this is subversion.

It is coming up to the ten-year anniversary of Emmanuelle Alt's sovereignty at the legacy title. Paris represents fashion and Alt has to translate that message and interpret it for the rest of the world. By now, Alt has been editor-in-chief long enough for her definition of Frenchness, fashion and *Vogue Paris* to be recognisable. She expresses it by being creatively adventurous while remaining accessible. This requires a delicate equilibrium of past and present; balancing the importance of archives with the necessity for fresh blood; pleasing old-school subscribers while luring new online followers. Only one quality is still as true to the modern *parisienne* identity as it was to the historical. Exclusivity. When Jonathan

Newhouse informed editors that taking freelance commissions on top of *Vogue* duties was against company policy,[755] Alt apparently replied there could be no question on the matter: she was entirely exclusive to *Vogue Paris*.[756]

CHAPTER 17

'Vogue *Will Always Be* Vogue'

Right Now and What Next

From Shulman to Enninful

In Britain, a shake-up was coming. The edition had historically distinguished itself with a kind of oddball English eccentricity that was eyebrow raising but aesthetically pleasing. A little off the beaten track, a little romantic, a little quirky. Those times were long gone. Although Anna Wintour is often held accountable for the euthanising of British *Vogue*'s personality during her tenure there in the mid-1980s, the truth is both Wintour's and her successor Tilberis' magazines still had a brightness and stylishness, a pinch of old-world glamour and a visible eighties dance influence. But when Liz Tilberis was poached by Hearst to move to *Harper's Bazaar* in America, the very last remnants of what made British *Vogue* a whacky, one-of-a-kind masterpiece were wiped away for ever. In 1992, Alexandra Shulman was appointed editor-in-chief of British *Vogue*, a post she held on to till 2017. Her tenure is the longest of any editor in the London office, totalling twenty-five years and representing a quarter of the edition's life.

The public had initially felt warmly towards Shulman; she seemed relatively down to earth, a bastion of normality in an excessively ornamental industry. Preferring messy hair and down-to-earth clothes to high-octane glamour, she's pretended not to play the fashion editor part. With interviewers she discusses her love of roast chicken,[757] her weakness for croissants[758] and the amount of times she got fired in her youth,[759] told in a self-deprecating way. The press appeared to like Shulman for being neither very thin nor conventionally pretty. A long and stable tenure such as hers resulted in Shulman being accepted as a mainstay of the fashion industry and the *Vogue* representative in Britain, so it was a bolt from the blue when she resigned, citing a desire to experience a different life. When she handed in her notice, her years fronting the glossy were suddenly being re-examined and the conclusions drawn this time round were none too friendly. A different age had dawned, one which lambasted her magazine for not being inclusive[760] and accused her of 'nepotism hiring'.[761]

After Shulman announced her imminent departure in 2017, supermodel Naomi Campbell tweeted a picture of the *Vogue* editorial staff of that year, featuring fifty-odd team members with not one person of colour among them.[762] Campbell called Shulman out on the lack of diversity and expressed her wish for a different future under new management. Further examination revealed that Shulman had only given two black models solo covers since 2002, yet had featured Kate Moss a total of thirty-seven times. Her 1990s covers tend to feature semi-identical headshots of actresses and models on plain backgrounds with their hair blown outwards in the dated wind-machine look. They are more *Women's Health* than *Vogue*. In the early 2000s some soul appears, with a few party touches like David Bowie make-up on Kate Moss in May 2003[763] and the New Year's Eve cover with Elton John and Elizabeth Hurley in a shower of confetti,[764] but this quickly subsides back into the repetitive shots which endure – with the odd exception – till the end of her tenure.

She has also been condemned in newspapers from the right-wing *Spectator* to the left-wing *Guardian* for her use of extremely thin girls. This might not have looked so bad for Shulman, except that in various interviews she has openly said she's 'bored' of discussing her editorial choices and insists readers don't want to see 'real women' representing fashion.[765] She goes so far as to say on BBC Radio 2 in 2014 that women could look at themselves in the mirror for free and didn't want to pay for a magazine full of people who looked like them.[766]

In the 1990s she was blamed for propagating the 'heroin chic' look of waifish girls with dark circles under their eyes to the extent that even fashion advertisers – usually indifferent to weight issues – became squeamish enough to pull ads. *Vogue* was blamed for contributing to a national rise in eating disorders and for propagating unrealistic expectations for women. Shulman remained indifferent to this too, claiming few people had told her they'd stopped eating as a direct result of her magazine.[767] On the other hand, *Vogue* is an extremely easy target. As the best-known fashion magazine and one of the most prominent globally, it is frequently blamed for any negative trends concerning women or body image and it's hard to find solid evidence to back the accusations.

Regarding her own image, Shulman has been a victim of female expectations too. From an early age she was criticised for her weight and during her many years in the public eye almost every article in the press made reference to her size. However, it's hard to feel sympathetic towards a woman who could have influenced social outlook. Shulman attempts to defend herself by saying her British *Vogue* never published diet tips or anything on cosmetic surgery, yet even the most cursory of searches on Vogue.co.uk will reveal that this is not quite the case.[768] Often diet tips are just disguised as 'Model Health Tips'.[769] Some of the straplines on the front covers, especially in the 1990s, come across extremely anti-feminist according to our standards today. One cover of 1996 reads, 'Don't hate me because I'm thin';[770] another in 2000 runs 'Eat Fat, Get Thin'.[771] However, again it is worth noting that in the 1990s, the skinny ideal reached its peak. The thinner the better was the mantra for the decade and images of tiny women proliferated everywhere from TV shows to adverts to movies. *Vogue* was reflecting the norms of the day. Unfortunately for Shulman her work was being judged through the lens of the 2010s, removed from the historical framing it was conceived in.

The more her career was examined in 2017, the more heat Shulman received. The result was some particularly malicious pieces, such as one written for *The Spectator* under the pseudonym Pea Priestly titled 'Alexandra Shulman's reign at Vogue will be defined by mediocrity, idiocy and flip-flops' and which began with:

The outpouring of love following Alexandra Shulman's departure from Vogue was truly touching; she was described as 'unpretentious' and 'very British' (code for overweight and posh) as the UK mourned the loss of this affable leader. Though I'm sure she was a very nice lady, there is something quite perverse about celebrating a fashion editor who could barely find the time to comb her hair and was too busy glugging wine to look in the mirror before leaving the house. As the UK's number one representative for fashion it was her responsibility to look presentable and deliver interesting work and she failed to do either.[772]

This article is by no means the only one; hundreds exist with similarly bilious criticisms. The thousands of comments on social media have also leaned towards character assassination. Although Shulman refused to take risks, it is also important to remember she was responsible for a huge hike in circulation and revenue thanks to the period of stability cemented by her long reign. Regardless, onlookers were dying for change and rumours about the replacement were rife. It was in the midst of this international buzz that Edward Enninful stepped on to the scene.

Fashion's burning topic in 2017 was the newcomer at British *Vogue*. Everybody waited with bated breath for the announcement of the heir apparent and when Enninful was named, it was to the sound of collective cheering. He is the first non-white and openly gay person to occupy the post and the first male editor-in-chief in the history of the UK edition. Enninful has had a long and salubrious career as a stylist and came to *Vogue* from *W* magazine where he was known for his cutting-edge visuals. Before taking the post there, he had already been contributing editor at *Vogue Italia*, contributing fashion editor at American *Vogue* and was well known to Condé Nast. Many had expected a promotion to occur within the company, with the title going to one of Shulman's set of Chelsea girls.

During Shulman's time, *Vogue* was again accused of awarding the daughters of the rich preferential treatment. It was only just before Shulman became EIC that they abolished the 'private income' question from job application forms; previously, all candidates had to fill out forms for HR stating where they went to school and disclose the exact sum of the monthly allowances awarded to them by trust or loving relative. Much as Shulman seemed 'normal', she was actually the daughter of theatre critic Milton Shulman and journalist Drusilla Beyfus (both of whom were fired from *Vogue* by Anna Wintour), who grew up in Belgravia and attended St Paul's Girls' School.

Nepotism was rife at Condé Nast and Shulman benefitted from it. She had been editing *GQ* (another Condé Nast title) when a new editorial director, Nicholas Coleridge, arrived. Coleridge had already known Alexandra Shulman for some time. From his youth he'd been friends with her sister, Nicola, and had hired her to work for him before. When the seat of British *Vogue* was left empty by Tilberis, it was he who handed it to Alex Shulman. This cliquey atmosphere is said to have endured at *Vogue* and many hoped Edward Enninful, who was outspoken about his diversity agenda, would be the one to disperse it.

As happens so frequently under new management, a series of fall-outs and firings followed in the months after Enninful was named. There was a mass exodus of the posh-girls and a mass influx of celebrities on the masthead. Enninful made Naomi Campbell, Kate Moss and Steve McQueen contributing editors. Emily Sheffield, who was made redundant in this process, recalls the fight between the old guard and the new guard raging so ferociously in the office that it spilled over into the public eye.[773] Sheffield, who was Shulman's deputy editor, is the daughter of Sir Reginald Sheffield and the sister of Samantha Cameron, wife of David Cameron. Some of these 'redundancies' made the news, with the biggest splash orchestrated in a post-*Vogue* interview with Lucinda Chambers, who'd spent thirty-six years at British *Vogue*, published on the niche platform *Vestoj*.[774] The widely circulated interview is candid in the extreme. Chambers boldly admits to being fired (not made 'redundant') and rails against an industry so focused on appearances she'd even been encouraged to lie about the firing to save face. She goes so far as to say, 'fashion can chew you up and spit you out' and claims, 'Truth be told, I haven't read Vogue in years'.[775] She continued her musings on the glossy media, explaining her belief that it leaves customers more anxious than empowered:

It's a shame that magazines have lost the authority they once had. They've stopped being *useful*. In fashion we are always trying to make people buy something they don't need. We don't *need* any more bags, shirts or shoes. So we cajole, bully or encourage people into continue buying. I know glossy magazines are meant to be aspirational, but why not be both aspirational *and* useful? That's the kind of fashion magazine I'd like to see.[776]

Fans of Enninful would argue there is an irony to this statement: his *Vogue*, the one Chambers is no longer part of, aims to be exactly this kind of magazine.

In his first editor's letter Enninful introduces us to 'your new Vogue' (spawning the hashtag #NewVogue), the December issue of 2017, intended as a celebration of Britain despite recent Brexit turmoil.[777] The cover shows British-born, mixed-race model Adwoa Aboah wearing a silk turban in hues of pink and orange with sparkling diamond pendants, producing a beautiful vintage look that strongly recalled the glamour of the 1950s.[778] Instead of captions concerning shoes or seasons, on the left-hand side runs a list of British power players in fields ranging from politics, represented by London's mayor Sadiq Khan; to literature, represented by Zadie Smith and Salman Rushdie; to music, represented by grime artist Skepta; and the usual fashion royalty, including Cara Delevingne, Naomi Campbell, Kate Moss. The issue is packed with 'down-to-earth' features written by big names: John Galliano catches the no. 12 bus in Elephant and Castle[779] and Victoria Beckham is photographed in her childhood bedroom talking about bullies.[780] Some features are obviously supposed to show *Vogue* as anti-establishment and daring, with Zadie Smith calling the Queen 'distinctly lower middle-class' and derisively referring to her as 'Mrs Windsor' not HRH.[781] Elsewhere, Salman Rushdie writes about Christmas in a multi-faith family,[782] while Skepta discusses the black British experience.[783] These harder-hitting conversations are diluted with corgis, Lady Jean Campbell photographed wearing Chanel[784] and Cara and Poppy Delevingne rhapsodising on the excruciatingly trite.[785] The Mayor of London talked to 'fellow South Londoner' (note: not global supermodel) Naomi Campbell on their experiences growing up.[786]

The issue makes a huge and admirable effort to bring a new message to *Vogue*, with heavy emphasis on inclusivity and topics which land decidedly outside of fashion's standard remit. In his editor's letter Enninful wrote of the British: 'there is surely one thing we can all agree on: We are a talented bunch.'[787] By tracing the early lives and birthplaces of mega-celebrities like Victoria Beckham and Naomi Campbell, Enninful is obviously trying to make a pitch for talent against all odds or success in spite of where you come from, a sort of counter-response to Shulman's promotion of the rich and beautiful just because they are rich and beautiful. Yet these efforts might feel more sincere if there wasn't still a whiff of nepotism.

Enninful's cover star Adwoa Aboah is described as a Ghanaian model and activist in the media, however, a frequently omitted fact is that her parents are extremely well-connected fashion insiders. Her mother is Camilla Lowther, a former model and daughter of a viscount, who runs a top talent agency. Aside from her aristocratic lineage, Aboah has the added advantage of being the god-daughter of Ronnie Cooke Newhouse, the wife of Jonathan Newhouse, chairman of Condé Nast International. In short, she has an intimate relationship with the family that owns *Vogue*. If anything, she is more privileged than any of Shulman's staff or even the A-list actresses that have appeared in British *Vogue*. Meanwhile supermodels Cara Delevingne and Edie Campbell are the god-daughters of Nicholas Coleridge, now president of Condé Nast International. As much as it is #NewVogue, it is still *Vogue*, and as journalist Jess Cartner-Morley astutely commented, 'Vogue is dead, long live Vogue'.[788]

Since the first issue, Enninful has continued to showcase his commitment to diversity, although even he has run into trouble. Bystanders were unimpressed when his second cover featured white celebrity Taylor Swift[789] and were even more so when the third cover, in February 2018, showed Margot Robbie and Nicole Kidman with the strapline 'WHY WE NEED TO TALK ABOUT RACE'.[790] Sarcastic comments proliferated on social media, expressing disappointment in Enninful for producing a strong first cover then apparently reverting to the standard *Vogue* recipe. Belief in Enninful was revived with his cover of May 2018, which featured nine trailblazingly diverse models: from Paloma Elsesser, the popular plus-size model; to Halima Aden, who wears a hijab in her shoots.[791] Here were women breaking the mould of the traditional modelling industry and representing minorities. Oprah made a spectacular appearance in August 2018;[792] feel-good singer and body-positivity advocate Lizzo shone on the cover in December 2019;[793] Rihanna has taken the front spot twice, with her 2020 cover highly lauded as it was the first in the history of British *Vogue* in which a woman has worn a durag.[794]

Enninful seems to have made a play at checking off as many firsts as he can, although this hasn't been hard since so much of the magazine has been extremely conservative. Perhaps the greatest splash since his debut issue was the September edition of 2019, which was guest-edited by Meghan Markle, the newly minted Duchess of Sussex. Given the pompous title, 'Forces for Change', Markle's magazine proved intensely divisive. On the surface Markle's professed beliefs align with Enninful's mission statement for *Vogue*. For the theme Markle chose to focus on activism and the cover features fifteen personalities with some connection to advocacy or charity. There is a sixteenth square with a reflective mirror effect meant for the reader of *Vogue* to see themselves in it and enter the conversation, becoming a 'force for change' too.

This cover misses an opportunity to feature anyone who isn't already a celebrity or include any businesswomen or scientists. We see the usual set of A-list faces including six actresses and three models. Adwoa Aboah appears yet again. There is no wild card, no eye-opening insight, just another list of famous names we've all heard a hundred times, except here they appear under the guise of being social justice warriors. Even inside, the only contributors are people with vast social media followings, down to the author Matt Haig, whose addition to the publication is a fatuous swear-word laden poem. Even the mirror trick of the empty sixteenth square, which seems clever, is a stolen concept. *Time* magazine already did this in 2006 when their Person of the Year was 'You'. At no point does it feel like Markle set out to find and reward pioneering campaigners; rather, it feels a lot like she threw in anyone with a big platform just to show she could draw them in.

The cover aside, Markle faced harsh criticism over her decision to get involved with *Vogue* in the first place. Although other royals have guest-edited publications before, the problem seems to be that Markle did not remain apolitical. As a representative of Buckingham Palace it's not really fair to her subjects, who might hold differing views. This is further complicated since so much social activism is sponsored by huge corporations which may be at odds with each other, or our governing political systems. Others have said that *Vogue* is not the right platform: it is still uncomfortable to see feminism nestled beside Gucci dresses retailing for upwards of £2,000 and designed for tiny women on extreme diets; just as it is hard to talk about sustainability when fashion is one of the most polluting industries on the planet. Markle does acknowledge this in her introduction:

There is one caveat for you to remember: this is a magazine. It's still a business, after all. I share that to manage expectations for you: there will be advertising sections that are requisite for every issue, so while I feel confident that you'll feel my thumbprint on most pages, please know that there are elements that just come with the territory.[795]

Markle's magazine was a sell-out – which makes it a success for Condé Nast's bottom line – and there is a great deal of prestige attached to a publication which can get a duchess to work with them. British *Vogue* has a long history of pairing up with the royals, including featuring Kate Middleton on the cover of their centenary issue. However, Markle's issue cannot be declared an out-and-out triumph. It might even have been one of the final nails in her coffin in the eyes of the British public. The marketing blitz surrounding this edition could not stamp out the sense of virtue-signalling and nar-cissism with which commentators felt Markle's attempt at publishing was laced. The legitimacy of fighting for equality is further dimin-ished by descriptions of Enninful ducking in and out of clandestine meetings with the duchess over mint tea, while Markle herself makes a top-secret rendezvous with Michelle Obama, all relayed in a hush-hush tone as though they were dealing with the ins and outs of global economies rather than a few pages in a monthly glossy.[796] The elite setting is at odds with the issues like classism. Once again, we come back to the difficulty of an exclusive magazine trying to be inclusive. At least Enninful and Markle shared the same 'woke' tone which has become a staple of the new *Vogue*. Enninful represents the new mainstream, a world where everything – especially fashion – has become highly politicised.

Enninful has to respond to a tricky contemporary landscape: it is a world of social media 'likes' justified by unproved good causes, popular opinion repressing solid facts and youth with a cause seeking to override experienced professionals. It is also a moment where corporations and people alike are anxious to promote their moral values, sometimes at odds with the way they continue to operate behind the scenes. It is not an easy epoch to interpret and since he has only held the position since 2017, there are bound to be teething problems. Occasional hypocrisy in the material might be a temporary evil while Enninful works out a strategy to convert *Vogue* into a more transparent operation. Enninful preaches inclusivity but a substantial number of his favourite stars have links to the Condé Nast directors. His covers are often shot by veteran *Vogue* photographers like Steven Meisel (who has worked for the magazine some three decades), Mario Testino (two and a half decades) and Juergen Teller (two and a half decades). Of the thirty issues he has worked on so far, there are only two covers shot by a photographer under the age of fifty and only one cover by a relative newcomer with no prior experience working with *Vogue*. When it comes to photography at least, Enninful clearly prefers his talent established rather than emerging and repetitive rather than diverse. The exception to this rule is Nadine Ijewere, a London-born photographer of Nigerian–Jamaican descent, who shot pop singer Dua Lipa for the cover of January 2019.

It was a shock to Ijewere when a friend told her that across all its international editions, there had never been a *Vogue* cover shot by a woman of colour; Ijewere was about to take that title at the age of twenty-six. The call had come out of the blue, though a fleeting glance at Ijewere's portfolio shows how closely her personal vision aligns with Enninful's. From her university days she has photographed women outside fashion industry standards and uses the lens to explore her own identity, explaining to me that she wished to represent African and Caribbean cultures without the tribal stereotypes which they are often attached to in fashion shoots.[797] Living in London, one of the world's most multicultural cities, also helped broaden her outlook on beauty. Ijewere is friendly, cheerful and refreshingly forthright when we meet to discuss her experience at *Vogue*. Of Enninful's office she only has positive things to say. Key to the enjoyment of the commission was the measure of creative freedom: 'They kept saying don't make it look like a *Vogue* image, make it yours'.

For her, the most interesting thing British *Vogue* is doing now is appealing to the younger generation. 'I've seen it change and the topics it approaches are relevant, it's not wishy-washy fantasy fashion, there's more of a meaning to it.'[798] Hopefully Ijewere's inclusion among the seasoned photographers is a sign of good things to come. It follows that using younger image-makers will bring an exciting new look to the magazine, one which might get the attention of the millennials, digital natives and teenagers which *Vogue* is working hard to attract. The work of Testinos and Tellers may be incredible, but if Enninful is making a magazine for future generations it is time to give more space to new talent.

Soon after leaving, Alexandra Shulman wrote an opinion piece for *The Business of Fashion* entitled 'What Makes a Great Magazine Editor?', which was generally received as a thinly veiled swipe at her successor at British *Vogue*.[799] Shulman's article addressed the importance of trained staff, noting that big-name stars are seldom keen to put in actual work and merely like the esteem of being connected to a publication like *Vogue*. As for editors, she writes: 'It is certainly not a job for someone who doesn't wish to put in the hours and thinks that the main part of their job is being photographed in a series of designer clothes with a roster of famous friends.'[800]

Enninful is not shy in posting frequent shots across social media of him and pals like Naomi Campbell and Kate Moss, who made it to the masthead as contributors, but whose actual contribution is hard to evaluate. Shulman also makes the point that:

> The digital curveball thrown at print is powerful, but that doesn't mean that magazine brands don't require editors who actually edit. Who sweat the small stuff. There is no point in their magazines becoming imitators of experiences that can be found elsewhere, chasing clickbait that is mirrored in a zillion websites and cravenly following a small pool of short-term celebrity names.[801]

These quotes underline the trouble publishing faces. Enninful has been accused on numerous occasions of firing highly skilled staff to pay for bigger photoshoots and A-list contributors with huge followings to lend little more than their names to his pages. *Vogue* continues to be criticised for consolidating their budgets around an online presence, settling on a played-out format of listicles and other repetitive pieces. This one-size-fits-all approach has been something *Vogue* typically avoided, always preferring to tailor material to different audiences, exemplified by their preference for launching separate editions in each country rather than trying to enter different markets with one landmark edition. The internet has pushed the powers at *Vogue* to produce online content which is both expensive and time-consuming. It may maintain the brand's visibility, but at the cost of its voice of authority.

Edward Enninful is stuck between a rock and a hard place: since margins are squeezed he is more or less forced to sacrifice some quality of the print. For all the criticism of Shulman's unimaginative front covers, she can really write. The words in Enninful's issues are sparse, mostly snippets of copy and celeb Q&As. Enninful is a stylist, not a journalist by trade and his *Vogue* reflects this by showcasing the street style of today, a frequently unisex, athletic-driven look, which does not fit within the elegant legacy of *Vogue*. But times have changed. *Vogue* is a mass-circulation magazine and Enninful obliges by displaying what is currently in fashion. As Shulman points out in her piece 'Magazines are a business',[802] and evidently Enninful is the EIC that Condé Nast thinks will bring them the most money at this point in time, and they're probably right. He is extremely popular and has revived interest in the British edition by targeting a younger crowd and serving as a worthy role model.

The Consequences of Digital Disruption

There was a second, more far-reaching event which shook *Vogue* to the core in 2017: the death of Si Newhouse. Lauded as a media titan, he had presided over the magazine since the early sixties, meaning that for over half a century he had been the central figure at *Vogue* and its many sisters. With competition from online media only heating up, he left his legion of luxury print publications during a particularly rough patch. It was a bad year all round for Condé Nast. Aside from the death of their benevolent patron, there was the resignation of Graydon Carter, master editor of *Vanity Fair*, who'd held the post for twenty-five years and, more devastating still, the company reportedly lost $120 million.[803]

In 2018, they were still in the red, but by 2019 a clear direction for the company began to emerge. Long-time CEO Bob Sauerberg was replaced by Roger Lynch, formerly head of Pandora, a music-streaming service, with a strong entertainment and tech background. It was the first appointment of an outsider CEO in Condé Nast's hundred-plus years. Lynch's lack of publishing experience didn't matter; his brief was to create a twenty-first century media company, not a print empire.[804] A difficult task indeed, since by Lynch's own admission nobody knows what that ought to look like. The proof of this is in the continued development of the many branches at Condé Nast which have little to do with the print artefacts at the heart of the corporation.

Condé Nast Entertainment (CNE) contributed little to its parent company initially. It was created in 2011 as a video-production department, intended to safeguard their earnings should articles published by Condé Nast be developed into films or TV shows (*Brokeback Mountain*, for instance, had started as a piece in *The New Yorker* and they were bitter about not getting a cut from the movie). However, CNE produced no hits and, languishing in the doldrums, mostly ended up focusing on YouTube. Many of these videos were expensive to produce and did not convert into views. One series for *Vogue* interviewed models at the Hôtel Plaza Athénée in Paris and cost roughly $250,000 to make, yet each clip had only been watched a couple of hundred times.

The company found its niche by churning out repetitive format recordings like '73 Questions' in which a celebrity walks around, answering a random interrogation; and 'Go Ask Anna!' in which *Vogue*'s biggest star is pumped by strangers to reveal her personal thoughts. These result in a plethora of trite, celeb-heavy content which *do* get millions of viewers, but the margins are slim. To make CNE work, the department has to exercise a lean, bean-counting policy. These kinds of difficulties do not stop the media from believing video is the way forward and Condé Nast seems especially determined to keep this adventure going.

CNE is not the only part of Condé Nast that is engaged in a belt-tightening policy. This now applies across the company – the famous days of profligacy are well and truly over. Amid the difficulties of 2017, Condé Nast began breaking down and merging their various brands. In a process of 'hubbing', each publication was taken apart and centralised, meaning every design team was combined into Creative Group; copy-editors and fact-checkers were folded into something called Content Integrity Group; and the tech and website staffers were gathered into the mysteriously named Co/Lab.[805] Meanwhile, sales were coalesced into seemingly random clusters, with one cluster assuming responsibility for both *The New Yorker* and *Teen Vogue*. Although costs were cut and old rivalries between magazines disappeared, new rivalries between departments bubbled to the surface.

The Co/Lab personnel, who, as representatives of the digital side, suddenly assumed a great importance, began to receive typical tech start-up perks. Their floor of the building was duly kitted out with ping-pong tables and their fridges stuffed with string cheese and guacamole, which rankled the editorial teams when they found out, since their supplies had been cut. Soon, writers and graphic designers were making expeditions upstairs to loot the fridges and according to one source *The New Yorker* fact-checkers made a habit of materialising on Fridays to stuff their bags full of free beer.[806] Developers and programmers now saw themselves at the top of the food chain, just as once *Vogue* and *Vanity Fair* had looked down at the more prosaic girls of *Brides* or *Self*. Eventually the Co/Lab members complained, creating a curious rift where some people were allowed posh drinks and crisps, and others weren't. The sense of injustice was pervasive enough for a Creative Group employee to write 'WE ARE CREATIVES, NOT 2ND CLASS CITIZENS' on a Post-it note and stick it on a wall.[807]

In the squeezing of staff, Condé Nast has found the twenty-three floors it originally assigned itself at their headquarters at One World Trade Center too generous and they no longer occupy the whole building. Of course, Anna Wintour still has a vast private office.

Some readers have expressed concerns that Condé Nast boasts about its brands but undermines them by constant cost-cutting. In all the pruning of once lavish budgets, *Vogue* was still the headlining brand and the creative and editorial teams found themselves increasingly pressured to emulate *Vogue*'s format, wording and imagery no matter which magazine they were working on. After all, *Vogue* brings in 28 per cent of the entire global revenue of Condé Nast.[808]

What comes next is anybody's guess. It's fascinating to see a company like Condé Nast, who built their reputation on creative talent, step away from this and hone in on operational logistics and algorithms. *Vogue*, many say, took too long to get online, a rare misstep for the mammoth corporation. A lack of understanding led to a half-baked product and even after the formation of Co/Lab, numerous technical glitches made the user experience frustrating and unfriendly. Yet the earliest internet attempts still fell under the remit of editors-in-chiefs like Anna Wintour and Alexandra Shulman, who perhaps did not grasp the importance of the digital terrain. And as the politics of 'hubbing' demonstrate, editors, writers and image-makers are only falling lower on the ladder, their skills seemingly less valued.

This new social hierarchy dictates that magazines are now governed by computer programmers, not journalists. To this industry backdrop it does not seem surprising that Edward Enninful was made editor-in-chief of British *Vogue*; he is in the digital camp, not the traditional one. This has its side effects; for one, editors have become as fetishised as the handbags and shoes in *Vogue*'s pages. Wintour, for example, runs a membership programme charging $100,000 per annum and those willing to pay are offered access to Wintour and given special invites to *Vogue* events, including cosy get-togethers such as group breakfasts with Wintour and other related *Vogue* celebrities. Equally, so many Condé Nast employees are approached to post sponsored content on their personal social media pages that in 2019 management introduced a new company policy stipulating such deals had to be brokered by Condé Nast. They would also be taking a cut.

There is the concern that consumers will tire of digital subscriptions and being bombarded with information. Another worry is whether digital advertising will hold out. Steven Newhouse, the 62-year-old nephew of Si Newhouse who was made co-president of Advance Publications Inc. (which owns Condé Nast) after his death, reiterated the old Newhouse mantra of the bottom line. In a conversation with one of his former journalists, he pointed out that neither *Vogue* nor any other Condé Nast magazines were a vanity project, they were there to churn profit.[809] Yet the perpetual race towards dollar signs is no longer a clearly marked path. Much as the digital strategy seems like the right idea, the 'cool' and 'socially responsible' voice they believe we want these days is not that easy to monetise.

Teen Vogue, which had been pioneering a very Enninful strategy of 'wokeness', had to go online-only in 2017. Since then, it has refocused on fashion: being 'real' wasn't reeling in the big bucks. It is interesting that this formula is being retested with British *Vogue*. In this volatile landscape, the Newhouses are hedging their bets by spending their riches on surer things. In 2019 there was a funding round for Reddit (which Condé Nast bought for $20 million in 2006, and where it still remains the majority stakeholder) which brought Reddit's valuation to $3 billion; and the purchase of Turnitin (the anti-plagiarism software used by universities) for $1.7 billion. How far these and other investments will go to cushion the blows to Condé Nast remains to be seen. Without Si Newhouse to protect the magazines, there is still the danger that they could become collateral damage in the war of internet disruption if they do not perform.

Guessing the Futures of *Vogue*

People seem divided about the future of *Vogue*, although they split quite easily into two camps: those who think *Vogue* is on its last legs, and those who think *Vogue* is immortal. Sometimes, to decide who is in which camp, I had to sift through quite a lot of polite, indirect answers. *Vogue* is not a subject people discuss freely – whether they are involved with Condé Nast or not. Industry insiders, whether they believe in the power of *Vogue* or otherwise, are at least clear on the purpose of the magazine. Vanessa Friedman of the *New York Times* put it most succinctly when she called it a 'filtering and translating role' that helps 'connect fashion and the fashion world to readers'.[810] By 'translating' fashion for an audience and promoting designers they think are talented, *Vogue* and its ilk stand in between critical newspaper coverage, and blogs and social media, which connect brands to consumers directly. Most see *Vogue*'s function as supportive, it acts as cheerleader for the whole sector. Defining fashion magazines in a league of their own should eliminate some of the worry that they are in direct competition with blogs, e-zines, newsletters, etc. but it won't do much for the broader implications of general competition. More platforms mean consumers have options, and their attention span is shortened. *Vogue* could still be drowned out in the crowded media space.

The founder, CEO and editor-in-chief of the global media company *The Business of Fashion* Imran Amed proposes the idea that *Vogue* caters to two different kinds of readers:[811] the consumers who buy the magazine and the consumers who read the website. The print and the digital editions differ significantly enough to hint at separate target groups. This approach would allow the physical product to engage in more substantial fare, while the snippets of Kardashian gossip and fifty ways to wear a white T-shirt can snare fast-scrolling browsers. Yet, to say that *Vogue* is catering to just these two audiences is massively oversimplifying. *Vogue* is now a much bigger brand, a multi-pronged beast that services casual onlookers, diehard fans, creative professionals and everyone in between. Whether you're watching catwalk shows on YouTube, having a tea at Vogue Café or taking out a subscription to the archive for your PhD, you are a customer of Condé Nast.

One cannot help but wonder what Amed really thinks about all this. In 2019, Condé Nast launched *Vogue Business*, a future-focused newsletter which provides analytical and market insights to the fashion industry. It bears striking similarities to Amed's *The Business of Fashion*, which has been running since 2007. *Vogue Business* is said to have sprung out of Condé Nast's incubator and aims to harness a more niche, high-value audience, since large-scale, ad-supported readership is getting harder and harder to monetise. Currently, they are nowhere near overtaking *The Business of Fashion* in subscriber numbers.

Meanwhile Anja Aronowsky Cronberg, the founder and editor-in-chief of *Vestoj*, a Paris-based sartorial publication part-funded by the London College of Fashion, is dubious about how much value *Vogue* even attributes to their audience. 'Sometimes I'm wondering if the readership is at all important. I think maybe the magazine just goes from the publisher straight onto the desks of various PRs, you know? So the PRs can then show their clients, look, your garment is on page so and so in *Vogue*.'[812] She is someone who is not optimistic about their survival: 'that way of working doesn't work in the long-term, not when you have budgets as large as I think *Vogue* is used to having.'

Vestoj, which typically focuses on academic pieces, came into the mainstream when Cronberg interviewed Lucinda Chambers, the fashion director fired from British *Vogue*. Long after the piece went viral, Cronberg was ruminating on Chambers' comments, including the statement that although she worked for *Vogue* she no longer read it. Cronberg speculates that her peers believe *Vogue* is 'a bit silly, definitely irrelevant. Who takes it seriously? Nobody really. At the same time it's a form of status to get to work for *Vogue*.' This creates a complicated relationship: 'not respecting *Vogue* as a publication, but at the same time knowing that it's good for your professional career to work with them'.[813]

A lack of respect for the product among those employed in its making can hardly spell a happy future. Nor does Cronberg necessarily have faith in the Newhouses' desire to keep it running. Cronberg believes that *Vogue* is a good example of the power shift happening in the fashion industry right now. Whether *Vogue* will be the last glossy standing remains to be seen. 'It could be any glossy really because they're all very similar. I'm sure it won't have very much to do with what they actually publish, but more to do with who's lucky enough to have a patron. Someone that thinks they are worth investing in.'[814]

There are other viewpoints. *Sunday Times* columnist and broadcaster Katie Glass responds to fashion publications with enormous enthusiasm: 'I love glossy magazines! Especially when you're doing something like going to a hotel or taking a flight or having a weekend away or getting in the bath, I associate it with that state. It's a luxury. And part of the luxury is the touch and the quality, but also being able to read something.'[815] To Glass, the attraction of print media is the lengthy, long-form pieces, penned for the beauty of the written word, not for the sake of getting hard facts in. 'I like the unreality of *Vogue*. I can't afford any of the clothes and I can't possibly buy a Rolls-Royce Phantom. No one's reading it for that. They're reading it for all that lovely indulgent stuff, the magazine itself becomes a luxury.'[816] It is interesting to think that *Vogue*, in its incarnation as a mass-media magazine, has become the luxury it sells in its pages. It is both a physical replacement, and a peephole, for a world most of us can't live in, but enjoy looking at.

Award-winning journalist Flora Carr is also on the side of print, saying 'I certainly find that there's a shift, particularly in my generation and the generation below me – my sister is Generation Z – and she subscribes to magazines where she is sent a physical copy. I think it's nice to have a tangible copy in your hands'. Along with the draw of the product is Carr's opinion on the power of the brand itself: 'I really doubt that it will suffer in the same way that perhaps lesser known titles might.'[817]

Even Alexandra Shulman defends the format by saying, 'I remain convinced that the appeal of the tangible experience of a thick glossy magazine remains strong.'[818] Along with the conviction that people have come to see reading as a luxury, came the insistence from this camp that *Vogue* is still widely consumed. I found interviewees keen to impress upon me that their mothers read *Vogue* and always had, along with the hope that their daughters would too. I also found, in passing conversation, people from all walks of life who still collect *Vogue*. Teenagers and housewives. Corporate lawyers and investment bankers. Graphic designers, art dealers, freelance writers, bloggers and gardeners. There is clearly still something to be said for its appeal. Glass's comment 'I have friends who even love the ads' is particularly telling.[819]

Flora Carr, who won the Vogue Talent Contest in 2015, still describes the lunch held at Vogue House for shortlisted entrants with what seems to be a sense of wonder. Included in the prize is an internship at *Vogue* itself, and Carr recalls the positive response from staff to her writing, the supportive nature of the office and an overall pleasant, bustling, friendly environment.[820] Although as an

intern there was much she wasn't privy to, she still felt close enough
to the action for a lot of surreal, 'pinch me' moments, from Alexa
Chung swinging through for meetings to transcribing an interview
with Victoria Beckham.[821] She believes winning the competition
was her launchpad; a vital foundation to her subsequent career in
journalism. She has no doubt that the prestige of *Vogue* on her CV
opened doors.

Both *The Business of Fashion* and *Vestoj* are new publications
which deal with fashion in new ways, altering traditional formats.
They are made diverse not just by including ethnic minorities on
front covers, but by the entire structure of their media companies.
In speaking to Miles Socha, editor-in-chief of *Women's Wear Daily*
(*WWD*), one sees the approach of a legacy brand. *WWD* appeared
in 1910 and so has almost as long a history as *Vogue*, although it
is a trade publication. *WWD* is currently experiencing a boom in
subscriber numbers, and Socha underlines the ongoing importance
of experts, saying, 'Twitter was the first one to explode, as I think
consumers looked to *WWD* as a benchmark of truth and journalistic
integrity in a sea of questionable info and sponsored content.'[822]

The steep competition from digital platforms is not something
Socha feels can rival his output, explaining, 'The differentiating
factor, of course, is journalistic know-how, because it requires specialised skills and yields unique and valuable content. In the case
of *WWD*, we were always a specialised media and the explosion of
influencers has only thrown that into sharper relief.'[823] So there are
vast fashion media companies that still rank professional writing
high on the list of employee must-haves. In recent years there has
been a steady return of readers to 'serious' publications, as people
bore of clickbait and hunger for the educated opinions of experts. The
niche, journalist-led model is back, servicing smaller audiences who
are prepared to pay higher prices for quality material. How *Vogue*

negotiates this latest movement will be challenging, considering it is so mainstream. Manoeuvring a company this big to fit changing trends is tough.

To manage these tricks of the trade and to shift its titanic being *Vogue* will always need its editors. These are the frontline people, the managers and the crucial links between shadowy directors, genuine talent and junior faces. It has never been an easy job. The longest-serving editor-in-chief, Edna Woolman Chase, described it as a nightmarish case of being a general dogsbody, dealing with everything from arguing employees to production lines, and needing 'a combination nursemaid, policeman, diplomat, psychiatrist technique'.[824]

The role of the editor is unique and the job description is forever in flux. We know EICs used to be art directors and reporters, in the future at Condé Nast they might be influencers, vloggers or tech nerds. Imran Amed from *The Business of Fashion* describes the changes like this:

> Once upon a time the editor was the arbiter of good taste and I think now there's lots of people who are arbiters of taste. I think an editor today is a facilitator of a conversation, someone who can bring talented teams of people together to create ideas and content and experiences, and it's still the role of the editor to be the face and representative of a media company.[825]

There's also the vital matter of how EICs respond to the world around them – fashion is not the only thing changing, we are all hurtling into darker unknowns. Less than a century ago there were editors in London and Paris who hid from the Nazis and put out a bestselling magazine during major bombings. Decisions to cover women's health and second-wave feminism propelled American

Vogue into becoming the highest-circulating glossy in the 1970s, a lofty position it has retained ever since. Edward Enninful's diversity campaign #NewVogue refreshed an entire country's outlook.

Freer in their operations and less beholden to the owners or other networks of old contacts, new *Vogue* magazines with fresh EICs are doing innovative work. During the COVID-19 pandemic of 2020, British *Vogue* featured Rihanna for May; American *Vogue* put a skinny figure in front of a sparkly sand dune. Meanwhile *Vogue Portugal*, edited by the magical touch of Sofia Lucas, put out an exquisite cover of a couple kissing while wearing face masks. In style, it is reminiscent of old photographs of sweethearts parting before war. The issue is called 'Freedom on Hold'. It is one of a long series of breath-taking covers featured under Lucas's direction, exploring fascinating topics with titles such as 'Twin Souls'[826] and 'Planet Earth is the New Trend'[827]. The environmental bent is strong, but so is a more egalitarian approach. Her photographers are younger, less famous, artistically focused and produce eerie, museum-worthy dreamscapes. *Vogue Portugal* under Sofia Lucas is low on celebrities and big on creativity; as such, it is close to the old *Vogue* spirit.

Other global issues have impacted fashion. When a spotlight was cast on Harvey Weinstein's crimes and the #MeToo movement, the sexual misconduct which went unreported in many industries was highlighted. By 2018, Condé Nast had to relinquish working with three of its biggest and longest-serving star photographers over multiple allegations (all denied) of coercion and sexual assault: Terry Richardson, Mario Testino and Bruce Weber. Equally, following the Black Lives Matter protests worldwide, *Vogue* was forced to take another look at its company politics. And, in an unprecedented apology, Anna Wintour acknowledged the printing of offensive and intolerant content, and for hiring too few black staff.[828] May it be the beginning of a thorough investigation into how Condé Nast is run.

'What next?' in the context of *Vogue* is a huge and impossible question. The past decade has been spent struggling with technology, grappling with an online world that is shooting ahead at the speed of light and forcing old-fashioned media companies to gasp for air. But *Vogue* has survived wars that toppled nations, suffered losses that could bankrupt entire states and sustained a brand legacy as well known as the royal family. In the letters, memoirs and biographies of various people involved with *Vogue* over the many years, there has always been the lingering speculation from jealous rivals that *Vogue* was on the verge of collapse. That it has flown too high for too long. That cry went up when the founder died in 1906, during the Depression of the 1930s, in the youth-led revolution of the 1960s and at the dawn of the blogger generation of the 2010s. But no one can truly believe there will be an end. *Vogue* will always be *Vogue*.

Endnotes

Chapter 1

1   E. Woolman Chase & I. Chase, *Always in Vogue*, Doubleday & Company, Inc., United States of America, 1954, p. 16

2   A. B. Turnure, 'STATEMENT', *Vogue*, vol. 1, issue 1, 17 December 1892, p. 16

3   L. Borrelli-Persson, '*Vogue* Fun Facts by the Numbers', *Vogue* [.com], Culture, 7 March 2017, <https://www.vogue.com/article/vogue-covers-models-facts-history>, accessed 1 February 2020

4   ibid.

5   Woolman Chase & Chase, op. cit., p. 16

6   E. Wharton, *The Age of Innocence*, The Modern Library, New York, 1920, p. 69

7   C. Seebohm, *The Man Who Was Vogue: The Life and Times of Conde Nast*, The Viking Press, New York, 1982, p. 40

8   Vogue, 'VOGUE', *Vogue*, vol. 1, issue 1, 17 December 1892, p. 1

9   ibid.

10   T. Peterson, *Magazines in the Twentieth Century*, 2nd edn, University of Illinois Press, Urbana, 1975, p. 2

11   ibid.

12   M. Beetham, *A Magazine of Her Own? Domesticity and Desire in the Women's Magazine 1800–1914*, Routledge, London, 1996, p. 5

13   Vogue, 'COMING EVENTS', *Vogue*, Vogue Society Supplement, vol. 1, issue 1, 17 December 1892, p. S2

14   ibid.

15   ibid.

16   ibid.

17   ibid., p. 3

18   Vogue, 'FLORAL GARNITURE', *Vogue*, Vogue Society Supplement, vol. 1, issue 1, 17 December 1892, p. 12

19   Vogue, 'SLIPPERS', *Vogue*, Vogue Society Supplement, vol. 1, issue 1, 17 December 1892., p. S4

20   ibid.

21   Vogue, 'LONDON', *Vogue*, Vogue Society Supplement, vol. 1, issue 1, 17 December 1892, p. S2

22   Woolman Chase & Chase, op. cit., p. 19

23   Vogue, 'BOTH KINDS', *Vogue*, vol. 1, issue 1, 17 December 1892, p. 16

24   Vogue, 'LONDON', *Vogue*, Vogue Society Supplement, vol. 1, issue 1, 17 December 1892, p. S2

25   ibid., p. 21

26   ibid.

27   ibid., p. 22

28   *Always in Vogue* by Woolman Chase, p. 32

29   ibid., p. 43

Chapter 2

30   C. Seebohm, *The Man Who Was Vogue: The Life and Times of Conde Nast*, The Viking Press, New York, 1982, p. 38

31   ibid.

32   E. Woolman Chase & I. Chase, *Always in Vogue*, Doubleday & Company, Inc., United States of America, 1954, p. 58

33   ibid., p. 49

34   ibid.

35   ibid., pp. 28–9

36   Woolman Chase & Chase, op. cit., p. 46

37   Seebohm, op. cit., p. 30

38   ibid.

39   ibid.

40   Woolman Chase & Chase, op. cit., p. 46

41   ibid.

42   ibid., p. 47

43   Vogue, 'Announcement', *Vogue*, vol. 35, issue 7, 12 February 1910, p. 7

44 ibid.

45 Woolman Chase & Chase, op. cit., pp. 54–5

46 ibid., p. 81

47 ibid., p. 26–7

48 ibid., p. 80

49 ibid., p. 78

50 ibid., p. 79

51 ibid.

52 ibid., p. 109

53 ibid., p. 53

54 ibid., pp. 129–31

55 ibid., pp. 140–1

56 Seebohm, op. cit., p. 88

57 ibid., p. 86

58 ibid., p. 88

59 Woolman Chase & Chase, op. cit., p. 53

60 Seebohm, op. cit., p. 86

61 Seebohm, op. cit., p.88

62 B. Ballard, *In My Fashion*, 1st edn 1960, V&A Publishing, London, 2017, [Apple Books e-book] pp. 12–13

63 Seebohm, op. cit., pp. 156–7

64 ibid., p. 41

65 ibid.

66 Woolman Chase & Chase, op. cit., p. 54

67 Ballard, op. cit., p. 13

68 ibid., p. 14

69 Woolman Chase & Chase, op. cit., pp. 109–10

70 ibid.

71 ibid.

72 ibid.

73 Seebohm, op. cit., p. 60

74 Woolman Chase & Chase, op. cit., p. 106

75 ibid., p. 282

76 Woolman Chase & Chase, op. cit., pp. 190–1

77 Ibid.

78 Seebohm, op. cit., p. 61

79 Woolman Chase & Chase, op. cit., p. 61

80 ibid., p. 71

81 ibid.

82 ibid.

83 Condé Nast, 'What We Do', Condé Nast, <https://www.condenast.com/about>, accessed 20 June 2020

84 Yoxall, H., *A Fashion of Life*, Taplinger Publishing Co., Inc., New York, 1967, p. 80

85 ibid., p. 81

Chapter 3

86 C. Seebohm, *The Man Who Was Vogue: The Life and Times of Conde Nast*, The Viking Press, New York, 1982, p. 76

87 D. Friend, '*Vanity Fair*: The One-Click History', *Vanity Fair*, Vintage V.F., 14 January 2008, <https://www.vanityfair.com/magazine/2008/01/oneclick-history>, accessed 5 February 2019

88 Seebohm, op. cit., pp. 260–1

89 ibid.

90 E. Woolman Chase & I. Chase, *Always in Vogue*, Doubleday & Company, Inc., United States of America, 1954, pp. 116–17

91 ibid.

92 Seebohm, op. cit., p. 123

93 ibid.

94 ibid., pp. 116–17

95 ibid.

96 L. Cohen, *All We Know: Three Lives*, Farrar, Straus and Giroux, United States of America, 2012, p. 231

97 Woolman Chase & Chase, op. cit., p. 116

98 D. Gilbert, 'The Looks of Austerity: Fashions for Hard Times', *Fashion Theory*, vol. 21, issue 4, 2017, pp. 477–99

99 A. de Warenne, *Vogue* (British), cover, Late January 1918

100 A. de Warenne, *Vogue* (British), cover, Early July 1918

101 H. Dryden, *Vogue* (British), cover, Early December 1918

102 G. Lepape, *Vogue* (British), cover, November 1918

103 Vogue, *Vogue* (British), Editor's Letter, Early October 1918

104 D. Edinger, *Vogue*, cover, vol. 51, no. 8, Late April 1918

105 J. R. Fernandez, '"IF YOU CAN'T be GAY be GALLANT" SAYS PARIS', *Vogue*, Fashion, vol. 52, issue 1, 1 July 1918, p. 38

106 Vogue, 'THESE ARE THE DEFENCES OF PARIS AGAINST THE WAR', *Vogue*, Fashion, vol. 52, issue 10, 15 November 1918, p. 39

107 Vogue, 'DRESSING ON A WAR INCOME', *Vogue*, Fashion, vol. 52, issue 1, 1 July 1918, p. 66

108 Clark's Thinning Bath Salts, *Vogue* (British), advertisements, Early September 1924

109 Woolman Chase & Chase, op. cit., pp. 89–91

110 ibid.

111 ibid., pp. 29–30

112 ibid., p. 91

113 ibid., pp. 91–2

114 ibid.

115 PortableNYC, 'Mamie Fish – the "Fun-Maker" of the Gilded Age', Portable NYC [blog], 9 May 2020, <https://portablenycblog.com/2020/05/09/mamie-fish-the-fun-maker-of-the-gilded-age/>, accessed 9 June 2020

116 Woolman Chase & Chase, op. cit., p.94

117 ibid., p. 94

118 ibid.

119 ibid., pp. 94–5

120 ibid.

121 ibid., p. 96

122 ibid., p. 97

123 ibid., p. 92

124 ibid., p. 83

125 ibid., p. 111

126 Woolman Chase & Chase, op. cit., p. 88

127 GREENWICHFREEPRESS, 'Fun Times Working at Condé Nast in Greenwich!', *Greenwich Free Press*, 14 February 2016, Around Town, <https://greenwichfreepress.com/around-town/fun-times-working-at-conde-nast-in-greenwich-58902/>, accessed 9 November 2019

128 ibid.

129 ibid.

130 Seebohm, op. cit., pp. 282–3

131 Woolman Chase & Chase, op. cit., p. 34

132 ibid., p. 109

133 Seebohm, op. cit., p. 261

134 ibid.

Chapter 4

135   O. Pentelow, 'Vogue Editors Through The Years', *Vogue* [.co.uk], News, 10 April 2017, <https://www.vogue.co.uk/gallery/past-british-vogue-editors-history>, accessed 1 February 2019

136   ibid.

137   E. Woolman Chase & I. Chase, *Always in Vogue*, Doubleday & Company, Inc., United States of America, 1954

138   L. Cohen, *All We Know: Three Lives*, Farrar, Straus and Giroux, United States of America, 2012, p. 235

139   P. Lewis, *The Cambridge Introduction to Modernism*, Cambridge University Press, New York, 2007, pp. xvii-3

140   Vanity Fair, 'IN VANITY FAIR', *Vanity Fair*, In Vanity Fair, March 1914, p. 15

141   Vogue, 'Early Paris Openings and Brides', *Vogue* (British), Contents, Early April 1925

142   Cohen, op. cit., pp. 242-3

143   ibid., p. 243

144   ibid.

145   ibid., p. 245

146   O. Todd, *Year of the Crab*, Aidan Ellis, London, 1975, p. 265

147   Cohen, op. cit., p. 254

148   Woolman Chase & Chase, op. cit., p. 118

149   Cohen, op. cit., pp. 230-1

150   ibid., p. 230

151   ibid., pp. 232-3

152   ibid.

153   ibid., p. 236

154   ibid., p. 237

155   M. Garland, conversation with Hilary Spurling, 29 March 1989, cited in Cohen, op. cit., p. 241

156   Cohen, op. cit., p. 238

157   N. Luckhurst, *Bloomsbury in Vogue*, Cecil Woolf Publishers, London, 1998, p. 24

158   Fish, 'A BACHELOR AT BAY', *Vogue*, Early May 1925, p. 72

159   C. Reed, 'A *Vogue* That Dare Not Speak its Name: Sexual Subculture During

the Editorship of Dorothy Todd, 1922–26', *Fashion Theory*, vol. 10, issue 1/2, 2006, p. 64

160 Vogue, 'SEEN on the STAGE', *Vogue*, Late November 1924, p. 62

161 Luckhurst, op. cit.

162 Cohen, op. cit., p. 267

163 ibid., p. 252

164 Woolf, V., *The Letters of Virginia Woolf, Volume III, 1923 – 1928*, ed. N. Nicholson & J. Trautmann, Mariner Books, United States of America, 1978, p. 170.

165 ibid.

166 Reed, op. cit., p. 57

167 Woolman Chase & Chase, op. cit., p. 118

168 Yoxall, H., *A Fashion of Life*, Taplinger Publishing Co., Inc., New York, 1967, p. 124.

169 ibid.

170 Vogue, *Vogue*, Late October 1923, p. iv

171 Cohen, op. cit., p. 265

172 ibid.

173 ibid., p. 266

174 C. Derry, 'Lesbianism and Feminist Legislation in 1921: the Age of Consent and 'Gross Indecency between Women', *History Workshop Journal*, vol. 86, Autumn 2018, p. 245

175 A. Parkes, 'Lesbianism, History, and Censorship: The Well of Loneliness and the Suppressed Randiness of Virginia Woolf's Orlando', *Twentieth Century Literature*, vol. 40, no. 4, 1994, pp. 434–60

176 Woolman Chase & Chase, op. cit., p. 119

177 Yoxall, op. cit., p. 107

178 Woolf, V., *The Letters of Virginia Woolf, Volume III, 1923 – 1928*, ed. N. Nicholson & J. Trautmann, Mariner Books, United States of America, 1978, pp. 478–9

179 M. Garland, memoir drafts, cited in L. Cohen, op. cit., p. 270

180 Cohen, op. cit., p. 343

181 ibid., pp. 343–4

182 Todd, loc. cit.

183 Cohen, op. cit., p. 344

184 A. J. Carrod, '"A plea for a renaissance": Dorothy Todd's Modernist experiment in British *Vogue*, 1922–1926', Doctor of Philosophy Thesis in English Literature, Keele University, Keele, Newcastle, 2015, p. 255

185 Woolman Chase & Chase, op. cit., pp. 119–21

186 ibid., p. 119

187 ibid., p. 122

188 ibid., pp. 121–5

189 Yoxall, op. cit., p. 81

Chapter 5

190 Yoxall, H., *A Fashion of Life*, Taplinger Publishing Co., Inc., New York, 1967. p. 123

191 ibid.

192 ibid., p. 125

193 ibid.

194 ibid.

195 ibid.

196 ibid.

197 M. D. Harmon, 'A war of words: the *British Gazette* and *British Worker* during the 1926 General Strike', *Labor History*, vol. 60, issue 3, 2019, p. 193

198 Yoxall, op. cit., p. 125

199 Harmon, op. cit., pp. 194–8

200 Yoxall, op. cit., pp. 125–6

201 ibid., p. 126

202 ibid.

203 ibid., p. 127

204 ibid.

205 ibid.

206 E. Woolman Chase & I. Chase, *Always in Vogue*, Doubleday & Company, Inc., United States of America, 1954, p. 131

207 D. Chambers & L. Steiner, 'The Changing Status of Women Journalists', in S. Allan ed., *The Routledge Companion to News and Journalism*, Routledge, London and New York, 2010, pp. 49–60

208 I. Coser, 'Alison Settle, Editor of British Vogue (1926–1935): Habitus and the Acquisition of Cultural, Social, and Symbolic Capital in the Private Diaries of Alison Settle', *Fashion Theory*, vol. 21, issue 4, 2017, pp. 477–99

209 Vogue, 'THE CHIC WOMAN'S DAY ON THE RIVIERA', *Vogue*, Features, vol. 77, issue 8, 15 April 1931, p. 112–40

210 A. Settle, 'Alison Settle Remembers . . .', *The Observer*, 24 June 1973, p. 27

211   A. Settle [diary entry], Spring–Summer 1932, Journals 1930–4, Charles Wakefield Private Archive, Canada

212   ibid.

213   A. Settle, 'Alison Settle Remembers . . .', *The Observer Review*, 1 July 1973

214   A. Settle [private notes], Alison Settle Archive, University of Brighton Design Archives, Brighton, R14

215   ibid., R6/R7

216   ibid., R14

217   A. Settle [private notes], Alison Settle Archive, University of Brighton Design Archives, Brighton, R16

218   ibid.

219   Yoxall, op. cit., p. 124

220   C. Geisst, *Wall Street*, Oxford University Press, Oxford, 1997, p. 147

221   C. Seebohm, *The Man Who Was Vogue: The Life and Times of Conde Nast*, The Viking Press, New York, 1982, p. 282

222   ibid.

223   ibid.

224   ibid.

225   Woolman Chase & Chase, op. cit., p. 193

226   Yoxall, op. cit., p. 81

227   ibid., p. 93

228   ibid., pp. 92–4

229   ibid.

230   ibid.

231   Woolman Chase & Chase, op. cit., pp. 131–2

232   ibid., p. 204

233   ibid., pp. 205–6

234   Seebohm, op. cit., pp. 264–5

Chapter 6

235   E. Woolman Chase & I. Chase, *Always in Vogue*, Doubleday & Company, Inc., United States of America, 1954, p. 128

236   ibid., p. 85

237   ibid.

238   ibid., p. 127

239   ibid.

240 ibid.

241 B. Ballard, *In My Fashion*, 1st edn 1960, V&A Publishing, London, 2017, [Apple Books e-book], pp. 158–87

242 Woolman Chase & Chase, op. cit., p. 127

243 Ballard, op. cit., p. 34

244 ibid., p. 45

245 M. McAuliffe, *Paris on the Brink: The 1930s Paris of Jean Renoir, Salvador Dalí, Simone de Beauvoir, André Gide, Sylvia Beach, Léon Blum, and their Friends*, Rowman & Littlefield, United States of America, 2018, p. 1

246 ibid., p. 39

247 Ballard, op. cit., p. 45

248 ibid.

249 ibid., p. 82

250 ibid., p. 36

251 ibid., p. 97

252 ibid., p. 44

253 ibid., pp. 46–7

254 Woolman Chase & Chase, op. cit., p. 121

255 ibid.

256 ibid.

257 ibid., p. 175

258 Ballard, op. cit., p. 47

259 Woolman Chase & Chase, op. cit., p. 178

260 ibid., p. 48

261 ibid., p. 54

262 ibid., p. 55

263 ibid.

264 Ballard, op. cit., p. 55

265 ibid.

266 Woolman Chase & Chase, op. cit., p. 212

267 Ballard, op. cit., p. 266

268 ibid., p. 58

269 Woolman Chase & Chase, op. cit., p. 213

270 ibid., p. 214[delete repeated note 36]

271 ibid.

272 Ballard, op. cit., p. 83

273 ibid.

274 ibid.

275   ibid., p. 85
276   ibid.
277   ibid., pp. 85–6
278   ibid.
279   ibid.
280   ibid., p. 86
281   ibid., pp. 86–7
282   ibid., p. 87
283   ibid.
284   ibid., pp. 90–1
285   ibid., p. 84

Chapter 7

286   Yoxall, H., *A Fashion of Life*, Taplinger Publishing Co., Inc., New York, 1967, p. 179
287   ibid.
288   E. Woolman Chase & I. Chase, *Always in Vogue*, Doubleday & Company, Inc., United States of America, 1954, p. 255
289   ibid., p. 249
290   ibid., p. 246
291   Yoxall, op. cit., p. 183
292   Woolman Chase & Chase, op. cit., p. 246
293   B. Ballard, *In My Fashion*, 1st edn 1960, V&A Publishing, London, 2017, [Apple Books e-book], p. 302
294   ibid., p. 304
295   ibid., p. 305
296   Ballard, op. cit., p. 311
297   ibid., pp. 312–13
298   Woolman Chase & Chase, op. cit., p. 255
299   ibid., p. 291
300   Ballard, op. cit., p. 315
301   ibid., pp. 325–7
302   Yoxall, op. cit., p. 181
303   ibid.
304   ibid., p. 182
305   ibid.

306   ibid.

307   ibid., p. 183

308   ibid., p. 182

309   D. Beyfus, 'Audrey Withers', *The Guardian*, Obituaries, 31 October 2001, <https://www.theguardian.com/news/2001/oct/31/guardianobituaries>, accessed 09 December 2018

310   ibid.

311   ibid.

312   ibid.

313   A. Withers, 'British Vogue Weathers the Storm', *Vogue*, People and Ideas, vol. 96, issue 11, 1 December 1940, pp. 80, 81, 138, 139, 140, 141

314   ibid., p. 80

315   ibid.

316   Vogue, 'Sorry If We're Late . . .', *Vogue*, Advertisement, vol. 103, issue 5, 1 March 1944, p. 192

317   Yoxall, op. cit., p. 125

318   Yoxall, op. cit., pp. 180–1

319   ibid.

320   Ministry of Information, *Home Front Handbook*, Balding and Mansell, Great Britain, 2005 [1945], p. 50–1

321   A. Withers, *Lifespan: An Autobiography*, Peter Owen, London and Chester Springs, 1994, p. 51

322   J. Summers, *Fashion on the Ration: Style in the Second World War*, Profile Books LTD, Great Britain, 2015

323   ibid.

324   J. Kron, 'When Beauty Was a Duty', *New York Times*, Arts, 8 February 1991, <https://www.nytimes.com/1991/02/08/arts/when-beauty-was-a-duty.html>, accessed 9 August 2019

325   Vogue, 'Nov. I: Sell Time-Savers, Beauty-Savers!', *Vogue*, Vogue Advance News For Retailers, vol. 100, issue 9, 1 November 1942, p. A1

326   Vogue, 'In this Issue', *Vogue* (British), September 1939, p. 11

327   ibid.

328   P. Roy, *Vogue* (British), cover, March 1942

329   Vogue, 'General Economy Issues his Orders of the Day', *Vogue* (British), May 1942, p. 21

330   ibid.

331   C. Beaton, *Vogue* (British), cover, September 1943

332   C. Beaton, 'The Stuff of Vogue', *Vogue* (British), March 1942, p. 25

333 Ballard, op. cit., p. 420

334 K. Nelson Best, *The History of Fashion Journalism*, Bloomsbury, London, New York, 2017, pp. 95–6

335 Woolman Chase & Chase, op. cit., p. 263

336 ibid., p. 261

337 ibid., p. 262

338 ibid. pp. 262–3

339 ibid.

340 ibid.

341 ibid., p. 263

342 ibid.

343 Yoxall, op. cit., p. 59

344 Woolman Chase & Chase, op. cit., p. 264

345 ibid.

346 ibid. pp. 264–5

347 ibid.

348 ibid.

349 ibid.

350 ibid. p. 277

351 ibid. p. 279

352 C. Beaton, 'The Honourable Scars of London', *Vogue*, People and Ideas, vol. 98, issue 7, 1 October 1941, p. 120

353 C. Beaton, 'Fashion is Indestructible', *Vogue* (British), Fashion, September 1941, p. 32

354 A. Withers, *Lifespan: An Autobiography*, Peter Owen, London and Chester Springs, 1994, p. 53

355 The Telegraph, 'Audrey Withers', *The Telegraph*, News, Obituaries, 1 November 2001, <https://www.telegraph.co.uk/news/obituaries/1361993/Audrey-Withers.html>, accessed 11 October 2018

356 A. Penrose, *The Lives of Lee Miller*, 2nd edn, Thames & Hudson, London, 2002, p. 193

357 L. Blanch, 'How British Vogue Editors Live, Dress, Work, in Robot-bombed London', *Vogue*, People and Ideas, vol. 104, issue 6, 1 October 1944, p. 127

358 The Telegraph, 'Audrey Withers', *The Telegraph*, News, Obituaries, 1 November 2001, <https://www.telegraph.co.uk/news/obituaries/1361993/Audrey-Withers.html>, accessed 11 October 2018

359 Ballard, op. cit., p. 402

360 ibid., p. 409

361 Woolman Chase & Chase, op. cit., p. 287

362 ibid. p. 275

363 ibid. p. 291

364 ibid. p. 295

365 ibid.

366 ibid.

Chapter 8

367 B. Ballard, *In My Fashion*, 1st edn 1960, V&A Publishing, London, 2017, [Apple Books e-book], p. 480–515

368 E. Woolman Chase & I. Chase, *Always in Vogue*, Doubleday & Company, Inc., United States of America, 1954, p. 306

369 ibid., p. 307

370 ibid., pp. 307–10

371 F. du Plessix Gray, *Them: A Memoir of Parents*, Penguin Press, New York, 2005, pp. 398–9

372 ibid.

373 ibid., p. 396

374 Vogue, *Vogue*, 10th Americana Issue, vol. 109, issue 3, 1 February 1947

375 A. Whitman, 'Jessica Daves of Vogue Is Dead; Favored Ready-To-Wear Trend', *New York Times*, Obituaries, 24 September 1974, <https://www.nytimes.com/1974/09/24/archives/jessica-daves-of-vogue-is-dead-favored-readytowear-trend-went.html>, accessed 9 August 2018

376 R Tuite, 'Rediscovering Vogue's Jessica Daves', Thames and Hudson, News, 20 November 2019, <https://thamesandhudson.com/news/article-rediscovering-jessica-daves/>, accessed 13 December 2019

377 Vogue, 'More taste than money – and more 1955 fashion per dollar', *Vogue*, Fashion, vol. 125, issue 3, 15 February 1955, p. 62

378 Vogue, *Vogue*, Vogue's Eye-view of the Museum of Modern Art, vol. 106, issue 1, 1 July 1945

379 K. Nelson Best, *The History of Fashion Journalism*, Bloomsbury, London, New York, 2017, p. 134

380 ibid.

381 I. Penn, *Vogue*, cover, vol. 113, no. 7, Late April 1949

382 H. Ketchum, *American Fabrics*, Doric Publishing Company, Fall 1949, p. 96

383 L. McClean, 'Do You Think You're a Snob?', *Vogue*, People, vol. 138, issue 8, 1 November 1961, p. 150

384   J. Mason Brown, 'What Makes A Woman Memorable', *Vogue*, Features –
      Articles – People, vol. 128, issue 9, 15 November 1956, pp. 100, 101, 159

385   ibid.

386   Vogue, 'The Summer Figure: Topic for Today', *Vogue*, Fashion, vol. 123, issue
      9, 15 May 1954, pp. 82–3

387   Vogue, 'Mrs. Exeter's List', *Vogue*, Mrs. Exeter, vol. 126, issue 4, 1 September
      1955, p. 256

388   Vogue, 'Who is Mrs. Exeter?', *Vogue*, Mrs. Exeter, vol. 124, issue 1, 1 July
      1954, p. 94

389   G. Mirabella, *In and Out of Vogue*, Doubleday, New York, 1995, p. 63

390   A. Whitman, 'Jessica Daves of Vogue Is Dead; Favored Ready-To-Wear
      Trend', New York Times, Obituaries, 24 September 1974, <https://www.
      nytimes.com/1974/09/24/archives/jessica-daves-of-vogue-is-dead-favore-
      dreadytowear-trend-went.html>, accessed 9 August 2018

391   Mirabella, op. cit., p. 72

392   Ibid.

393   J. Daves, *Ready-Made Miracle; The American Story of Fashion for the Mil-
      lions*, G. P. Putnam's Sons, New York, 1967, p. 69

394   Mirabella, op. cit., p. 20

395   A. Fine Collins, 'The Cult of Diana', *Vanity Fair*, Culture, November 1993,
      <https://www.vanityfair.com/culture/1993/11/diana-vreeland-199311>,
      accessed 11 January 2019

396   Yoxall, H., *A Fashion of Life*, Taplinger Publishing Co., Inc., New York, 1967,
      p. 96

397   C. Felsenthal, *Citizen Newhouse; Portrait of a Media Merchant*, Seven Stories
      Press, New York, 1998, p. 25

398   du Plessix Gray, op. cit., pp. 405–6

399   du Plessix Gray, op. cit., pp. 349

400   A. Fine Collins, 'The Cult of Diana', *Vanity Fair*, Culture, November 1993,
      <https://www.vanityfair.com/culture/1993/11/diana-vreeland-199311>,
      accessed 11 January 2019

401   ibid.

402   B. Leser cited in S. Homewood, 'Publishing icon Bernie Leser passes away',
      AdNews, News, 15 October 2015, <https://www.adnews.com.au/news/
      publishing-icon-bernie-leser-passes-away>, accessed 11 February 2019

403   Homewood, loc. cit.

404   Ballard, op. cit., p. 549

Chapter 9

405   B. Ballard, *In My Fashion*, 1st edn 1960, V&A Publishing, London, 2017, [Apple Books e-book], p. 472

406   ibid., p. 472

407   F. du Plessix Gray, *Them: A Memoir of Parents*, Penguin Press, New York, 2005, p. 408

408   ibid.

409   Horwell, V., 'Edmonde Charles-Roux obituary', *The Guardian*, Books, 25 January 2016, <https://www.theguardian.com/books/2016/jan/25/edmonde-charles-roux>, accessed 11 June 2019

410   du Plessix Gray, op. cit., p. 409

411   Ballard, op. cit., p. 529

412   ibid., pp. 526–8

413   A. Garland, *Lion's Share*, Michael Joseph Ltd., New York, 1970, p. 38

414   ibid., p. 48

415   H. Cox and S. Mowatt, 'Monopoly, Power and Politics in Fleet Street: the Controversial Birth of IPC Magazines, 1958–63', paper presented to the BHC Annual Conference, Frankfurt, 14–15 March 2014, pp. 1–20 <http://orapp.aut.ac.nz/bitstream/handle/10292/6787/Cox%20and%20Mowatt%20BHC%20paper%20Monopoly%2c%20Power%20and%20Politics.pdf?sequence=2&isAllowed=y>, accessed 11 March 2020

416   Garland, op. cit., p. 37

417   ibid., p. 141

418   ibid.

419   ibid.

420   ibid.

421   ibid., p. 140

422   ibid., pp. 140–5

423   ibid., p. 145

424   ibid., pp. 148–52

425   ibid.

426   ibid.

427   ibid., p. 149

428   ibid.

429   ibid.

430 ibid.

431 ibid.

432 ibid., p. 150

433 ibid., p. 175

434 ibid., p. 147

435 ibid., p. 178

436 Office for National Statistics, 'Trends in births and deaths over the last century', 15 July 2015, <https://www.ons.gov.uk/peoplepopulationandcommunity/birthsdeathsandmarriages/livebirths/articles/trendsinbirthsanddeathsoverthelastcentury/2015-07-15>, accessed 11 January 2020

437 Vogue, *Vogue* (British), Young Idea, January 1953

438 Garland, op. cit., p. 155

439 B. Conekin, 'From Haughty to Nice: How British Fashion Images Changed from the 1950s to the 1960s', *Photography and Culture*, vol. 3, issue 3, 2010, p. 285

440 Yoxall, H., *A Fashion of Life*, Taplinger Publishing Co., Inc., New York, 1967, pp. 108–9

441 Garland, op. cit., p. 143

442 R. Muir, 'Two take Manhattan', *The Guardian*, 17 March 2007, <https://www.theguardian.com/theguardian/2007/mar/17/weekend7.weekend1>, accessed 11 June 2019

443 ibid.

444 ibid.

445 Garland, op. cit., pp. 180–2

446 The Telegraph, 'Beatrix Miller – obituary', *The Telegraph*, News, Obituaries, 23 February 2014, <https://www.telegraph.co.uk/news/obituaries/10656743/Beatrix-Miller-obituary.html>, accessed 11 June 2019

447 ibid.

448 ibid., p. 224

449 P. Knapp, 'Vogue's new beauty etiquette', *Vogue* (British), Fashion, June 1971

450 ibid.

451 ibid.

452 Coddington, G., *Grace: A Memoir*, Chatto & Windus, London, 2012, p. 229

453 ibid., p. 302

Chapter 10

454   G. Mirabella, *In and Out of Vogue*, Doubleday, New York, 1995, p. 133

455   ibid.

456   ibid.

457   ibid.

458   Vogue, 'The Explorers. Fashion that's all yours for the discovery . . .', *Vogue*, Fashion, vol. 152, issue 7, 15 October 1968, pp. 108–29

459   Mirabella, op. cit., p. 132

460   ibid., p. 131

461   ibid., p. 132

462   ibid.

463   ibid.

464   M. Evans, 'The Great Fur Caravan', *Vogue*, Fashion, vol. 148, issue 7, 15 October 1966, pp. 88–113, 175

465   ibid., p. 88

466   D. Vreeland, 'Why Don't You . . .', *Harper's Bazaar*, 1936

467   ibid.

468   A. Fine Collins, 'The Cult of Diana', *Vanity Fair*, Culture, November 1993, <https://www.vanityfair.com/culture/1993/11/diana-vreeland-199311>, accessed 11 January 2019

469   Mirabella, op. cit., p. 128

470   Vogue, 'Youth Quake', *Vogue*, Fashion, vol. 145, issue 1, 1 January 1965, pp. 112–19

471   Fine Collins, op. cit.

472   Vreeland, D., *D.V.*, ed. G. Plimpton & C. Hemphill, Alfred A. Knopf, Inc., New York, 1984, p. 118

473   ibid., p. 106

474   ibid.

475   ibid.

476   ibid.

477   ibid.

478   ibid.

479   *Diana Vreeland: The Eye Has to Travel* [documentary], dir. L. Immordino Vreeland, Submarine Entertainment; New York, 2012.

480   T. Maier, *All That Glitters: Anna Wintour, Tina Brown, and the Rivalry*

Inside America's Richest Media Empire, Skyhorse Publishing, New York, 2019, [Apple Books e-book] pp. 109–10

481   F. du Plessix Gray, *Them: A Memoir of Parents*, Penguin Press, New York, 2005, p. 308

482   ibid., p. 309

483   ibid.

484   ibid.

485   ibid., p. 442

486   Fine Collins, op. cit.

487   Mirabella, op. cit., p. 103

488   ibid., p. 119

489   Mirabella, op. cit., p. 131

490   ibid.

491   ibid.

492   du Plessix Gray, op. cit., p. 442

493   Mirabella, op. cit., p. 142

494   ibid.

495   ibid.

496   ibid., p. 136

497   ibid., p. 141

498   A. Talmey, 'Power is a Boy's Best Friend: Senator John Sparkman', *Vogue*, Vogue Politics, vol. 164, issue 2, 1 August 1974, p. 32

499   M. Weber, 'Vitamin E/Christmas Blues . . .', *Vogue*, Vogue Health, vol. 164, issue 6, 1 December 1974, p. 130

500   ibid.

501   Mirabella, op. cit., pp. 159–60

502   ibid., p. 161

503   ibid., p. 162

504   ibid., pp. 193–6

505   ibid., p. 195

506   ibid., p. 198

507   ibid., p. 201

508   ibid.

509   ibid., p. 204

510   ibid.

511   ibid., p. 203

512   ibid., p. 207

Chapter 11

513   G. Mirabella, *In and Out of Vogue*, Doubleday, New York, 1995, p. 215

514   S. Stewart, 'LION IN WINTOUR – HOW ANNA HISSED, CLAWED & FLIRTED HER WAY TO THE TOP; CALL HER CRUELLA DE VOGUE', *New York Post*, Entertainment, 1 February 2005, <https://nypost.com/2005/02/01/lion-in-wintour-how-anna-hissed-clawed-call-her-cruella-de-vogue/>, accessed 8 January 2019

515   J. Oppenheimer, *Front Row: Anna Wintour: What Lies Beneath the Chic Exterior of Vogue's Editor in Chief*, St Martin's Griffin, New York, 2005, p. 11

516   ibid., p. 22

517   ibid., pp. 12–27

518   ibid., pp. 78–9

519   ibid., p. 70

520   ibid., p. 67

521   ibid., p. 170

522   Adweek, 'The Up-and-Comers: Wintour Displays Knack for the New', *Adweek*, November, 1983

523   Oppenheimer, op. cit., pp. 214–15

524   G. Mahon, 'S.I. Newhouse and Conde Nast; Taking Off The White Gloves', *New York Times Magazine*, section 6, 10 September 1989, <https://www.nytimes.com/1989/09/10/magazine/si-newhouse-and-conde-nast-taking-off-the-white-gloves.html>, accessed 8 January 2019

525   H. Marriott, '4am starts and no apologies: could Anna Wintour's master class transform my life and career?', *The Guardian*, Shortcuts, 24 September 2019, <https://www.theguardian.com/fashion/shortcuts/2019/sep/24/4am-starts-no-apologies-anna-wintour-masterclass-vogue-editor-in-chief-creativity-leadership>, accessed 20 January 2019

526   ibid., pp. 313–14

527   ibid.

528   ibid.

529   ibid., pp. 135–6

530   Oppenheimer, op. cit., pp. 236–46

531   S. Heller Anderson, 'HG Magazine Is Not What It Used to Be', *New York Times*, Arts, 8 June 1988, <https://www.nytimes.com/1988/06/08/arts/hg-magazine-is-not-what-it-used-to-be.html>, accessed 8 January 2019

Chapter 12

532   J. J. Buck, *The Price of Illusion, A Memoir*, Washington Square Press, New York, 2017, p. 84

533   H. Newton, *Vogue* (French), 'Rue Aubriot / Le Smoking', September 1975

534   S. Mower, 'The "King of Kink" Made Naughty Fashionable, *New York Times*, Arts, 21 September 2003, <https://www.nytimes.com/2003/09/21/style/the-king-of-kink-made-naughty-fashionable.html>, accessed 8 June 2020

535   G. Bourdin, Charles Jourdan advertisement, 1977

536   G. Bourdin, Charles Jourdan advertisement, 1975

537   Buck, op. cit., pp. 84–7

538   ibid., p. 87

539   C. Pringle, telephone interview with author, 06 February 2020

540   ibid.

541   ibid.

542   ibid.

543   E. Novick, *Vogue* (French) Special Issue, cover, December–January 1988

544   P. Demarchelier, *Vogue* (French), cover, August 1988

545   Pringle, loc. cit.

546   ibid.

547   ibid.

548   ibid.

549   ibid.

550   ibid.

551   ibid.

552   ibid.

553   ibid.

554   ibid.

555   ibid.

556   ibid.

557   ibid.

558   N. Vreeland, *Vogue* (French) Special Issue, 'The Beauty Rules of a Monk', December–January 1993

559   ibid.

560   ibid.

561   ibid.

562 ibid.

563 ibid.

564 I. Berry, J. Nachtwey, *Vogue* (French) Special Issue, 'Violence', December–January 1994

565 T. Motswai, *Vogue* (French) Special Issue, cover, December–January 1994

566 P. Lindbergh, *Vogue* (French) Special Issue, 'Nelson Mandela', December–January 1994

567 Pringle, loc. cit.

568 ibid.

569 ibid.

570 T. Willis, 'Nelson's Columns', *The Sunday Times*, Style & Travel, 5 December 1993, p. 26

571 ibid.

572 Willis, loc. cit.

573 Pringle, loc. cit

574 ibid.

575 ibid.

576 ibid.

Chapter 13

577 W. Norwich, 'An Affair to Remember', *Vogue*, Fashion, vol. 196, issue 7, 1 July 2006, pp. 128–35, 176

578 W. Norwich, 'A Grand Affair', *Vogue*, Features, vol. 197, issue 7, 1 July 2007, pp. 158–67

579 J. Shi, 'How the Met Gala Avoided Chinese Clichés', BizBash, Style & Decor, 13 May 2015, <https://www.bizbash.com/style-decor/event-design/media-gallery/13481016/how-the-met-gala-avoided-chinese-cliches>, accessed 25 September 2019

580 V. Friedman, 'It's Called the Met Gala, but It's Definitely Anna Wintour's Party', *New York Times*, Style, 2 May 2015, <https://www.nytimes.com/2015/05/03/style/its-called-the-met-gala-but-its-definitely-anna-wintours-party.html>, accessed 8 January 2019

581 ibid.

582 Tilberis, L., *No Time To Die*, Weidenfeld & Nicolson, London, 1998, p. 136.

583 G. Fabrikant, 'THE MEDIA BUSINESS: Advertising; Tough Year for Harper's Bazaar', *New York Times*, Business, 26 August 1988, <https://www.

nytimes.com/1988/08/26/business/the-media-business-advertising-tough-year-for-harper-s-bazaar.html>, accessed 13 May 2019

584 J. Kron, 'Style Setter: Fashion's Resurgence Means Wealth, Power for *Vogue* Magazine', *Wall Street Journal*, 30 January 1986

585 P. Demarchelier, *Vogue*, 100th Anniversary Special, vol. 182, issue 4, 1 April 1992

586 Rourke, M., 'Money. Power. Prestige. With so much at stake, Anna Wintour of Vogue and Liz Tilberis of Harper's Bazaar are locked in a . . . : Clash of the Titans', *Los Angeles Times*, Style, 17 May 1992, <https://www.latimes.com/archives/la-xpm-1992-05-17-vw-356-story.html>, accessed 08 May 2019.

587 M. Gross, 'War of the Poses', *New York* magazine, Contents, 27 April 1992, p. 3

588 Coddington, op. cit., p. 512

589 J. Brown, 'Liz Tilberis', *Salon*, 22 April 1999, <https://www.salon.com/1999/04/22/tilberis/>, accessed 11 May 2019

590 B. Weber, *Blood Sweat and Tears, Or, How I Stopped Worrying and Learned to Love Fashion*, teNeues, UK, 2005, p. 31

591 Vogue, 'Anna Wintour's Favorite *Vogue* Images of All Time', *Vogue* [.com], Fashion, 13 August 2012, <https://www.vogue.com/slideshow/anna-wintour-favorite-images-photos>, accessed 9 May 2019

592 P. Lindbergh, *Vogue*, vol. 178, issue 11, 1 November 1988

593 P. Demarchelier, *Vogue*, vol. 179, issue 5, 1 May 1989

594 P. Demarchelier, 'Enter the Era of Elegance', *Harper's Bazaar*, 1 September 1992

595 T. Maier, *All That Glitters: Anna Wintour, Tina Brown, and the Rivalry Inside America's Richest Media Empire*, Skyhorse Publishing, New York, 2019, [Apple Books e-book], p. 285

596 ibid.

597 ibid.

598 Gross, op. cit. p. 24

599 G. Dullea, 'Liz Tilberis's Kind of September', *New York Times*, Style, 23 August 1992, <https://www.nytimes.com/1992/08/23/style/liz-tilberis-s-kind-of-september.html>, accessed 27 January 2019

600 Rourke, loc. cit.

601 A. Wintour, 'Up Front: Remembering Liz Tilberis (1947 – 1999)', *Vogue*, vol. 189, issue 6, 1 June 1999, p. 72

602 J. Kron, 'Style Setter: Fashion's Resurgence Means Wealth, Power for *Vogue* Magazine', *Wall Street Journal*, 30 January 1986

603   ibid.

604   Rourke, loc. cit.

605   ibid.

606   Maier, op. cit. p. 94

607   G. Mahon, 'S.I. Newhouse and Conde Nast; Taking Off The White Gloves', *New York Times Magazine*, section 6, 10 September 1989, <https://www.nytimes.com/1989/09/10/magazine/si-newhouse-and-conde-nast-taking-off-the-white-gloves.html>, accessed 8 January 2019

608   Maier, op. cit., pp. 126–53

609   ibid., p. 289

610   ibid., p. 49

611   T. Brown, *The Vanity Fair Diaries 1983–1992*, Weidenfeld & Nicolson, New York, 2017, [Apple Books e-book], p. 83

612   D. Plotz, 'Let Si Get This', *Slate*, News & Politics, 6 December 1997, <https://slate.com/news-and-politics/1997/12/let-si-get-this.html>, accessed 12 May 2019

613   W. Henry III, 'A Search for Glitz', *Time*, 4 June 1990

614   R. Mead, 'The Truman Administration', *New York* magazine, 23 May 1994, p. 48

615   Maier, op. cit., p. 499

616   E. Kolbert, 'How Tina Brown Moves Magazines', *New York Times Magazine*, 5 December 1993, <http://www.maryellenmark.com/text/magazines/new%20york%20times%20magazine/904Z-000-015.html>, accessed 27 January 2019

617   Mahonop. cit.,

618   Spy, 'The New British Invasion', *Spy*, February 1993

Chapter 14

619   Buck, J. J., *The Price of Illusion, A Memoir*, Washington Square Press, New York, 2017, p. 164

620   ibid.

621   ibid.

622   ibid., p. 171

623   ibid., pp. 171–3

624   ibid., p. 172

625   ibid., p. 180

626   ibid., p. 201

627   ibid.

628   ibid., p. 263

629   Buck, loc. cit.

630   ibid., pp. 207–9

631   ibid., p. 207

632   ibid., p. 206

633   M. Hispard, *Vogue Paris*, 'La Femme Française', September 1994

634   Buck, op. cit., p. 218

635   ibid.

636   M. Thompson, *Vogue Paris*, 'Cinéma', December 1994–January 1995

637   Buck, op. cit., p. 226

638   M. Thompson, *Vogue Paris*, 'Le fabuleux album des 75 ans', December 1995–January 1996

639   Buck, op. cit., pp. 246–9

640   ibid.

641   ibid., p. 204

642   J-B. Mondino, *Vogue Paris*, 'Musique', December 1996–January 1997

643   S. Mazeaud, 'Madame Claude', *Vogue Paris*, 'Spécial Haute Couture', September 1997

644   J-B. Mondino, *Vogue Paris*, 'Mode et Science: Archives de l'Avenir', December 1999–January 2000

645   Buck, op. cit., p. 301

646   A. Barrett, 'French Vogue Combines Fashion With – Surprise – Quantum Physics', *Wall Street Journal*, 21 January 1999, <https://www.wsj.com/articles/SB916866770745531000>, accessed 16 October 2019

647   ibid.

648   Buck, op. cit., p. 321

649   ibid., p. 347

650   ibid., pp. 351–4

651   ibid., p. 362

652   ibid., pp. 349–52

653   ibid., p. 356

654   ibid.

655   ibid., p. 357

656   J. J. Buck, 'Joan Juliet Buck: My Vogue Interview With Syria's First Lady', *Newsweek*, World, 30 July 2012, <https://www.newsweek.com/joan-juliet-buck-my-vogue-interview-syrias-first-lady-65615>, accessed 27 April 2020

657   J. J. Buck, 'A Rose in the Desert', *Vogue*, Fashion & Features, vol. 201, issue
       3, 1 March 2011, pp. 528–33, 571

658   ibid.

659   ibid., p. 531

660   J. J. Buck, 'Joan Juliet Buck: My Vogue Interview With Syria's First Lady',
       Newsweek, World, 30 July 2012, <https://www.newsweek.com/joan-juliet-
       buck-my-vogue-interview-syrias-first-lady-65615>, accessed 27 April 2020

661   ibid.

662   ibid.

663   ibid.

Chapter 15

664   K. Nelson Best, *The History of Fashion Journalism*, Bloomsbury, London,
       New York, 2017, p. 218

665   ibid.

666   *Moving Fashion* [video], SHOWstudio, 29 September 2005, <https://show-
       studio.com/projects/moving_fashion>, accessed 27 June 2019

667   M. Echeverri, 'Essay: The Sound of Clothes', SHOWstudio, 9 October
       2013, <https://showstudio.com/projects/the_sound_of_clothes/essay_the_
       sound_of_clothes>, accessed 17 June 2019

668   C. McDowell, 'The CFDA and the Bloggers: Why?', Colin McDowell [blog],
       16 March 2010, <https://colin-mcdowell.blogspot.com/2010/03/cfda-and-
       bloggers-why.html>, accessed 17 June 2019

669   S. Singer, 'Ciao, Milano! Vogue.com's Editors Discuss the Week That Was',
       Vogue [.com], Runway, 25 September 2016, <https://www.vogue.com/article/
       milan-fashion-week-spring-2017-vogue-editors-chat>, accessed 27 June 2019

670   S. Mower, ibid.

671   N. Phelps, ibid.

672   A. Codinha, ibid.

673   ibid.

674   A. Belonsky, 'Condé Nast, McKinsey and the Death of Endless Dreams',
       Gawker [blog], 9 September 2009, <https://gawker.com/5355309/conde-nast-
       mckinsey-and-the-death-of-endless-dreams>, accessed 27 June 2019

675   J. Koblin, 'Condé Nast Hires McKinsey, Staffers Suffer Shock', *New York
       Observer*, 21 July 2009, <https://observer.com/2009/07/cond-nast-hires-
       mckinsey-staffers-suffer-shock/>, accessed 27 June 2019

676 J. Goldberg, 'McKinsey Draft Report on Rethinking Conde Nast', *The Atlantic*, Global, 22 July 2009, <https://www.theatlantic.com/international/archive/2009/07/mckinsey-draft-report-on-rethinking-conde-nast/21839/>, accessed 27 June 2019

677 CZJFan87, 'Rank of Meryl Streep's movies by Box Office performance', IMDB, 7 January 2015, <https://www.imdb.com/list/ls073278870/>, accessed 27 June 2019

678 Coddington, G., *Grace: A Memoir*, Chatto & Windus, London, 2012, pp. 32–5

679 V. Friedman, 'Planning for the future in Milan', *Financial Times*, 23 September 2010, <https://www.ft.com/content/d297e2bd-e93e-3d0c-9f67-55404f1b3d25?kbc=e8a1fafb-292f-3334-897a-7dca06ee2b2b>, accessed 27 June 2019

680 K. Carter, 'Anna Wintour's whims worry Italy's fashion pack', *The Guardian*, Fashion, 11 February 2010, <https://www.theguardian.com/lifeandstyle/2010/feb/11/anna-wintour-italy-fashion>, accessed 27 June 2019

681 Web Desk, 'Vogue editor Anna Wintour under fire for being "icy" towards mag's first Black model', *The News*, 16 June 2020, <https://www.thenews.com.pk/latest/673490-vogue-editor-anna-wintour-under-fire-for>, accessed 27 June 2020

682 M. Bustillos, 'Is Anna Wintour Satan?', *Vintage Voice*, 11 February 2003, <http://pix.popula.com/items/0224/vintage/wintour.html>, accessed 27 June 2019

683 B. Sowray, 'Today In History – April 7', *Vogue* [British], News, 7 April 2010, <https://www.vogue.co.uk/article/anna-wintour-was-attacked-with-a-pie-by-anti-fur-protesters>, accessed 1 July 2019

684 J. Safran Foer, *Eating Animals*, Penguin Random House, UK, 2009, p. 71

685 D. Tartt, 'The Power of Words: Rebel Spirit', *Vogue*, Up Front, vol. 196, issue 1, 1 January 2006, p. 62–4

686 C. Gandee, 'Under the Influence', *Vogue*, Features, vol. 184, issue 3, 1 March 1994, pp. 380–3, 436, 437

687 A. Wicks, Z. Turner, 'Tough Times at the Newsstand', *WWD*, 9 August 2011, <https://wwd.com/business-news/media/fashion-magazines-fall-at-news-stand-5048220/>, accessed 25 April 2019

688 ibid.

689 J. W. Peters, 'Power Is Always in Vogue', *New York Times*, Fashion, 15 June 2012, <https://www.nytimes.com/2012/06/17/fashion/for-anna-wintour-power-is-always-in-vogue.html/>, accessed 8 January 2019

690   L. McCalmont, 'Obama, Wintour spotlight workshop', *Politico*, 5 May
       2014, <https://www.politico.com/story/2014/05/michelle-obama-anna-win-
       tour-106365>, accessed 8 March 2019

691   Vogue, '*Vogue* Endorses Hillary Clinton for President of the United States',
       Vogue [.com], Magazine, 18 October 2016, <https://www.vogue.com/article/
       hillary-clinton-endorsement-president-united-states-democrat>, accessed 3
       February 2019

692   I. Amed, A. Berg, L. Brantberg, S. Hedrich, 'The State of Fashion 2017',
       McKinsey & Company, Our Insights, 1 December 2016, <https://www.
       mckinsey.com/industries/retail/our-insights/the-state-of-fashion#>,
       accessed 8 March 2019

Chapter 16

693   M. Foley Sypeck, J. J. Gray and A. H. Ahrens, 'No longer just a pretty face:
       Fashion magazines' depictions of ideal female beauty from 1959 to 1999',
       International Journal of Eating Disorders, vol. 36, issue 3, 2004, pp. 342–7

694   B. McNair, *Striptease Culture: Sex, Media and the Democratisation of Desire*,
       Routledge, London and New York, 2002, pp. 24–6

695   J. J. Buck, *The Price of Illusion, A Memoir*, Washington Square Press, New
       York, 2017, p. 199

696   J. A. Wright, 'The Imp Wears Blue Jeans: Former *Vogue Paris* Chief Carine
       Roitfeld Talks Feminism, Nudity and Why Anna Wintour Isn't a Fashion
       Editor', *New York Observer*, 9 June 2013, <https://observer.com/2013/09/
       the-imp-wears-blue-jeans-former-vogue-paris-chief-carine-roitfeld-talks-
       feminism-nudity-and-why-anna-wintour-isnt-a-fashion-editor/>, accessed
       20 April 2018

697   ibid.

698   The Business of Fashion, 'Carine Roitfeld', *The Business of Fashion*, BoF
       500, 2013, <https://www.businessoffashion.com/community/people/carine-
       roitfeld>, accessed 5 January 2020

699   C. Long, 'Lunch with the FT: Carine Roitfeld', *Financial Times*, 20 May 2011,
       <https://www.ft.com/content/aa714ad8-8266-11e0-8c49-00144feabdc0>,
       accessed 19 April 2018

700   ibid.

701   Buck, op. cit., p. 349

702   ibid.

703 Inez & Vinoodh, *Vogue Paris*, cover, August 2003

704 P. Demarchelier, *Vogue Paris*, 'No Smoking', April 2009

705 M. Testino, *Vogue Paris*, 'Corps & Lames', February 2005

706 D. Sims, *Vogue Paris Calendar*, Calendar, 2007

707 M. Healy, 'We're French! We smoke, we show flesh, we have a lot of freedom . . .', *The Guardian*, *The Observer*, 25 February 2007, <https://www.theguardian.com/media/2007/feb/25/pressandpublishing.fashion>, accessed 23 April 2018

708 M. Testino, *Vogue Paris*, 'La Decadanse', May 2010

709 T. Richardson, *Vogue Paris*, 'Festine', October 2010

710 S. Klein, *Vogue Paris*, 'LARA', October 2009

711 M. Sawyer, 'Commentary: Blackface is never okay', CNN, World, 14 October 2009, <https://edition.cnn.com/2009/WORLD/asiapcf/10/14/sawyer.blackface/>, accessed 29 April 2018

712 S. Hamza, *Vogue Paris*, 'Cadeaux', December 2010–January 2011

713 X. Jardin, 'Pedocouture: In Vogue Magazine, 6-Year-Olds Are Sex Vixens', Boing Boing [blog], 5 January 2011, <https://boingboing.net/2011/01/05/in-vogue-magazine-6.html>, accessed 8 September 2019

714 elizabeth, 'RE: Pretty Babies', Frockwriter [blog], 17 December 2010, <https://frockwriter.blogspot.com/2010/12/pretty-babies.html>, accessed 17 September 2018

715 A Mother, ibid.

716 E. Maree, 'Is Fashion Now All About The Shock Factor?', Emily Fashion Fiend [blog], 26 April 2013, <https://emilyfashionfiend.wordpress.com/tag/vogue-paris/>, accessed 17 September 2018

717 J. Sauers, 'French *Vogue*'s Sexy Kiddie Spread is Misunderstood', Jezebel [blog], 1 May 2011, <https://jezebel.com/french-vogues-sexy-kiddie-spread-is-misunderstood-5725707>, accessed 23 April 2018

718 M. Reimer, C. Tosenberger and L. Wodtke, '"*Je suis fatigué par le culte de la jeunesse*": Or, Walking on Ice in High Heels', *Jeunesse: Young People, Texts, Cultures*, vol. 3, issue 1, summer 2011, pp. 1–10

719 T. Ford, *Vogue Paris*, 'Forever Love', December 2010–January 2011

720 M. Msa, *Vogue Paris*, 'La Panthère Ose', December 2010–January 2011

721 A. Heath, 'Vogue Paris = CARINE ROITFELD', *032C*, 1 December 2005, <https://032c.com/vogue-paris-carine-roitfeld/>, accessed 23 April 2018

722 Wright, op. cit.

723 S. Klein, *Vogue Paris*, 'Crystal Taillee', May 2010

724 B. Weber, *Vogue Paris*, cover, November 2007

725   Wright, op. cit.

726   D. Garnett, 'Guest Editor: Carine Roitfeld Is the Fashion Stylist's Stylist. . .',
      Vogue, Vogue Beauty, vol. 189, issue 12, 1 December 1999, p. 328

727   ibid.

728   S. Mower, 'Sexy Classic', *Vogue*, Fashion, vol. 191, issue 8, 1 August 2001,
      pp. 244–51

729   ibid.

730   S. Kilcooley-O'Halloran, 'Today in History – December 17', *Vogue* [.co.uk],
      17 December 2012, <https://www.vogue.co.uk/article/carine-roitfeld-re-
      signed-as-editor-of-french-vogue>, accessed 23 April 2019

731   J. Diderich, S. Conti, J. Weil, 'Carine Roitfeld to Depart French Vogue',
      WWD, 17 December 2010, <https://wwd.com/business-news/media/carine-
      roitfeld-is-to-leave-french-vogue-3405583/>, accessed 23 April 2019

732   D. Lo, 'Rumor: Was Carine Roitfeld Fired From Vogue? Le Figaro's Fashion
      Director Virginie Mouzat is Frontrunner for the Job', Racked, 20 December
      2010, <https://www.racked.com/2010/12/20/7778903/rumor-was-carine-
      roitfeld-fired-from-vogue-le-figaros-fashion>, accessed 23 April 2019

733   ibid.

734   ibid.

735   Heath, op. cit.

736   Standen, D., 'The Future of Fashion, Part Seven: Carine Roitfeld', *Vogue.
      com*, Trends, 12 February, 2011, <https://www.vogue.com/article/the-fu-
      ture-of-fashion-part-seven-carine-roitfeld>, accessed 24 April 2019

737   L. Guilbault, 'Can Carine Roitfeld Become a Brand?', *The Business of
      Fashion*, Professional, 16 May 2019, <https://www.businessoffashion.com/
      articles/professional/can-carine-roitfeld-become-a-brand>, accessed 24
      April 2019

738   J. Diderich, S. Conti, J. Weil, op. cit.

739   A. Larocca, 'The Anti-Anna', *New York* magazine, Fashion, 14 February 2008,
      <https://nymag.com/fashion/08/spring/44215/>, accessed 23 April 2019

740   M. Tungate, *Fashion Brands: Branding Style from Armani to Zara*, 2nd edn,
      Kogan Page Publishers, London and Philadelphia, 2008

741   L. Indvik, 'Emmanuelle Alt: "Vogue is more than a magazine"', *Vogue Business*,
      8 August 2019, <https://www.voguebusiness.com/talent/articles/emmanuelle-
      alt-editor-in-chief-vogue-paris-interview/>, accessed 2 January 2020

742   Indvik, op. cit.

744   P. Martin, 'Emmanuelle Alt: Conversation with Penny Martin', *Aperture
      'Fashion'*, Words, issue 216, fall 2014, p. 43

745   C. Horyn, 'Fashion Director Is Named New Editor of French Vogue', *New York Times*, Business, 7 January 2011, <https://www.nytimes.com/2011/01/08/business/media/08vogue.html>, accessed 23 April 2019

746   Anne, 'French Woman Carine Roitfeld Knows Sensuality Is Not a Sin', thebkmag [blog], 17 April 2011, <https://thebkmag.com/2011/04/17/french-woman-carine-roitfeld-knows-sensuality-not-sin/>, accessed 17 May 2019

747   ibid.

748   Mert & Marcus, *Vogue Paris* Special Issue, 'Inès de La Fressange', December 2014–January 2015

749   D. Sims, Inez & Vinoodh, K. Sadli, *Vogue Paris* Special Issue, 'Vanessa Paradis', December 2015–January 2016

750   Mert & Marcus, *Vogue Paris*, cover, March 2017

751   E. Alt, *Vogue Paris*, 'Editor's Letter', March 2017

752   Martin, loc. cit.

753   ibid.

754   Indvik, loc. cit.

755   J. Diderich, S. Conti, J. Weil, 'Carine Roitfeld to Depart French Vogue', op. cit.

756   C. Horyn, 'New Star in the Front Row', *New York Times*, 9 February 2011, <https://www.nytimes.com/2011/02/10/fashion/10ALT.html>, accessed 23 April 2019

Chapter 17

757   C. Edwardes, 'Alexandra Shulman: the British Vogue editor on fashion, her candid memoir and standing by Philip Green', *Evening Standard*, 20 October 2016, <https://www.standard.co.uk/lifestyle/esmagazine/alexandra-shulman-the-british-vogue-editor-on-fashion-her-candid-memoir-and-standing-by-philip-green-a3372576.html>, accessed 11 September 2019

758   ibid.

759   A. Shulman, 'My first boss: Vogue's Alexandra Shulman and editor Shirley Lowe', *The Guardian*, 4 April 2014, <https://www.theguardian.com/lifeandstyle/2014/apr/04/first-boss-alexandra-shulman-shirley-lowe>, accessed 11 September 2019

760   O. Petter, 'Alexandra Shulman's Vogue Might Not Have Shown "Ethnic Diversity" but Edward Enninful May Make Up for Lost Time', *Independent*, 13 November 2017, <https://www.independent.co.uk/

life-style/fashion/vogue-ethnic-diversity-alexandra-shulman-edward-enninful-change-black-minority-models-fashion-a8052706.html>, accessed 11 September 2019

761 Petter, op. cit.

762 BBCNewsEnts, 'Naomi Campbell shames Vogue over diversity', Entertainment & Arts, BBC, 23 August 2017, <https://www.bbc.co.uk/news/entertainment-arts-41022264>, accessed 13 September 2019

763 N. Knight, *Vogue* (British), cover, May 2003

764 M. Testino, *Vogue* (British), cover, December 2002

765 'Alexandra Shulman chats with Lily [Allen]' [online audio], BBC Radio 2, 16 March 2014, <https://www.bbc.co.uk/programmes/p01vb37l>, accessed 10 December 2019

766 ibid.

767 "Fat" FrontLine (PBS), 17 March 2014

768 A. Roberts, 'Alexandra Shulman: "I won't tell women they need surgery or diets to be attractive"', *Evening Standard*, London Life, 3 April 2012, <https://www.standard.co.uk/lifestyle/london-life/alexandra-shulman-i-won-t-tell-women-they-need-surgery-or-diets-to-be-attractive-7614732.html>, accessed 13 January 2020

769 L. Niven-Phillips, 'Model Health Tips', Celebrity Beauty, *Vogue* [.co.uk], 18 December 2013, <https://www.vogue.co.uk/gallery/model-health-tips-diet-and-wellbeing-quotes>, accessed 5 January 2020

770 R. Erdmann, *Vogue* (British), cover, June 1996

771 M. Testino, *Vogue* (British), cover, October 2000

772 P. Priestly, 'Alexandra Shulman's reign at Vogue will be defined by mediocrity, idiocy and flip-flops', *The Spectator*, 2 February 2017, <https://www.spectator.co.uk/article/alexandra-shulman-s-reign-at-vogue-will-be-defined-by-mediocrity-idiocy-and-flip-flops>, accessed 14 September 2019

773 E. Sheffield, 'Emily Sheffield: from Vogue to ThisMuchIKnow, with help from her sister Samantha Cameron', *The Times*, 1 February 2020, <https://www.thetimes.co.uk/article/emily-sheffield-from-vogue-to-thismuchiknow-with-help-from-her-sister-samantha-cameron-hf7c6gwv7>1 February 2020

774 A. Aronowsky Cronberg, 'Will I Get A Ticket?', interview, *Vestoj*, <http://vestoj.com/will-i-get-a-ticket/>, accessed 5 January 2020

775 L. Chambers, cited in Aronowsky Cronberg, ibid.

776 Ibid.

777 E. Enninful, 'Editor's letter', *Vogue* (British), 1 December 2017, pp. 69–70

778 S. Klein, *Vogue* (British), cover, December 2017

779 ACM, 'Back to my roots', *Vogue* (British), Fashion and features, 1 December 2017, p. 282

780 CC, ibid., p. 290

781 Z. Smith, 'Mrs Windsor', *Vogue* (British), Viewpoint, ibid, p. 136

782 S. Rushdie, 'In The Spirit', ibid., pp. 143–4

783 Skepta, 'Love letters to Britain', ibid., p. 210

784 B. Weber, 'The secret garden', *Vogue* (British), Fashion and features, ibid., p. 295

785 C. Delevingne, P. Delevingne, 'Love letters to Britain', *Vogue* (British), Viewpoint, ibid., p. 208

786 S. Khan, N. Campbell, '"What's the secret of every great city? Talent"', *Vogue* (British), interview, ibid., pp. 185–8

787 Enninful, op. cit.

788 J. Cartner-Morley, 'Edward Enninful's new Vogue – a bit more cool, a bit less posh', Fashion, *The Guardian*, 8 November 2017, <https://www.theguardian.com/fashion/shortcuts/2017/nov/08/edward-enninfuls-new-vogue-a-bit-more-cool-a-bit-less-posh>, accessed 24 December 2019

789 Mert and Marcus, *Vogue* (British), cover, January 2018

790 J. Teller, *Vogue* (British), cover, February 2018

791 C. McDean, *Vogue* (British), cover, May 2018

792 Mert and Marcus, *Vogue* (British), cover, August 2018

793 Kloss Films, *Vogue* (British), cover, December 2019

794 S. Klein, *Vogue* (British), cover, May 2020

795 HRH the Duchess of Sussex, 'HRH The Duchess of Sussex Introduces The September Issue In Her Own Words', *Vogue* [.co.uk], 29 July 2019 <http://vestoj.com/will-i-get-a-ticket/>, accessed 12 January 2020

796 HRH the Duchess of Sussex, op. cit.

797 N. Ijewere, in-person interview with author, 23 January 2020

798 ibid.

799 A. Shulman, 'What Makes a Great Magazine Editor?', *The Business of Fashion*, Opinion, 4 October 2017, <https://www.businessoffashion.com/articles/opinion/what-makes-a-great-magazine-editor>, accessed 15 January 2020

800 ibid.

801 ibid.

802 ibid.

803 C. Fernandez, 'Condé Nast's Results Show Its Future Lies Outside Europe', *The Business of Fashion*, 25 March 2019, News & Analysis, <https://www.businessoffashion.com/articles/news-analysis/conde-nasts-results-show-its-future-lies-outside-europe>, accessed 9 January 2020

804   Communications Team, 'Condé Nast announces new global leadership struc-
      ture', Condé Nast, 14 August 2019, Announcements, <https://www.condenast.
      com/news/conde-nast-announces-new-global-leadership-structure>,
      accessed 13 January 2020

805   R. Wiedeman, 'What's Left of Condé Nast', *New York* magazine *Intelligencer*,
      Media, 28 October 2019, <https://nymag.com/intelligencer/2019/10/conde-
      nast-anna-wintour-roger-lynch.html>, accessed 3 October 2019

806   ibid.

807   ibid.

808   K. Hays, 'Condé's Roger Lynch Talks Video, Acquisitions and Layoffs', *WWD*,
      Business / Media, 15 August 2019, <https://wwd.com/business-news/media/
      roger-lynch-conde-nast-ceo-talks-business-video-future-1203239888/>,
      accessed 13 January 2020

809   ibid.

810   V. Friedman, telephone interview with author, 19 November 2019

811   I. Amed, telephone interview with author, 6 March 2020

812   A. Aronowsky Cronberg, telephone interview with author, 31 January 2020

813   Ibid.

814   Ibid.

815   K. Glass, telephone interview with author, 4 February 2020

816   ibid.

817   ibid.

818   Shulman, A., 'What Makes a Great Magazine Editor?', *Business of Fashion*,
      Opinion, 04 October 2017, <https://www.businessoffashion.com/articles/
      opinion/what-makes-a-great-magazine-editor>, accessed 15 January 2020

819   Glass, op. cit

820   F. Carr, telephone interview with author, 06 February 2020

821   ibid.

822   M. Socha, email interview with author, 22 November 2019

823   ibid.

824   Woolman Chase & Chase, op. cit., p. 200.

825   Amed, loc. cit.

826   S. Lucas, Twin Souls, *Vogue* (Portugal), November 2019

827   S. Lucas, Planet Earth is the New Trend, *Vogue* (Portugal), September 2019

828   M. Ferrier, 'Anna Wintour apologises for not giving space to black people
      at Vogue', *The Guardian*, 10 June 2020, Fashion, <https://www.theguardian.
      com/fashion/2020/jun/10/anna-wintour-apologises-for-not-giving-space-
      to-black-people-at-vogue>, accessed 20 July 2020

Select Bibliography

Aronowsky Cronberg, A., 'Will I Get A Ticket?', *Vestoj*, interview, <http://vestoj.com/will-i-get-a-ticket/>, accessed 5 January 2020.

Ballard, B., *In My Fashion* (1st edn. 1960), V&A Publishing, London, 2017.

Buck, J. J., *The Price of Illusion, A Memoir*, Washington Square Press, New York, 2017.

Carrod, A., '"A plea for a renaissance": Dorothy Todd's Modernist experiment in British *Vogue*, 1922–1926', Doctor of Philosophy Thesis in English Literature, Keele University, Keele, Newcastle, 2015.

Coddington, G., *Grace: A Memoir*, Chatto & Windus, London, 2012.

Cohen, L., *All We Know: Three Lives*, Farrar, Straus and Giroux, USA, 2012.

Conekin, B., 'From Haughty to Nice: How British Fashion Images Changed from the 1950s to the 1960s', *Photography and Culture*, vol. 3, issue 3, 2010, pp. 283–96.

Coser, I., 'Alison Settle, Editor of British *Vogue* (1926–1935): Habitus and the Acquisition of Cultural, Social, and Symbolic Capital in the Private Diaries of Alison Settle', *Fashion Theory*, vol. 21, issue 4, 2017, pp. 477–99.

Cox, H. & Mowatt, S., 'Vogue in Britain: Authenticity and the creation of competitive advantage in the UK magazine industry', Business History, vol. 54, issue 1, 2012, pp. 67–87.

Delis Hill, D., As Seen in Vogue: A Century of American Fashion in Advertising, Texas Tech University Press, USA, 2007.

Endres, K. & Lueck, T., Women's Periodicals in the United States: Consumer Magazines, Greenwood Press, USA, 1995.

Felsenthal, C., Citizen Newhouse: Portrait of a Media Merchant, Seven Stories Press, New York, 1998.

Fine Collins, A., 'The Cult of Diana', Vanity Fair, Culture, November 1993, <https://www.vanityfair.com/culture/1993/11/diana-vreeland-199311>, accessed 11 January 2019.

Friend, D., 'Vanity Fair: The One-Click History', Vanity Fair, VINTAGE V.F., 14 January 2004, <https://www.vanityfair.com/magazine/2008/01/oneclickhistory>, accessed 5 February 2019.

Garland, A., Lion's Share, Michael Joseph Ltd., New York, 1970.

Hemmings, R., 'Beautiful objects, dutiful things: waste, ruins and the stuff of war', Word & Image, vol. 32, issue 4, 2016, pp. 360–74.

Lynge-Jorlen, A., Niche Fashion Magazines: Changing the Shape of Fashion, I. B. Tauris, London, New York, 2017.

Maier, T., All That Glitters: Anna Wintour, Tina Brown, and the Rivalry Inside America's Richest Media Empire, Skyhorse Publishing, New York, 2019.

Mirabella, G., In and Out of Vogue, Doubleday, New York, 1995.

Nelson Best, K., The History of Fashion Journalism, Bloomsbury, London, New York, 2017.

Plessix Gray, F. du, Them: A Memoir of Parents, Penguin Press, New York, 2005.

Reed, C., 'A Vogue That Dare Not Speak its Name: Sexual Subculture During the Editorship of Dorothy Todd, 1922–26', Fashion Theory, vol. 10, issue 1/2, 2006, pp. 39–72.

Seebohm, C., *The Man Who Was Vogue: The Life and Times of Condé Nast*, Viking Press, New York, 1982.

Settle, A., Alison Settle Archive, University of Brighton Design Archives, Brighton.

Shulman, A., *Inside Vogue: My Diary of Vogue's 100th Year*, Fig Tree, Great Britain, 2016.

Steele, V., ed., *Paris, Capital of Fashion*, Bloomsbury Visual Arts, Great Britain, 2019.

Taylor, L., & McLoughlin, M., ed., *Paris Fashion and World War Two: Global Diffusion and Nazi Control*, Bloomsbury Visual Arts, London, Oxford, 2020.

Tilberis, L., *No Time To Die*, Weidenfeld & Nicolson, London, 1998.

Vreeland, D., *D.V.*, ed. G. Plimpton & C. Hemphill, Alfred A. Knopf, Inc., New York, 1984.

Woolman Chase, E. & Chase, I., *Always in Vogue*, Doubleday & Company, Inc., USA, 1954.

Yoxall, H., *A Fashion of Life*, Taplinger Publishing Co., Inc., New York, 1967.

Acknowledgements

My first thanks go to my agent, Juliet Pickering, for believing in my idea, and to my editors Jane Sturrock and Charlotte Fry for their endless patience in transforming this idea into the best book possible. Thank you also Sam Hodder of the Blake Friedmann Agency and the rest of the team at Quercus.

The following people helped me with either encouragement or information or both: Prosper Assouline, for your searing criticism; Mark Heywood and Rupert Heath for the early and invaluable advice; and my dearest friends Dean Merali and Lina Viktor, who have been there from the beginning of this adventure. Thank you also: Rik Ubhi, Ashleigh Smith, Sophie Foan, Elly Goldsmith, James Crump, Christopher Denruyter, Bradley Reynolds, Ruth Peterson, the Worshipful Company of Stationers and Newspaper Makers, The Hospital Club and everyone at Londnr who held the fort while I was writing.

I'm particularly grateful to Colombe Pringle, for opening up her home and a window to the past, for her time and generosity, and for her lively conversation. Her contribution has been one of the most valuable. Thank you also to Ilaria Coser for answering my pleas for information, to Lesley Whitworth at the Alison Settle University of

Brighton Design Archives, Vanessa Friedman, Katie Glass, Flora Carr, Imran Amed and his PR team Kerry and Paloma, Anja Aronowsky Cronberg, Nadine Ijewere, Miles Socha and the countless others who prefer to remain unnamed but supplied me with insights on the topic of *Vogue* in particular, and fashion magazines in general. I'm also deeply indebted to The Vogue Archive at the National Art Library and the Condé Nast Archive.

My final thanks go with love to Elena Guinea and Christoph Miralles.

Picture Credits